Lecture Notes in Computer Science 7703

Commenced Publication in 1973
Founding and Former Series Editors:
Gerhard Goos, Juris Hartmanis, and Jan van Leeuwen

Michael Grossniklaus   Manuel Wimmer (Eds.)

Current Trends in Web Engineering

ICWE 2012 International Workshops
MDWE, ComposableWeb, WeRE, QWE,
and Doctoral Consortium
Berlin, Germany, July 23-27, 2012
Revised Selected Papers

 Springer

Volume Editors

Michael Grossniklaus
Portland State University, Department of Computer Science
P.O. Box 751, Portland, OR 97207-0751, USA
E-mail: grossniklaus@cs.pdx.edu

Manuel Wimmer
Vienna University of Technology
Institute of Software Technology and Interactive Systems
Favoritenstrasse 9-11/188-3, 1040 Vienna, Austria
E-mail: wimmer@big.tuwien.ac.at

ISSN 0302-9743   e-ISSN 1611-3349
ISBN 978-3-642-35622-3   e-ISBN 978-3-642-35623-0
DOI 10.1007/978-3-642-35623-0
Springer Heidelberg Dordrecht London New York

Library of Congress Control Number: 2012954000

CR Subject Classification (1998): H.5, H.4, H.3, K.6, D.2, C.2, H.3.5, H.5.3

LNCS Sublibrary: SL 3 – Information Systems and Application, incl. Internet/Web
and HCI

Typesetting: Camera-ready by author, data conversion by Scientific Publishing Services, Chennai, India

Printed on acid-free paper

Springer is part of Springer Science+Business Media (www.springer.com)

Foreword

ICWE 2012 marked the 12th edition of the International Conference on Web Engineering and was held during July 23–27, 2012, in Berlin, Germany. As in previous years, the conference's main program was complemented by a number of co-located workshops, tutorials, and a doctoral consortium. All of these satellite events are designed to give researchers and practitioners an opportunity to interact in a setting that is both more informal and focused at the same time. This volume presents revised contributions to the workshops and the doctoral consortium, while summaries of the tutorials have been published in the main conference proceedings (LNCS Volume No. 7387).

Workshops have always played an important role in the ICWE community as they are a vessel both to explore new trends and for in-depth discussions on core topics of Web engineering. While this year's workshop program did not include any newcomers, most of the well-established workshops broadened their focus to harbor contributions addressing novel and emerging requirements and opportunities, such as cloud computing, agile development, end-user development, linked data management, or social data and networks. At the same time, classic themes, such as Web modeling, the semantic Web, service-oriented architectures and mashups, or rich Internet applications, were also represented in the workshop program.

A total of nine workshop proposals were submitted and reviewed by the workshop Program Committee with respect to topicality and chance of success. Based on their recommendations, the Workshop Chairs accepted seven workshops. Of these seven workshops one had to be canceled as it did not meet the expected number of submissions. Another two workshops were withdrawn by their organizers. The final four workshops, which are listed below, all share a long-standing tradition in the Web engineering community and were successfully held once again at ICWE 2012.

- *MDWE 2012*: 8th International Workshop on Model-Driven and Agile Engineering for the Web
- *ComposableWeb 2012*: 4th International Workshop on Lightweight Integration on the Web
- *WeRE 2012*: Third Workshop on the Web and Requirements Engineering
- *QWE 2012*: Third International Workshop on Quality in Web Engineering

The doctoral consortium, which featured five presentations, complemented the conference and workshop program. In contrast to previous editions of ICWE, the format of the doctoral consortium was revised this year to put more emphasis on mentoring. Each participating PhD student was assigned two mentors to whom they presented their poster. This formal part was followed by a lunch that provided an opportunity for informal discussion.

This proceedings volume would not have been possible without the work of the enthusiastic and committed workshop and doctoral consortium organizers. Therefore, our first thank you is to all our colleagues who dedicated their time and skills to making the ICWE 2012 satellite events a success. In particular, we would like to thank the members of the workshop Program Committee whose careful evaluations of the submitted workshop proposals were an invaluable asset in assembling the ICWE 2012 workshop program. The success of any individual workshop largely depends on the quality and quantity of submissions. Keeping this reality in mind, our thanks also go out to the researchers, practitioners, and PhD students who contributed their work to this volume. Finally, we would like to thank the General Chair of ICWE 2012, Robert Tolksdorf, and the Program Chairs, Marco Brambilla and Takehiro Tokuda, for their feedback and constant support.

August 2012   Michael Grossniklaus
                                                   Manuel Wimmer

Organization

Workshop Program Committee

Nora Koch	Ludwig-Maximilians-Universität München and NTT DATA, Germany
Maristella Matera	Politecnico di Milano, Italy
Moira C. Norrie	ETH Zurich, Switzerland
Luis Olsina	Universidad Nacional de La Pampa, Argentina
Óscar Pastor	Universidad Politécnica de Valencia, Spain
Werner Retschitzegger	Johannes Keppler Universität Linz, Austria
Gustavo Rossi	Universidad Nacional de La Plata, Argentina
Antonio Vallecillo	Universidad de Málaga, Spain
Erik Wilde	University of California, Berkeley, USA
Marco Winckler	Paul Sabatier University, France

8th International Workshop on Model-Driven and Agile Engineering for the Web (MDWE 2012)

The 8th International Workshop on Model-Driven and Agile Engineering for the Web (MDWE 2012) continued with the successful series of the Model-Driven Web Engineering workshops that have been held jointly with ICWE conferences since 2005, with exception of MDWE 2008 that was held jointly with MoDELS 2008 in Toulouse.

MDWE promotes a more systematic development of Web applications, i.e., focusing on methods, techniques, and tools that support the development process. This year we invited submissions of original high-quality papers on both model-driven and agile approaches covering different steps of the software development life cycle.

In response to the call for papers, a total of nine submissions were received. Each submitted paper was anonymously peer reviewed by at least three referees, and six papers were finally accepted for presentation at the workshop and publication in the proceedings. The workshop was the occasion for very lively discussions following the presentations, covering current and critical topics in the model-driven Web engineering domain. Some glimpses of the discussion are available online on the Instant Community website that was set up as support to the workshop.[1] The community site contains all the presentations, papers, and issues that were raised during the discussion.

The workshop also included a keynote talk by Arne Berre, from SINTEF, Norway, entitled "An Agile Model-Based Framework for Service Innovation for the Future Internet." The selected papers address, among others, the improvement of the model-driven approaches introducing new concerns such as non-functional requirements for cloud computing applications, social network elements, and an ontology perspective. The focus of other contributions are the improvement of MDWE processes with software engineering techniques such as test-driven modeling, aspect-orientation, and reverse engineering for converting a traditional Web into a RIA. Further information about the presented papers and all the information relevant to the workshop is available on the website of the event: http://mdwe2012.pst.ifi.lmu.de/.

The most important contribution of MDWE is the open discussion space that provides for solid theory work with practical on-the-field experience in model-driven approaches. In these proceedings you can find the papers that reflect this spirit, and how different approaches respond to the new challenges in the

---

[1] http://ic.kspaces.net/#!event/10749

development of Web applications. We hope you find these papers useful reading material for your research in model-driven software engineering.

We would like to thank the ICWE 2012 organization team for giving us the opportunity to organize this workshop, especially to the Workshop Chairs, Manuel Wimmer and Michael Grossniklaus, who were always very helpful and supportive. Many thanks to all those who submitted papers, and particularly to the presenters of the accepted papers and to Arne Berre for his interesting keynote talk. Our thanks go to the reviewers and the members of the Program Committee, too, for their timely and accurate reviews and for their help in choosing and suggestions for improving the selected papers.

August 2012   The Organizers

Organizers

Nora Koch	Ludwig-Maximilians-Universität München and NTT DATA, Germany
Marco Brambilla	Politecnico di Milano, Italy
Santiago Meliá	University of Alicante, Spain

Steering Committee

Nora Koch	Ludwig-Maximilians-Universität München and NTT DATA, Germany
Antonio Vallecillo	Universidad de Málaga, Spain
Gustavo Rossi	Universidad Nacional de La Plata, Argentina
Geert-Jan Houben	Technische Universiteit Delft, The Netherlands

Program Committee

Luciano Baresi	Politecnico di Milano, Italy
Hubert Baumeister	Technical University of Denmark, Denmark
Jordi Cabot	INRIA École des Mines de Nantes, France
Jorge Cuéllar	Siemens AG, Germany
Jutta Eckstein	IT Communication, Germany
Marina Egea	ATOS Origin, Spain
Piero Fraternali	Politecnico di Milano, Italy
Geert-Jan Houben	Technische Universiteit Delft, The Netherlands

Gerti Kappel	Vienna University of Technology, Austria
Alexander Knapp	Universität Augsburg, Germany
Maristella Matera	Politecnico di Milano, Italy
Alfonso Pierantonio	Università di L'Aquila, Italy
Vicente Pelechano	Universidad Politécnica de Valencia, Spain
Gustavo Rossi	Universidad Nacional de La Plata, Argentina
Fernando Sánchez	Universidad de Extremadura, Spain
Antonio Vallecillo	Universidad de Málaga, Spain
Manuel Wimmer	Vienna University of Technology, Austria
Marco Winckler	Paul Sabatier University, France
Agustín Yagüe	Universidad Politécnica de Madrid, Spain
Gefei Zhang	arvato Systems Technologies GmbH, Germany

4th International Workshop
on Lightweight Integration on the Web
(ComposableWeb 2012)

ComposableWeb focuses on research, practical experiences, and novel ideas in the context of component-based development of Web applications, lightweight composition on the Web, and Web mashups. The goal of the workshop is to provide a discussion forum for researchers and practitioners working in these areas and to jointly advance the state of the art. The workshop typically attracts enthusiastic people that like to play with novel technologies and that try to make application development accessible also to less-skilled developers or—as envisioned by many—even to end-users.

ComposableWeb 2012, the fourth edition of the workshop, was again held in conjunction with the International Conference on Web Engineering (ICWE), which it complements with a more experimental and technology-centric focus.

The scientific program of this year's edition of the workshop consisted of six papers and one keynote. All submissions went through a rigorous review process by our Program Committee, and only submissions with positive feedback were selected for publication. Among the accepted papers, the reader will find a model-driven approach to data mashups, an extension of the W3C widget model for inter-widget communication, an approach for the development of cooperative mobile mashups, a natural language-based development paradigm for mashups, a visualization technique for RSS feeds, and work on how to extract API models from API documentations. The keynote was held by Oscar Díaz from the University of the Basque Country in Spain and concentrated on Web augmentation, the practice of enhancing existing Web applications with new features and functionalities inside the client browser.

ComposableWeb 2012 was a full-day workshop. It started with a short intro by the organizers, followed by the keynote by Oscar Díaz. The second and third sessions of the workshop were dedicated to the presentation and discussion of the selected papers. Thanks to the lively participation of the audience (40–50 people), the last session turned into an interesting debate of the topics related to the presented papers as well as of some considerations regarding the scientific approach and rigor that characterizes the specific area of mashups and that of Web engineering in general. The main outcome of this discussion is the identification of the need for rigorous validation and evaluation of proposals, and, related, the comparison of approaches and results. This comparison may come in different forms, such as the implementation of a common reference scenario by different authors (as known from the various scientific 'challenges' competitions) or the availability of benchmark data for specific application areas (as know from database research). Both options may be taken into account in the next edition of the workshop.

Concluding, we would like to thank all the authors who contributed to the workshop with their papers and presentations, Oscar Díaz for his insightful keynote speech, our Program Committee for the constructive and competent feedback, and the audience for participating and actively contributing to the final discussion. We thank the ICWE organizers and Workshop Chairs for hosting the workshop and for providing a nice, relaxed, and constructive environment.

August 2012   The Organizers

Organizers

Florian Daniel	University of Trento, Italy
Sven Casteleyn	Universidad Politécnica de Valencia, Spain
Geert-Jan Houben	Delft University of Technology, The Netherlands

Program Committee

Luciano Baresi	Politecnico di Milano, Italy
Boualem Benatallah	University of New South Wales, Australia
Fabio Casati	University of Trento, Italy
Olga De Troyer	Vrije Universiteit Brussel, Belgium
Schahram Dustdar	Vienna University of Technology, Austria
Peep Küngas	University of Tartu, Estonia
Maristella Matera	Politecnico di Milano, Italy
Tobias Nestler	SAP, Germany
Moira C. Norrie	ETH Zurich, Switzerland
Gustavo Rossi	Universidad Nacional de La Plata, Argentina

Third Workshop on the Web and Requirements Engineering (WeRE 2012)

Nowadays, the advance of the Internet and the increasing need for high-performing information systems that agree with user expectations advise highlighting the requirements engineering tasks in the software development lifecycle. In the context of Web engineering, end users are frequently unknown, maintenance and traceability requirements are complex, and aspects such as navigation, safety, or interface acquire a high level of criticality. Therefore new technologies, tools, and methodological solutions are needed to ensure the quality of the results according to the elicited requirements.

The International Workshop on Web and Requirements Engineering (WeRE) aims to bring together experts interested in the proposal and development of solutions that help to improve the quality of work requirements in the environment of Web engineering. In this third edition, we received a total of eight papers, four of which were accepted, representing a 50% acceptance rate. The contributions belong to authors of seven countries from both academia and industry. As in previous years, we put a special emphasis in the relationship with the enterprise environment and the need to involve the business community. Therefore, we invited Pilar Calvo Charneco, in charge of the Administration and Finance Office of Everis Seville, Spain. She presented a keynote on the relevance of motivation in the field of requirements engineering. The companies Everis and Sadiel Inc. demonstrated their interest in the workshop by sponsoring the event.

The workshop was a meeting point that allowed for discussion and debate on different crucial aspects in the field of Web requirements engineering. We focused the discussion on traceability of requirements, application of early testing and its advantages and drawbacks, and the use of the model-driven paradigm for monitoring. These points attracted great interest from the audience. All editions of the workshop showed the need to continue with research in the WeRE area and seek better solutions for the treatment, maintenance, and management of software requirements in the context of Web engineering.

We would like to thank the ICWE 2012 organization for giving us the opportunity to organize this workshop, especially the Workshop Chairs, Manuel Wimmer and Michael Grossniklaus. Many thanks to all those that submitted papers and, in particular, to Pilar Calvo Charneco for presenting the point of view of her company in her keynote talk. Our thanks also go to the reviewers and the members of the Program Committee, for their timely and accurate reviews, for their help selecting the papers, and for their constructive comments that allowed for improvement of the contributions. Finally, we would like to mention that WeRE 2012 was partially organized within the context of the MANTRA project (GV/2011/035) from Valencia Government (Spain) and the Tempros project of the Ministerio de Educación y Ciencia (TIN2010-20057-C03-02).

August 2012   The Organizers

Organizers

María José Escalona	University of Seville, Spain
Irene Garrigós	University of Alicante, Spain
Nora Koch	Ludwig-Maximilians-Universität München and NTT DATA, Germany
Jose-Norberto Mazón	University of Alicante, Spain

Program Committee

José Alfonso Aguilar	Universidad Autónoma de Sinaloa, Mexico
João Araújo	Universidade Nova de Lisboa, Portugal
Davide Bolchini	Indiana University, USA
Sven Casteleyn	Universidad Politécnica de Valencia, Spain
Florian Daniel	University of Trento, Italy
Xavi Franch	Universitat Politècnica de Catalunya, Spain
Piero Fraternalli	Politecnico di Milano, Italy
Athula Ginige	University of Western Sydney, Australia
Paolo Giorgini	University of Trento, Italy
Emilio Insfran	Universidad Politécnica de Valencia, Spain
Ivan Jureta	University of Namur, Belgium
David Lowe	University of Technology, Sydney, Australia
María Angeles Moraga	Universidad de Castilla-La Mancha, Spain
Ana Moreira	Universidade Nova de Lisboa, Portugal
Gustavo Rossi	Universidad Nacional de La Plata, Argentina
Ambrosio Toval	University of Murcia, Spain
Roel Wieringa	University of Twente, The Netherlands
Eric Yu	University of Toronto, Canada
Didar Zowghi	University of Technology, Sydney, Australia

Third International Workshop
on Quality in Web Engineering
(QWE 2012)

The development of Web applications is continuously increasing. In fact, they enable companies to deliver services and products at a distance. The main goal of such applications should be the satisfaction of the customer needs, and thus quality aspects should be one of the main factors of Web application projects. Recent studies have instead found that quality features are scarcely considered.

New methods and techniques that help to improve the quality of delivered Web applications are needed. This is the motivation that led us to organize the third edition of the International Workshop on Quality in Web Engineering (QWE 2012) that was held in conjunction with the 12th International Conference on Web Engineering (ICWE 2012).

The purpose of the workshop was to discuss the effectiveness of existing approaches for evaluating and managing the quality of Web resources (e.g., quality models, quality evaluation methods, information quality tools, logging tools, automatic metric capture tools), with the final objective of allowing researchers and practitioners to discuss recent trends and open issues. Special emphasis was placed on Web engineering methods, and the way in which their early artifacts (process and product models) can improve both the quality of the development process and the quality of the final applications and content. This includes, among other aspects, discussing the way in which Web engineering methods can be further empowered by taking into account quality principles and by integrating sound quality assessment techniques that have proven their effectiveness (review guidelines, usability models, usability evaluation methods, usability checkers, accessibility verifiers, information quality tools, logging tools, automatic metric capture tools, statistical tools, etc.). The accepted papers mainly contribute to this direction. In fact, they focus on the quality assessment of courseware Web applications and on the quality measurement and evaluation strategies of generic Web applications, the latter also providing guidelines for improvement. Furthermore, the workshop also tried to encourage a discussion on the current trends in the creation of modern Web applications, commonly referred to as Web 2.0 applications. Such discussion was also facilitated by the invited talk, which, in particular, highlights issues related to the knowledge that can be retrieved from Web 2.0 sources. The talk confirms that the coverage and quality of the Web sources are important issues, but it is also necessary to consider that much of the knowledge they contain is uncertain. Methods to quantify this uncertainty are needed.

We would like to thank the invited speaker Gjergji Kasneci from the Hasso-Plattner-Institut and the authors for submitting their papers to the workshop and contributing to the interesting discussion during the workshop. We are also grateful to the members of the Steering Committee for their support and advice, to the members of the workshop Program Committee for their efforts in the reviewing process, and to the ICWE organizers for their support and assistance in the production of these proceedings. More details on the workshop are available on its website http://users.dsic.upv.es/workshops/qwe12/.

August 2012   The Organizers

Organizers

Cinzia Cappiello   Politecnico di Milano, Italy
Adrián Fernández   Universidad Politécnica de Valencia, Spain
Luis Olsina   Universidad Nacional de La Pampa, Argentina

Steering Committee

Silvia Abrahão   Universidad Politécnica de Valencia, Spain
Cristina Cachero   University of Alicante, Spain
Cinzia Cappiello   Politecnico di Milano, Italy
Maristella Matera   Politecnico di Milano, Italy

Program Committee

Shadi Abou-Zahra   W3C Web Accessibility Initiative
Carlo Batini   Università di Milano-Bicocca, Italy
Giorgio Brajnik   University of Udine, Italy
Paolo Buono   Università degli Studi di Bari, Italy
Ismael Caballero   University of Castilla-La Mancha, Spain
Coral Calero   University of Castilla-La Mancha, Spain
Tiziana Catarci   University of Rome, Italy
Sven Casteleyn   Universidad Politécnica de Valencia, Spain
Florian Daniel   University of Trento, Italy
Bernd Heinrich   University of Innsbruck, Austria
Emilio Insfran   Universidad Politécnica de Valencia, Spain
Sergio Luján   University of Alicante, Spain
Vicente Luque Centeno   University Carlos III, Spain
Geert Poels   Ghent University, Belgium
Roberto Polillo   Università degli Studi di Milano-Bicocca, Italy
Gustavo Rossi   Universidad Nacional de La Plata, Argentina
Carmen Santoro   ISTI-CNR, Italy
Monica Scannapieco   University of Rome, Italy
Marco Winckler   Paul Sabatier University, France

ICWE 2012
Doctoral Consortium

The ICWE 2012 Doctoral Consortium aim was to improve the research of PhD students and broaden their perspectives by giving them the opportunity to share and develop their research ideas in a critical but supportive environment in an international atmosphere. This event brought together PhD students working on topics related to the Web engineering field. They got feedback from mentors who are senior members of the Web engineering community, they improved their communication skills, exchanged ideas, and built relationships with other international Web engineering PhD students.

We received a total of nine papers; five of them were accepted, representing a 55% of acceptance. The submissions were from seven different countries: Germany, Slovakia, Japan, Tunisia, France, Spain, and Argentina.

Participants discussed their research ideas and results and they received constructive feedback from an audience consisting of their peers as well as more senior researchers experts in the field. After the presentation of the work, there was a further discussion during lunch in a relaxed atmosphere, with the support of Doctoral Consortium PC members.

We would like to thank the support of the ICWE 2012 organization team, especially the Workshop Chairs, Manuel Wimmer and Michael Grossniklaus. Also we would like to thank the students participating and the Doctoral Consortium PC members for their accurate reviews and constructive comments. We would especially like to thank the PC members who acted as mentors, who did an excellent job and gave very good feedback to students.

August 2012   The Chairs

Doctoral Consortium Chairs

Irene Garrigós   University of Alicante, Spain
Óscar Pastor   Universidad Politécnica de Valencia, Spain

Program Committee

Sven Casteleyn   Universidad Politécnica de Valencia, Spain
Florian Daniel   University of Trento, Italy
Olga De Troyer   Vrije Universiteit Brussel, Belgium
Oscar Díaz   University of the Basque Country, Spain
Peter Dolog   Aalborg University, Denmark
Martin Gaedke   Chemnitz University of Technology, Germany
Geert-Jan Houben   Delft University of Technology, The Netherlands

Gerti Kappel	Vienna University of Technology, Austria
Jose-Norberto Mazón	University of Alicante, Spain
Gustavo Rossi	Universidad Nacional de La Plata, Argentina
Daniel Schwabe	PUC-RIO, Brazil
Francisco Valverde	Universidad Politécnica de Valencia, Spain

Table of Contents

Third Workshop on the Web and Requirements Engineering (WeRE)

Third International Workshop on Quality in Web Engineering (QWE)

ICWE 2012 Doctoral Consortium

An Agile Model-Based Framework
for Service Innovation for the Future Internet

Arne J. Berre

SINTEF, Oslo, Norway
arne.j.berre@sintef.no

Abstract. Service innovation for the future internet, with service design and service engineering, can benefit from a combination of an agile and model-based development approach. An agile approach is focusing on early understanding of user needs and service touchpoints to optimise for the best user experience and rapid adaptation to emerging user needs. A model based approach allows for a combination of various domain specific language that are suited for expressing services on different abstraction levels, aimed at supporting higher productivity and quality in service engineering. This approach presents an agile model-based framework using the emerging OMG domain specific standard languages VDML, BPMN, IFML and SoaML for service design and engineering, relating value models, process models, user interface and interaction flow models, and service architectures and service contract models. The associated methodology and set of practices can be supported by the emerging OMG FACESEM standard (a Foundation for the Agile Creation and Enactment of Software Engineering Methods).

Keywords: Future Internet, Agile, Model-based, Service Innovation.

1   Introduction and Motivation

To better support the creation of innovative services for the future internet, it is suggested to combine the practices and techniques of the service design [1] and the software engineering communities [2]. Service innovation for the future internet, with service design and service engineering, can benefit from a combination of an agile and model-based development approach. An agile approach is focusing on early understanding of user needs and service touchpoints to optimise for the best user experience and rapid adaptation to emerging user needs. A model based approach allows for a combination of various domain specific language that are suited for expressing services on different abstraction levels, aimed at supporting higher productivity and quality in service engineering. The different domain specific languages can be selected to support the different perspectives required for a holistic system specification, based on the perspectives identified in various Enterprise Architecture frameworks. These frameworks typically describes a system both on different abstraction levels and from different stakeholders view, as well as from different perspectives like structure, function, process, data etc.. In order to support agility, the description languages need to support different abstraction levels.

M. Grossniklaus and M. Wimmer (Eds.): ICWE 2012 Workshops, LNCS 7703, pp. 1–4, 2012.
© Springer-Verlag Berlin Heidelberg 2012

2   Agile Model-Based Framework

There is a number of Enterprise Architecture frameworks with a multi viewpoint approach for abstraction levels and perspectives (Zachman., RM-ODP, TOGAF, UPDM).   The ASD (Agile Service Development) framework [2] is one that also includes user interaction as a separate perspective in addition to structure, function, coordination, information and extra functional aspects. The abstraction levels goes from requirements to design, implementation and infrastructure. Figure 1 illustrates a proposal for how different recent modeling languages can be used to support the various perspectives. Each of these comes with associated development practices. The suggested modeling languages are all existing standards from OMG, OASIS or W3C, or emerging languages in this context. These languages are well suited for their particular perspectives, but currently not designed to work harmonised together, and sometimes also contains more concepts and complexity than needed for a certain abstraction level. It is thus suggested to start an effort to create a coherent set of co-working languages with a foundation in the conceptual model of the existing languages. The agility emphasizes strong interactions with users and practitioners in dynamically adapting the models to emerging user needs. The emerging FACESEM/ESSENCE standard [6] from OMG (Foundation for the Agile Creation and Enactment of Software Engineering Methods) can be used to support the composition and agile adaptation of such practices.

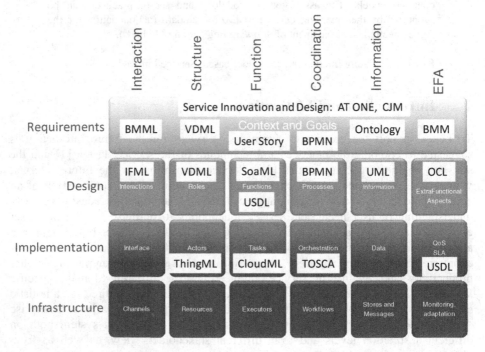

Fig. 1. Agile Service Development framework with modeling languages

3   Service Innovation and Service Design for the Future Internet

The community of service design has created a number of methods and practices independent from the software engineering community [1], they tend to focus more on interactive workshop activities and informal "sticky notes" for their documentation, rather than using formal modeling languages.

As an example the AT ONE method [1] takes an agile workshop-oriented approach to the identification of Actors, Touchpoints, Opportunities, Needs and Experiences, with a foundation in identifying innovative services with good user experiences. One integrated technique for this is CJM (Customer Journey Maps) [1], which illustrates the user experiences through the service journey between service provider and service user. This comes together with a number of creativity techniques to foster the innovation of services. The requirements engineering and software and service engineering communities could benefit well from integrating and adapting a number of the service design practices into their practices portfolio, and the service design community would benefit from the possibility to easier create prototype services for earlier and quicker user feedbacks. In particular for the creation of innovative services for the future internet it is of high importance to be able to do this as quickly as possible. Both a top down and a bottom up approach should be combined for this.

4   Business Level Requirements with Modeling Language Support

The following shows a number of modeling languages which are suitable for a direct language support for the various perspectives in the Agile Service Development framework [2].

Interaction can be supported with user interface mockups, as has been illustrated in [3], with mockups that also can be a basis for further generation of actual user interfaces through exchange languages such as BMML. Structure can be supported with VDML– Value Delivery Modeling Language [6] – an emerging standard from OMG focusing on value transfers in role collaboration and business activities. Function can be supported in an agile way by user stories in the spirit of agile requirements engineering [4] with a potential further refinement into use cases. Coordination can be supported by business level BPMN (Business Process Modeling Notation) [6]. Information can be supported by term definitions and relationships through ontologies, and representations in various graphical and textual forms as in ODM (Ontology Definition Metamodel) [6]. Extra functional aspects can be supported by BMM (Business Motivation Metamodel) [6], which focuses on identification of business vision and goals related to strategies with supporting processes and services.

5   Design and Implementation with Modeling Language Support

The following shows a number of modeling languages that are suitable for representation of the different design and implementation perspectives. Interaction can be supported through the emerging IFML (Interaction Flow Modeling Language) [6], which provides a platform independent approach for the specification of user interface dialogues. Structure with roles can be supported with VDML– Value Delivery Modeling Language [6] and the role models being related also to roles in SoaML for provisioning of services and further to the role of sensors in ThingML [7]. Function with services can be supported by service descriptions in SoaML (Service oriented architecture Modeling Language) from OMG, and also be further supported by USDL (Universal Service Description Language) which is being studied in W3C [8]. This can be supported further for realisation in Cloud environments using CloudML [7]. Coordination with processes can be supported by system level BPMN (Business Process Modeling Notation) [6], and further mappings to BPEL and TOSCA [9] for implementation level support for services and cloud environments. Information can be supported by further modeling through UML enhanced class diagrams, and have further mappings to representations in databases and semantic technologies. Extra functional aspects can be supported by constraints specification in various constraint languages, such as OCL (Object Constraint Language) [6].

6   Conclusion

Agile and model driven development for the Web and the Future Internet is a promising combination, in order to rapidly produce innovative services. Emerging modeling languages from OMG and others, with appropriate integration of language subsets, can be used as a good foundation for executable support for the various perspectives. There is a potential good synergy between the service design community and the software engineering community to foster the support for better service and software innovation. Thanks to partners in CSI, Center for Service Innovation, and the European projects NEFFICS, REMICS and ENVIROFI, for stimulating discussions and early experiments related to this approach.

References

1. Stickdorn, M., Schneider: This is Service Design Thinking. Wiley (2012), 1118156307
2. Lankhorst, M.: Agile Service Development. Springer (2012) ISBN 3642281877
3. Rivero, et al.: From mockups to user interface models. In: MDWE 2010 (2010)
4. Leffingwell, D.: Agile Software Requirements. Addison-Wesley (2010), 0321635841
5. Balsamiq – BMML, http://www.balsamiq.com/
6. OMG, OMG modeling standards, http://www.omg.org
7. SINTEF, ThingML and CloudML,
   http://www.thingml.org, http://www.cloudml.org
8. W3C, USDL, http://www.w3.org/2005/Incubator/usdl/
9. OASIS, TOSCA, https://www.oasis-open.org/committees/tosca

Web Engineering for Cloud Computing
(Web Engineering Forecast: Cloudy with a Chance of Opportunities)

Giovanni Toffetti

Faculty of Informatics, University of Lugano

Abstract. Web Engineering has always been concerned with modelling the *functional* aspects of Web applications. *Non-functional* (e.g., performance, availability) properties of Web applications have traditionally been a minor concern in the Web engineering community and have been seen as technology- or system-related issues. The advent of Cloud computing, with substantial delegation of "system concerns" to infrastructure or platform providers, seems at a first sight to confirm the validity of this choice. But is this really true?

We will argue that, in order to be able to actually profit from the Cloud computing paradigm, Web Engineering methodologies need several interventions transcending the platform-specific concerns of adapting to Cloud technologies.

In this position paper, we call for a long-due revamp of Web engineering methodologies to become more **sound engineering practices** with respect to both functional and non-functional aspects of Web applications. To this end, we propose a methodological framework that preserves the advantages of model-driven development, but also takes into account performance and cost considerations for Cloud-based applications.

1 Introduction

In a recent report Gartner predicts that by 2015 "most enterprises will have part of their run-the-business software functionally executing in the cloud, using PaaS services or technologies directly or indirectly" and "cloud-based solutions will be growing at a faster rate than on-premises solutions" [13]. Indeed, the pace of adoption of cloud-technologies is staggering, driven by the realization by companies that (at least for some applications) the advantages of the pay-per-use utility model of software, platform, and infrastructure as a service (SaaS, PaaS, IaaS) outweighs today the CAPEX and OPEX of traditional in-house data centres.

Cloud computing pledges to free Web application providers from the burden of managing the Web infrastructure and applications running on it. The direct emanation of a pay-per-use model is the focus on application *elasticity*, meaning that providers can at any time change the amount of resources (e.g., virtual machines, CPUs, disks) assigned to applications maintaining constant QoS (i.e., their performance) and adapting their cost to the incoming workload.

Some Cloud providers already advertise their platforms claiming that porting a traditional Web application to the Cloud is as simple as uploading its ".war" file

M. Grossniklaus and M. Wimmer (Eds.): ICWE 2012 Workshops, LNCS 7703, pp. 5–19, 2012.

to their systems. This is true, in the sense that the application will effectively run, but there is a small catch: generally **it will not scale**. Thus, this naive approach would only work for applications that do not need to support a considerable and varying number of users, hence probably have no real financial motivation behind Cloud adoption. For an enterprise application, where SLAs, serving multiple users, and data-intensive usage are the norm, moving to the Cloud means it will have to **support elasticity** in all its architectural constituents: from dynamic reconfiguration all the way to scalable technologies.

In this paper, we advocate that Cloud computing is a **great opportunity for the Web engineering community**. On one hand, Web engineering (WebEng) methodologies can become the enablers of new SaaS providers that design, test, deploy, and manage applications in a single online environment without requiring programming skills. On the other hand, and in order for these applications to scale, WebEng methodologies need to, at the very least, adapt their runtime and code generation mechanisms.

We go the full way and claim that also the modelling primitives and methodologies need a revamp. As main evidence to support this observation we will elaborate on the following two considerations: 1) some systemic trade-offs (e.g., consistency vs. availability vs. partition tolerance [4]) imply a *range of decisions that vertically span multiple modelling layers* through the complete application life-cycle; and 2) some of the main reasons to move to the Cloud are elasticity, the pay-per-use model, and the savings they imply: *non-functional aspects of Cloud applications reflect directly on their **cost and rentability**,* hence WebEng simply cannot afford not to consider them.

The main contributions of this paper are:

- An analysis of how to *enable Web engineering methodologies to address Cloud computing development* in terms of code generation, modelling primitives, Cloud patterns and elasticity;
- the prospect of *Web engineering as a service*, a viable opportunity to foster elastic application modelling;
- a *methodological framework* to address both the functional and *non-functional quality* of Web applications in the Cloud, preserving the advantages and flexibility of Web engineering methodologies.

The rest of this article is organized as follows: Section 2 gives a high level overview of cloud computing paradigms and common patterns; Section 3 justifies the need for adaptation, and describes the different integration scenarios between Cloud computing paradigms and Web engineering. Section 4 discusses whether the aspects currently covered by Web Engineering methodologies are still adequate for Cloud development, Section 5 proposes an extended methodological framework catering for non-functional aspect for continuous development in WebEng; Section 6 comments on the related work. Finally, Section 7 draws conclusions and illustrates our planned future work.

2   Cloud Computing in a Nutshell

The Cloud computing paradigm is typically characterized as either software, platform, or infrastructure *"as a service"*, respectively *SaaS*, *PaaS*, and *IaaS*, where being *a service* implies billing. Each characterization sees two actors: the cloud provider and the cloud user together with a different amount of responsibility and control.

In *SaaS*, the service being delivered is an application, a software accessed with a remote client, typically provided with some guarantees in terms of quality (QoS) expressed in terms of service level objectives (SLOs). The Cloud user normally pays a flat rate amount (monthly, yearly) to access the service and delegates the complete responsibility of managing the application, platform, and infrastructure upon which it runs to the service provider. For the client this is the simplest approach to cloud computing: it does not require any knowledge or experience about platforms and infrastructure technologies; the service offered is the application functionality and all non-functional aspects are delegated to the provider's responsibility. An example of a SaaS instance is the service offered by Salesforce.com, a company offering pre-packaged (and customizable) customer relationship management (CRM) solutions "as a service" to other companies.

In *PaaS*, the service being offered is a "platform" in the sense of an application runtime environment together with generic application functionalities (e.g., database storage, event buses, messaging, authentication). The cloud client pays for the service of utilizing a runtime (often also development) environment and delegates to the platform provider the activities of managing the elasticity and the infrastructure running the applications. Each platform in the PaaS sense is a coherent set of technologies selected and managed by the cloud provider. They are typically packaged in application programming interfaces (APIs) that are specific of the chosen PaaS provider. Currently this is one of the main obstacles to Cloud interoperability, since PaaS APIs are very heterogeneous due to the different technologies adopted by providers. Even though the PaaS market is supposed to be consolidating in a few years into a small numbers of "big" providers [13], this might of course still result in vendor lock-in situations. PaaS is intended for application developers, hence more advanced users with respect to SaaS, that are willing to pay cloud providers to manage the infrastructure and platform supporting their application logic. Two quite different examples of PaaS solutions are Google App Engine and CloudBees. The former allows developers to build applications using the same scalable solutions powering some Google products (e.g., BigTable, GFS) on the Google infrastructure; the latter is targeted at development and deploy of Java Web applications with additional generic services (e.g., monitoring, logging, storage) on top of third party infrastructure providers, for example Amazon EC2.

IaaS builds mainly on virtualization: Cloud providers offer infrastructural resources (e.g., CPUs, RAM, bandwidth) as a service for running third party applications typically packaged in virtual machines (VMs). The service level agreements between infrastructure providers and cloud users only deal with provisioning and availability of resources for the VMs. In this scenario, application developers have the most control on their application: apart from developing its functional logic, they can select the platform to use for development and deploy, and they have control on the number of virtual machines (and therefore on the amount and cost of resources) assigned to their application. Infrastructure providers retain the control on the actual physical data center infrastructure. Examples of IaaS are for instance Amazon EC2, Microsoft Azure, Rackspace, and GoGrid.

2.1 Cloud Patterns

Modern massively-scalable Web applications rely on different patterns and technological solutions with respect to traditional Web applications. While the three-tier architectural model still holds, each of the tiers had to undergo some restructuring in order to enable elasticity. Given the space limitations, here we give only a short list of the main issues addressed in elastic Cloud applications, they are:

Load balancing and HTTP sessions: Load balancers are used to spread the load across the multiple instances of VMs that compose an application. HTTP Sessions are typically stored at the application server layer, and load balancers have to forward requests for each user to the application server hosting the correct session (*"sticky sessions"*). Some PaaS providers (e.g., Cloudbees) do not support sticky sessions for some usage configurations, and suggest using session-specific datasources to persist all session-related variables so that they are shared by all VMs.

Dynamic reconfiguration: A common pattern for enterprise solutions is to realize Web applications as compositions of Web services offered by different components. When horizontally scaling any of this components by adding or removing a VM, all the components that directly communicate with it need to be notified and/or reconfigured. A typical solution is using enterprise service buses (ESB) to achieve de-coupling.

Storage, NoSQL, and sharding: This is probably the most notable paradigmatic change for Cloud-based Web applications. In his first conjecture of the CAP theorem, Brewer postulated [4] that it is impossible for a distributed system to provide at the same time consistency, availability, and partition tolerance. Much in this direction, Cloud application providers have soon realized that relational databases are able to scale only up to a point, then consistency (the 'C' in 'ACID') eventually has to be given up for improved availability and better partition-tolerance (i.e., ultimately for horizontal scalability). In other terms, the "blocking" needed for consistency might be negligible for small applications, but might become a hinderance when apps need to grow in size. One of the outcomes of these considerations is the thriving world of *NoSQL* approaches for "not-so-structured" storage of key-value pairs, documents, blobs. NoSQL is the term vaguely identifying the wide range of data management systems relaxing some of the ACID properties for the sake of horizontal scalability (i.e., adding instances). Several NoSQL solutions are widely adopted, for instance BigTable, Cassandra, Memcached, MongoDB, Apache CouchDB, and Voldemort. Apart from scalability, these solutions are typically adopted also because they offer very low latency and flexibility to schema changes or no predefined schemas at all. NoSQL solutions are no silver bullet: some application scenarios have hard consistency requirements and the best option in this case is still using RDBMS, but in some other cases (e.g. Web2 social applications) dirty reads might be tolerated and, if needed, recovery policies might be implemented at the application level. NoSQL solutions widen the spectrum of design choices for storage management. A recent comparison of scalable data stores is provided by Cattell in [6].

Multi-tenancy: a multi-tenant architecture is one that serves a single software to multiple "tenants". Tenants can be different organizations, company divisions, or generic clients. In a multi-tenant architecture data and processing for each client may have different ranges of sharing/isolation requirements (e.g., for data: dedicated physical servers, shared virtualized hosts, dedicated database on shared servers, dedicated schema within shared database, shared tables) as well as customization (e.g., schema customization, UI customization). Higher isolation translates into higher costs for the software (SaaS) provider. Multi-tenancy goes hand in hand with Cloud computing, since the SaaS provider can for instance leverage application elasticity to serve multiple global clients working across time zones with one customizable application and relatively few VM instances. A representative example is Salesforce.com that has "72,500 customers who are supported by 8 to 12 multi-tenant instances (meaning IaaS/PaaS instances) in a 1:5000 ratio. In other words, each multi-tenant instance supports 5,000 tenants who share the same database schema"[1]. Multi-tenancy is a key resource for software providers, since it allows optimizing and reducing costs for serving software to multiple clients.

MapReduce and large scale data processing: MapReduce [14] is a programming model for the *distributed* processing of large datasets. While its initial (and still main) purpose is to be used for the massive parallelization on commodity hardware of long-running tasks, in common practice it is also used in NoSQL databases for data processing and even simple aggregation queries over distributed datasets (e.g., in MongoDB[2]). The most widely known implementation of MapReduce is Apache Hadoop[3].

3   Web Engineering Concerns

Web engineering methodologies can potentially become the enablers of new Saas providers that use a single interface to *seamlessly model, deploy, run, manage, evolve, and sell* new Cloud-based Web applications. These SaaS providers will not need to own any computing infrastructure, but their only required assets will be modelling tools and the models of applications to be sold. This is very much in line with Gartner's expectations for the medium term: "By 2015, 50% of all

---

[1] http://www.computerworld.com/s/article/9175079/
Multi_tenancy_in_the_cloud_Why_it_matters_?
[2] http://www.mongodb.org/display/DOCS/MapReduce
[3] http://hadoop.apache.org

new application independent software vendors (ISVs) will be pure software-as-a-service (SaaS) providers" [13].

In order to do this, it is up to the WebEng community to seize the opportunity and update the current methodologies and tools. In the following paragraphs we will discuss why and how, but first, with the sole purpose of identifying the main areas of intervention, we need to briefly sketch what a WebEng approach looks like. Simplifying, we can roughly say that a generic Web engineering approach consists of:

- a *methodology* covering the complete Web application life-cycle;
- *platform-independent models* (data, "navigational", etc.);
- tools for model visualization and *editing*;
- tools for model transformation / *code generation*;
- libraries for the *runtime* support of the generated Web applications.

In WebEng, the separation between *platform independent* and *platform dependent* models and realizations is the abstraction that frees Web engineers from considering the technological details of the actual Web deployment letting them concentrate on the (core) functionality of their applications. The realization of platform-independent models (e.g., data and navigational models) into platform-dependent models (the application code / library configurations) is accomplished by the code-generation tools that embed the mapping / realization choices hiding them (and typically preventing changes) from developers.

We claim that for WebEng to support Cloud-based Web applications interventions are needed to:

1. adapt the runtime support and code generation techniques to Cloud APIs and technologies (platforms). This is a technological aspect required to address *elastic* Web applications;
2. include paradigmatic changes and patterns in the platform-independent models, and consequently update model editors. The aim is that of generalizing common patterns and make them available as clear design options to the application designer/analyst;
3. make modelling tools available for online usage, integrate with PaaS/IaaS providers realizing the view of *"Web modelling as a Service"*.

Admittedly, the third is not really a hard requirement, but rather a new and promising opportunity for WebEng approaches.

3.1   Code Generation

Current WebEng tools can generate Web application code for different platforms (e.g., Java, .NET) but are typically not concerned with systemic aspect of the production deployment, such as load balancing, scaling out, replication, and performances in general. In Section 2, we have seen how considerable effort has been invested in addressing application elasticity in Cloud development together with a brief list of the specific technologies that make this possible. These technologies can be accessed in different ways depending on the chosen Cloud model (PaaS or IaaS).

PaaS Deployment. In this scenario, the set of available elastic technologies is limited and depends on PaaS provider choices and expertise. This allows PaaS providers to control and manage the scaling out of applications. The biggest problem with PaaS is that in most cases access to scalable services and components needs to go through the PaaS provider API, *locking-in* applications to a single provider's infrastructure.

Considering that addressing all current PaaS providers' APIs is not a viable option, the first step in adapting a WebEng methodology for PaaS deployment would therefore be the choice of the (set of) PaaS provider(s) to support.

Then, for each PaaS provider API, the code generation and runtime support of every single modelling primitive (e.g., units in WebML [7]) would have to be rewritten and tested to invoke the correct provider methods. For instance, in Google App Engine the *default* data storage mechanism is the *"App Engine Datastore"*, an implementation of a NoSQL storage for objects that needs to be reached through a specific API in Java[4]. Only recently, Google extended the App Engine storage options with a relational offer (*"Google Cloud SQL"*) based on MySQL; for the moment being it is still in preview and with some limitations. It is a perfectly plausible scenario one in which, for reasons of opportunity, some application domain entities will be mapped to the relational data storage and some others to the NoSQL one. This is an example of design decision that will have to be made at model level, but needs to be supported by the code generation.

IaaS Deployment. In this scenario the atomic units of deployment are virtual machines (VMs). While each infrastructure provider supports its own VM specification (e.g., AMIs for Amazon EC2) and interoperability is not given as-is, lock-in issues are less severe in IaaS since application providers can freely choose their development platforms and OSs and can (re-)package them as disk images supported by each hypervisor technology.

The main problem instead is identifying and managing a set of components (load balancers, application servers, data storage implementations) so that they can be packaged in a coherent set of VMs, configured through code generation, and appropriately scaled out at runtime. Given the vast number of technologies currently available, it is by itself a challenging endeavour.

A sensible approach for adapting a Web engineering tool for IaaS might be building on pre-packaged (and modular) VMs adopting Cloud-specific patterns such as the ones provided by AppScale[5] [8]. A viable solution would then be updating code generation and runtime libraries to support for example at least one implementation per type of scalable storage (SQL vs NoSQL).

3.2 Model Extension

In our opinion, some of the aspects and patterns we introduced in Section 2.1 deserve to be promoted into platform-independent model concerns. We leave

---

[4] http://code.google.com/appengine/docs/java/datastore/queries.html
[5] http://appscale.cs.ucsb.edu/

the full proposal of how to include them and the evaluation of the possible alternatives to future work. In this paper, we want to give extensive justifications as to why and in which direction WebEng methodologies need to be updated.

For instance, the fact that some PaaS providers do not support sticky sessions can either be kept hidden in the code generation logic or explicitly taken into account at model level. In the first case, when generating code for a specific PaaS, all HTTP session-related logic has to be translated into storage queries and updates. Another option is to make designers aware of this choice by using warning mechanisms to prevent them from using HTTP session. The second choice impacts heavily on navigational modelling, and in case of multiple platforms might require model changes. The positive aspect is that the designer will have a clear perception of what the application actually does and will be aware of the eventual monetary costs and implications of the modelling choices, which might eventually lead to alternative designs.

As we stressed in Section 2, NoSQL storage is probably the Cloud-specific pattern with the most implications. Nowadays it is common for Cloud applications to use a combination of RDBMS and NoSQL data storage respectively to manage entities with hard consistency requirements (e.g., orders, item stocks, tickets, seats) and entities with eventual consistency (e.g., message chats, comments, events, logs). Designers will need to decide which kind of consistency they need for entities in their domain models. We argue this is not just a data mapping concern, since the type of entity (hard- or eventual- consistency) might need different navigational patterns.

We can give some practical examples. For instance, NoSQL objects are typically designed as self-contained elements to be accessed "in one scoop" with a query over a single collection (there are *no join operations* in NoSQL). For example, a blog post and all its comments can be stored and retrieved as a single navigable "object" (very much like beans in EJB) requiring a specific navigational pattern. Also giving up consistency for scalability (using NoSQL) one can find ways to mitigate transactionality: single object in NoSQL can support atomicity, and some failure and roll-back policies could be explicitly modelled at application level. For example, an online shop could use NoSQL data storage to manage items in stock and send out order cancellation notifications at a later time in case of stock depletion.

Multi-tenancy is another very interesting pattern for WebEng. Depending on the level of isolation, a SaaS provider could for example: 1) deploy multiple instances of the same application model with different UIs for each customer; or use the same application model and 2) explicitly trigger user-specific customizations at model level (e.g., add functionalities) as a sort of personalization, or 3) extend the modelling approach to add client customization (e.g., change UI with customer) as a separate/implicit concern to be dealt with at runtime. Many other possibilities are available and deserve some investigation, the message here is that WebEng can prove itself a powerful technique to achieve the rationalization of the SaaS provider multi-tenancy offering.

3.3   Web Engineering as a Service

The natural consequence of "everything as a service" is *Web engineering as a service*, where what is offered is a Web engineering approach as a modelling, development, and management platform. Let's not consider the practical impli-cations of realizing such an environment for the moment; the advantages "on paper" would be:

- no need to install any software, accessibility from everywhere and for every-one (possibly with a browser?);
- easier and more controlled user licensing model for the WebEng approach provider;
- a single interface for modelling, generation, deployment, management of Web application;
- integration with PaaS / IaaS providers, access to online monitoring and management of the deployment;
- one-click deploy of staging / production application models;
- online sharing of models, components, patterns;
- online consulting to solve, help with, signal issues with applications and models;
- immediate signalling and propagation of failure and bug warnings across all deployed applications (in a software product line way).

Clearly, considerable work to extend the current modelling tools would be needed in order to deliver the full functionality. Some of the above advantages are already within reach, some others require investments and a costs and benefits analysis. We believe that in the end it will prove being worth the effort, especially if the WebEng approach can yield measurable benefits when applied to the Cloud paradigm, as we will argue in the following paragraphs.

4   Putting Non-functional Aspects Back on the Map

The Cloud pay-per-use model yields the most financial benefits to companies providing elastic applications (or having flexible requirements). Following this consideration, it is clearly of tantamount importance for elastic applications to be able to *scale efficiently*, that is avoiding to waste resources (hence money) while offering elastic performance. In WebEng concerns, we argue that while it is a good idea to keep platform-specific aspects out of the way, now is a very good time to partially reconsider, since elastic scenarios make non-functional considerations critical. In this section and the next one we suggest how put these aspects back on the map in a non-intrusive (sort-of aspect-oriented) fashion.

As we have already said, platform-independent models in WebEng abstract from technological details to let designers focus on functionality. The downside to this is that, once the technological / system aspects are out of the way, it is very hard to put them back in the loop for an engineer to consider. As a consequence, Web engineering methodologies do not account for *non-functional* aspects (in particular performances) of the modelled applications.

In our opinion the fact that Cloud applications are elastic should be an **incentive**, rather than an excuse not to be concerned with the non-functional properties of Web applications. We try to contend in this direction with two examples.

Let's first consider a PaaS scenario, Google's App Engine for instance. Taking a look at the billing documentation[6] one can see that, apart from virtual machine usage, developers are charged also for datastore operations, and that, in order to limit running costs, they can set a maximum budget for running their apps. While a thorough look at how Google API high-level datastore operations map to low-level (billed) operations might save some money, a developer should make modelling decisions (and receive confirmatory feedback that they work by deploying) preventing the application from consuming its resource quotas and simply stop working[7]. In fact, application instance scaling is controlled by the number of requests in the queue of each machine instance[8]: complex pages mean higher latency, which means lower throughput, queues filling up, and *higher cost for running the application*. The trade-off is therefore between complex feature-rich pages and low latency and lower cost. In the end, given the relatively small control PaaS offer to developers, *fine tuning the application logic* and *knowing in detail the **performance profile*** of each of its page / operation / component are the only instruments available to achieve performance- and cost-effective applications.

For enterprise applications the predicted evolution is that they will partially move to the Cloud, keeping mission-critical resources on premises and following a hybrid (private/public cloud) approach [13]. In this case, a IaaS scenario can accommodate for more technological flexibility than PaaS since application providers can decide which components and platforms to use in their own virtual machines. This will be the most common requirement when adapting/migrating legacy applications to a hybrid cloud environment. In this case, non-functional aspects of applications become even more critical: enterprise applications have to deliver in terms of **QoS** (Quality of Service, e.g., with service level objectives on response times and availability) and face the risk of monetary penalties in case of violations. In IaaS, the design space for application logic, services, components, and VMs is considerable, and application elasticity (and their cost) is under the complete control of the application provider. Hence, in IaaS it is even more essential than in PaaS for application providers to have a **complete grasp of their application behaviour** in functional (F) and non-functional (NF) terms in order to make the right design decisions. The sought equilibrium is striking the balance between under- and over-provisioning, considering the effects that design decisions will have on performances, cost, and revenue.

In the following section we introduce the framework we foresee to support the all-around (F+NF) quality of Web applications deployed on the Cloud.

---

[6] http://code.google.com/appengine/docs/billing.html
[7] http://code.google.com/appengine/docs/quotas.html
[8] http://code.google.com/appengine/docs/adminconsole/instances.html

5   Model-Driven F+NF Quality Framework

The *functional quality* of model-driven applications is one of the **cornerstones** of Web engineering. It stems directly from *software product lines* [18] concepts combined with model-driven development and domain specific languages (DSLs). Briefly, WebEng DSLs allow modelling primitives to be implemented once by expert developers and then consistently reused by instantiating and configuring these primitives in the application models. In WebML [7] for example, the run-time service implementing each type of "unit" is a single parametric class that gets configured at runtime through unit descriptors: one descriptor specifying which attributes to show, how to sort, how to query for each unit instance in the model. The net result of this is that, once the parametric class for a unit has been thoroughly tested, the only way for one of its deployed instances to produce a failure is wrong configuration[9]. Simply said, WebEng DSLs strongly enforce **reuse**, a proven way of **reducing faults** and **improving quality**.

The other great advantage of WebEng approaches with respect to traditional development is **productivity**. Notwithstanding the (still) limited industrial adoption of WebEng techniques, it has been repeatedly proven in practice (see for instance the work by Acerbis et al. [1]) that, where the language primitives are sufficient to represent the needed application logic, model-driven approaches yield an advantage in terms of time and effort needed to design, develop, deploy, and maintain Web applications. There is a general trend that recognises the benefits of factoring out some concerns to be considered as separate aspects (e.g., CSS for style and appearance) in Web development, but so far only WebEng modelling has been able to offer instruments to do it effectively for Web application logic. In the end, increased productivity allows more **flexibility** in face of enterprise-specific and ever-changing requirements, maintenance, and continuous development of new features that are typical of the Web today. No need to recode, re-factor, or deal with software modules and artefacts, just update the model and generate the new code.

Cloud computing *complements the functional flexibility of WebEng DSLs with flexibility in the non-functional aspects*: application elasticity. In order to preserve and combine the benefits of both worlds, we propose an extension to WebEng methodologies that caters for quality (both functional and non-functional) of Cloud-based Web applications across their complete life-cycle. A high-level overview of the framework is shown in Figure 1. For space reasons, we only illustrate it considering the more complete and complex scenario of IaaS deployment. PaaS deployment would only use a subset of the considered activities, which are:

1. **DSL modelling:** to achieve reuse, quality, productivity, and flexibility of a model-driven approach.
2. **Model transformation:** in order to add elasticity to the equation, WebEng *model transformation*, code-generation, and runtime support need to leverage

---

[9] To mitigate this, most WebEng tools provide warning generation mechanisms to prevent misconfigurations by checking the models through language-specific rules.

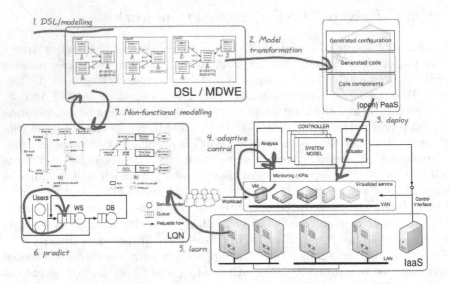

Fig. 1. Quality framework for Cloud-based Web applications

scalable technologies and patterns. Furthermore, appropriate monitoring probes need to be implemented and embedded in VMs to enable runtime monitoring and control [9].

3. **Cloud deployment:** the advantage of using Cloud computing in this case is the relative simplicity in setting up dynamic staging and production environments thanks to virtualization of resources.

4. **Adaptive control:** it consists in the management of the application elasticity. In production, most IaaS providers offer a user interface for dynamically adding and removing virtual machines at runtime, another common approach is to set up *auto-scaling rules* based on some low level metric (e.g., CPU load, memory usage). When considering enterprise applications, with several components and complex service mixes, manual scaling and rules can be too simplistic and model-based controllers are needed [2]. Traditional design-time capacity planning techniques (e.g., linear models, simple queues) also have drawbacks in a Cloud computing setting as they are unable to keep up with changes and emerging behaviour and tend to become unrealistic over time [3]. The solution we suggest is using system performance models to achieve *autonomic control*. For instance, a statistical model and an evaluation is proposed by Bodík et al. in [3]; while the authors propose an approach using Kriging models and their evaluation of model prediction quality in [17].

5. **Learning:** Autonomic controller models keep updating themselves at runtime. The knowledge gathered in this learning process makes the controllers *robust* to the environmental (e.g., workload peaks) and application changes to which Cloud-based systems are constantly exposed.

6. **Prediction:** Collected knowledge from the running system can be leveraged for parameter estimation of layered queue networks (LQN) or other models, allowing performance prediction across the whole application elasticity range.
7. **Non-functional modelling:** Finally, performance models from data obtained at runtime and LQNs can be combined with WebEng models to close the loop. This, as we proposed in [12], enables *modelling taking into account non-functional concerns*. For each modelling action, Web developers can receive an immediate feedback of the effects it will have in terms of system performances and costs. By providing a model of the expected workload range and performance service level objectives (SLOs) for each page / operation, a warning system can be implemented to explicitly signal when SLO violations or budget exceedances are predicted in the workload range.

The users of the framework are not required to be performance experts nor system engineers. In this aspect, all non-functional concerns can be considered separately using software automation. Given a formal set of SLOs, solutions like the ones we proposed in [12] and [17] can be integrated and work in a totally autonomous fashion. In this way, novice users will only receive warnings in case the modelled pages / operations might violate SLOs, while more advanced users will be able to get complete predictions and monitoring of the response time, throughputs, and system configurations. The advantage of this approach is that it allows Web engineers to **change their design incrementally and in a controlled way** keeping at all times application's performances and costs under strict supervision.

6   Related Work

To the best of our knowledge, this is the first work that addresses the problem of adapting Web engineering methodologies for the Cloud computing paradigm; some of its aspects are however not new. The concept of Model-Driven Performance Engineering, for instance, was introduced by Frietzsche and Johannes in [11] and consists annotating models with performance information to enable performance analysis, for example with LQNs as in [15]. As we discuss more extensively in [12] our approach is similar, but in our case we can benefit from a continuous online estimation of LQN parameters and an arbitrarily accurate definition of the LQN starting from WebEng and PaaS models.

Various authors have addressed the topic of migrating applications to the Cloud, focusing in particular on legacy applications as in [16]. With respect to these works, our proposed approach has the unique feature of dealing with model-driven methodologies that, by leveraging reuse, allow for a rationalized migration process. In fact, only the runtime primitives of each modelling language need to be migrated to Cloud-specific technologies (as we explain in Section 3), then model transformation can generate the rest of the needed configuration.

A relatively large amount of work has focused on automatic control of application elasticity, we cited some relevant works in Section 5. With respect to the framework we propose, these are all interchangeable solutions that can be adopted (e.g., different autonomic controller implementations), the paper claims no contribution in this area.

Escalona and Koch survey how WebEng approaches deal with capturing, specifying, and validating Web requirements [10]. However, the considered non-functional requirements are mainly concerning *usability* aspects; no formal specification or assurance of *performance* aspects is explicitly considered by any methodology at platform-independent model level. Instead, in this work, we claim that performance aspects directly reflect on application running costs in a Cloud computing scenario, and therefore should be explicit.

Finally, the concept of "Web engineering as a service" is not new, as it is introduced as "modelling as a service" in [5]. However, this is the first contribution that proposes (admittedly at very high level) a methodology for it that caters for functional, performance, and monetary aspects in the continuous-development life cycle of Web applications.

7 Conclusions

In this paper we discuss how to enable Web engineering methodologies to address Cloud computing development. We report that one of the main economical reasons for Cloud computing adoption is in the savings that the "pay-per-use" model enables for elastic applications.

We argue that current Web engineering methodologies do not make use of elastic technologies and would need an update to support Cloud development. More importantly, we sustain that Web engineering methodologies are generally too focused on functional concerns to be able grasp the main drivers of Cloud-based Web applications, which are performances and costs. To this end, we discuss the main interventions we deem necessary in order to combine the functional flexibility of WebEng DSLs with the flexibility in the non-functional aspects offered by the Cloud paradigm. In particular we relate on: 1) updating code generation and runtime libraries to support elastic technologies; 2) exposing Cloud-specific design decision in platform-independent models; 3) upgrading modelling tools to achieve Web engineering "as a service". Additionally, we propose a methodological framework to extend WebEng methodologies to consider non-functional (and in particular performance) concerns that are crucial in the Cloud pay-per-use model.

Acknowledgments. I wish to thank Florian Daniel at UniTN, Alessio Gambi at USI, Emanuele Molteni and Roberto Acerbis from WebRatio, and Piero Fraternali at PoliMi for the comments and discussions on the subject. I also wish to thank the anonymous reviewers for the valuable suggestions on how to improve the paper.

References

1. Acerbis, R., Bongio, A., Brambilla, M., Tisi, M., Ceri, S., Tosetti, E.: Developing eBusiness Solutions with a Model Driven Approach: The Case of Acer EMEA. In: Baresi, L., Fraternali, P., Houben, G.-J. (eds.) ICWE 2007. LNCS, vol. 4607, pp. 539–544. Springer, Heidelberg (2007)

2. Barna, C., Litoiu, M., Ghanbari, H.: Model-based performance testing: NIER track. In: ICSE, pp. 872–875. IEEE (2011)
3. Bodík, P., Griffith, R., Sutton, C., Fox, A., Jordan, M., Patterson, D.: Statistical machine learning makes automatic control practical for internet datacenters. In: Hot Topics in Cloud Computing, p. 12. USENIX Association (2009)
4. Brewer, E.: Towards robust distributed systems. In: ACM Symposium on Principles of Distributed Systems, pp. 1–12 (2000)
5. Brunelière, H., Cabot, J., Jouault, F.: Combining Model-Driven Engineering and Cloud Computing. In: Modeling, Design, and Analysis for the Service Cloud - MDA4ServiceCloud 2010, Paris, France (June 2010)
6. Cattell, R.: Scalable sql and nosql data stores. ACM SIGMOD Record 39(4), 12–27 (2011)
7. Ceri, S., Fraternali, P., Bongio, A.: Web Modeling Language (WebML): a modeling language for designing Web sites. In: WWW, pp. 137–157. North-Holland Publishing Co., Amsterdam (2000)
8. Chohan, N., Bunch, C., Pang, S., Krintz, C., Mostafa, N., Soman, S., Wolski, R.: Appscale: Scalable and open appengine application development and deployment. In: Cloud Computing, pp. 57–70 (2010)
9. Clayman, S., Galis, A., Toffetti, G., Vaquero, L.M., Rochwerger, B., Massonet, P.: Future Internet Monitoring Platform for Computing Clouds. In: Di Nitto, E., Yahyapour, R. (eds.) ServiceWave 2010. LNCS, vol. 6481, pp. 215–217. Springer, Heidelberg (2010)
10. Escalona, M., Koch, N.: Requirements engineering for web applications-a comparative study. Journal of Web Engineering 2, 193–212 (2004)
11. Fritzsche, M., Johannes, J.: Putting Performance Engineering into Model-Driven Engineering: Model-Driven Performance Engineering. In: Giese, H. (ed.) MoDELS 2007 Workshops. LNCS, vol. 5002, pp. 164–175. Springer, Heidelberg (2008)
12. Gambi, A., Toffetti Carughi, G., Comai, S.: Model-driven web engineering performance prediction with layered queue networks. In: Proceedings of Model-Driven Web Engineering Workshop (MDWE) (2010)
13. Gartner, Inc. Paas road map: A continent emerging (2011), Report ID Number: G00209751
14. Ghemawat, S., Dean, J.: Mapreduce: Simplified data processing on large clusters. In: Symposium on Operating System Design and Implementation (OSDI 2004), San Francisco, CA, USA (2004)
15. Gu, G.P., Petriu, D.C.: Xslt transformation from uml models to lqn performance models. In: WOSP 2002: Proceedings of the 3rd International Workshop on Software and Performance, pp. 227–234 (2002)
16. Hajjat, M., Sun, X., Sung, Y.-W.E., Maltz, D., Rao, S., Sripanidkulchai, K., Tawarmalani, M.: Cloudward bound: planning for beneficial migration of enterprise applications to the cloud. In: Proceedings of the ACM SIGCOMM 2010 Conference, SIGCOMM 2010, pp. 243–254. ACM, New York (2010)
17. Toffetti, G., Gambi, A., Pezzè, M., Pautasso, C.: Engineering Autonomic Controllers for Virtualized Web Applications. In: Benatallah, B., Casati, F., Kappel, G., Rossi, G. (eds.) ICWE 2010. LNCS, vol. 6189, pp. 66–80. Springer, Heidelberg (2010)
18. van der Linden, F.J., Schmid, K., Rommes, E.: Software Product Lines in Action: The Best Industrial Practice in Product Line Engineering. Springer (2007)

Developing Semantic Rich Internet Applications with the S^m4RIA Extension for OIDE

Jesús M. Hermida[1], Santiago Meliá[1], Jose-Javier Martínez[2],
Andrés Montoyo[1], and Jaime Gómez[1]

[1] Department of Software and Computing Systems, University of Alicante
Apartado de Correos 99, E-03080 Alicante, Spain
{jhermida,santi,montoyo,jgomez}@dlsi.ua.es
[2] InsideSoft IT Consulting, Spain
jjmartinez@insidesoft.es

Abstract. This paper introduces the S^m4RIA Extension for OIDE, which implements the S^m4RIA approach in OIDE (OOH4RIA Integrated Development Environment). The application, based on the Eclipse framework, supports the design of the S^m4RIA models as well as the model-to-model and model-to-text transformation processes that facilitate the generation of Semantic Rich Internet Applications, i.e., RIA applications capable of sharing data as Linked data and consuming external data from other sources in the same manner. Moreover, the application implements mechanisms for the creation of RIA interfaces from ontologies and the automatic generation of administration interfaces for a previously design application.

1 Introduction

The development of Rich Internet Applications (RIAs) has lead to the improvement of the user interfaces in Web applications increasing the interoperability of their components by means of an event-driven paradigm, and providing an appearance and user experience similar to a desktop interface. Nevertheless, due to technological issues, RIAs act as black boxes that show their contents in a user-friendly manner but complicate the access to the data to some types of Web clients, which require accessibility, such as, the search engines. This drawback is shared both by browser-oriented RIAs, whose data is visualized according to a list of events triggered by users, and plugin-oriented RIAs, which, in addition to being event-driven, are implemented as binary objects whose information can be only visualized using a plug-in specific for each technology and browser. In this context, the S^m4RIA approach (Semantic Models for RIA) [1] introduces a new model-driven methodology, extending OOH4RIA, for the development of Semantic Rich Internet Applications (SRIAs), i.e., a new type of RIA that facilitate the interconnection to external RIA systems and data sources by means of techniques and technologies from the Semantic Web. Specifically, these applications are capable of both sharing their internal data as Linked Data (*http://linkeddata.org/*) and exploiting data shared by other nodes of the Linked Data cloud.

M. Grossniklaus and M. Wimmer (Eds.): ICWE 2012 Workshops, LNCS 7703, pp. 20–25, 2012.
© Springer-Verlag Berlin Heidelberg 2012

This paper describes the main features of the S^m4RIA Extension for OIDE, which implements the S^m4RIA approach in OIDE [2] (OOH4RIA Integrated Development Environment, see Fig. 1) and, thus helping users to model SRIAs using the S^m4RIA models. Furthermore, this extension automates a transformation process (model-to-model and model-to-text) needed for the generation of SRIAs. Complementing the original S^m4RIA approach, the tool also includes mechanisms for the generation of RIA interfaces from ontologies and the generation of administration views for the designed applications.

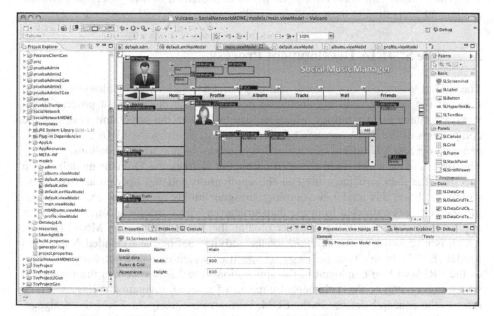

Fig. 1. Screenshot of the OIDE tool showing the OOH4RIA Presentation model

In order to contextualize the contribution of this paper, the next sections briefly introduce the concept of SRIA, the S^m4RIA methodology and its activities. For further explanations, Hermida et al. describe the approach in [1] in depth. Moreover, the following Web site *http://suma2.dlsi.ua.es/ooh4ria/sm4ria.html* also contains general information and a collection of demonstrative videos and use cases.

2   Introducing Semantic Rich Internet Applications

Due to technological restrictions, Rich Internet Applications behave as black boxes in a way that software agents, such as search engines, cannot access the data they share on the Web. RIAs usually include textual metadata that briefly describe the content of the application. However, the information contained in this metadata does not provide a realistic view of the RIA content. In several cases, the only manner of gaining access to all the content is to use the visual representation of the data produced by the

Web browser. Although there are currently some available solutions, they are still dependent on the technology chosen for the implementation of the RIA.

Semantic Rich Internet Applications (SRIA [1]) extensively use Semantic Web techniques and technologies in order to provide a representation of the contents managed by the application and facilitating the reuse existing knowledge sources on the Web. This solution is technologically independent since it can be adapted to any RIA framework. A schema of this type of application, the software modules it contains and the Social Network Site (SNS) case study are described in [1] or at the S^m4RIA Web site. The S^m4RIA Extension for OIDE, which is presented in this paper, supports the design and generation of these modules implementing the S^m4RIA methodology.

3   The S^m4RIA Development Process

The S^m4RIA methodology extends the original OOH4RIA methodology modifying some of the existing tasks and including new ones. The development process is divided into three main activities, which include tasks with the same aim: 1) design the components of the SRIA server; 2) design the components of the SRIA client; and 3) generate the SRIA by means of a collection of model-to-text transformations.

The first activity starts when the server designer defines the Domain model, which specifies the data structures used in the application and the operations over these structures. From this model, the ontology designer builds the domain ontology aligning the concepts extracted from the data structures with concepts of other sources or applications. As a result, the designer obtains the Extended Domain Model (EDM), which is a requisite of the next task of the activity: define the Extended Navigation Model (ENM). In this task, the designer specifies which data and ontology instances of the SRIA will be employed in the application. The EMN specifies the manner in which users navigate these elements by means of a set of navigational classes, which refer to the concepts defined in the EDM. Furthermore, using the ENM the designers can specify the access to external knowledge bases, using SPARQL queries, and the manner in which this information will be gathered and managed.

The second activity of the S^m4RIA process continues by transforming the Extended Navigational Model into a skeleton of the Presentation and Orchestration models using two model-to-model transformations: *Nav2Pres* and *NavPres2Orch*. The Presentation model describes the structure of the user interface (components and visualization) which is complemented by the Orchestration model, which defines the behavior of the interface.

Finally, the last activity of the method is aimed at generating the software components of the SRIA using the information captured in the S^m4RIA models by means of a collection of model-to-text transformation processes.

4 S^m4RIA Extension for OIDE: Main Features

OIDE is an application based on the Eclipse framework, developed as a set of Eclipse plug-ins, which supports the OOH4RIA methodology for the development of RIAs. Specifically, this application defines the OOH4RIA meta-models using the EMOF/Ecore meta-metamodel and, using the EMF/GMF framework, facilitates the definition using a graphical concrete syntax of the OOH4RIA models: Domain, Navigational and Presentation-Orchestration. Moreover, this tool supports the generation processes that obtain most of the RIA software components (both server and client modules). The generation rules are implemented as a set of Xpand rules, which, at present, transform the models into C# code using the Silverlight, WCF (Windows Communication Foundation) and NHibernate frameworks.

Using OIDE as platform, the S^m4RIA extension for OIDE implements the artifacts and processes of the S^m4RIA methodology as a new functionality of Eclipse. This section describes the elements developed and the modifications to the original tool that facilitate the design of the SRIA software components. More specifically, this extension includes the following features and components:

a) **New models.** Using the EMF and GMF libraries, three new models have been implemented, whose meta-models have been defined over the Ecore meta-model:

- *Extended Domain Model:* This model allows the designers to model lightweight ontologies using the tool and map the elements of domain model into ontology elements (represented in Fig. 2).
- *Extended Navigational Model:* This model extends the OOH4RIA navigational model in such a way that it facilitates the definition of new navigational classes from the EDM and external navigational links, which could be combined creating data/knowledge *mashups*. At present, the tool helps to access the main Linked Data services, i.e., the SPARQL endpoints. Fig 2 depicts an example of this model.
- *Visualization Ontology Model:* this model allows the designers to represent the characteristics of the structure and the behavior of the user interface from the point of view of the user (in contrast to the designer's viewpoint).

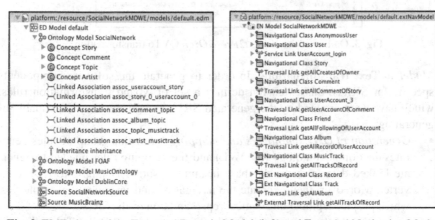

Fig. 2. EMF views of the Extended Domain Model (left) and Extended Navigation Model

b) **Model-to-Model transformations.** The tool includes a collection of M2M rules that facilitate and boost the design processes. The chosen specification language and rule engine was provided by the Eclipse QVT operational implementation. Specifically, the transformations defined in this extension are the following (M_a – M_b transformations are unidirectional, i.e., they transform model M_a into M_b):

- *Dom2ExtDom Transformation:* Domain model – Extended Domain Model. This transformation generates the basic elements of an ontology (concepts, properties, subclass axioms, etc.) from the Domain model. After the transformation process, the EDM generated can be modified/adapted/updated by the designer.
- *ExtDom2ExtNav Transformation:* Extended Domain Model – Extended Navigation Model. From the Extended Domain Model of the application, this transformation can generate a new view of the Extended Navigation Model for software agents.
- *NavExt2Pres&Orch Transformation:* Extended Navigation Model – Presentation Model. This transformation implements the S^m4RIA *Nav2Pres* and *Nav&Pres2Och* transformation, thus creating a predefined UI from the Navigation Model.

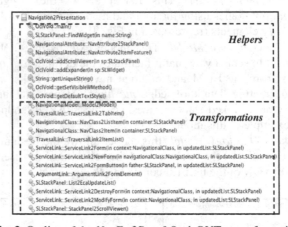

Fig. 3. Outline of the *NavExt2Pres&Orch* QVTo transformation

c) **Model-to-Text transformations.** In order to generate the software components specific for SRIAs, this extension defines a set of Xpand transformation rules, which have been grouped by the generated SRIA component they are capable of generating:

- *Generation of OWL ontologies and mapping rules:* this group of rules generates the domain ontology (in OWL) and the mapping rules needed to generate Linked data from the database instances using a Database-to-RDF converter. Moreover, they generate the navigation and visualization ontologies, which provide a global ontological representation of the SRIA.
- *Generation of the components for the access to Linked Data:* This subset of rules generates the components required to access SPARQL endpoints and retrieve Linked Data.
- *Generation of the components for the access to local data:* this rule group generates a HTML interface for RIA, which is accessible by any Web client, even those which cannot process the Silverlight UI.

d) New processes of software generation. The new implemented artifacts facilitate the adaptation of the S^m4RIA methodology to new processes of generation. Among them, it is worth highlighting the following:

- *Automatic generation of administrator views for applications.* Using the M2M transformations already defined, it is possible to automatically generate UIs for SRIA administrators (or facilitate the generation of most of their modules) from the S^m4RIA EDM or the OOH4RIA domain model. Fig. 4 shows an example of Presentation model that was automatically generated for a social network site.

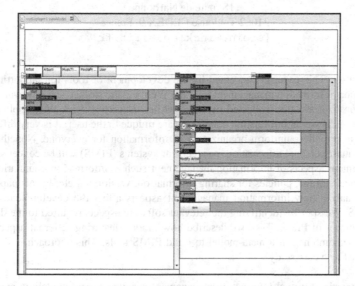

Fig. 4. Presentation model for administrative tasks of a social network site

As mentioned before, the screenshots and demonstrative videos of this tool are available at the OOH4RIA-S^m4RIA Web site: *http://suma2.dlsi.ua.es/ooh4ria/ sm4ria.html*

Acknowledgements. This paper has been supported by the Spanish Ministry of Education under the FPU program (ref. AP2007-03076) and the SONRIA project (ref. TIN2010-15789). The authors would also like to thank the University of Alicante for the economic support given through the DIMENRIA research project (ref. GRE10-23).

References

1. Hermida, J.M., Meliá, S., Montoyo, A., Gómez, J.: Developing Rich Internet Applications as Social Sites on the Semantic Web: A Model-Driven Approach. IJSSOE 2(4), 21–41 (2011)
2. Meliá, S., Martínez, J.-J., Mira, S., Osuna, J.A., Gómez, J.: An Eclipse Plug-in for Model-Driven Development of Rich Internet Applications. In: Benatallah, B., Casati, F., Kappel, G., Rossi, G. (eds.) ICWE 2010. LNCS, vol. 6189, pp. 514–517. Springer, Heidelberg (2010)

A Model-Based Approach for Supporting Aspect-Oriented Development of Personal Information Management Systems

Caio Stein D'Agostini and Marco Winckler

ICS-IRIT, University Paul Sabatier
118 route de Narbonne
31062 Toulouse CEDEX 9, France
{stein,winckler}@irit.fr

Abstract. This paper is concerned by the development of tools for supporting personal information management over the Web; i.e. the storage and retrieval of personal information collected by users whilst interacting with Web applications. As personal information collections are unique to the user, it is very difficult to provide a uniform organization of information for everyone. Nonetheless, most personal information management systems (PIMS) will be concerned by similar aspects of information management such as information granularity, physical storage, policies for sharing information, versioning, etc. In this paper we analyze how information management aspects affect the development of PIMS. We start by identifying the relevant software aspects required to the development of PIMS. Then we describe how models featuring different aspects can be combined in a meta-model to build PIMS tools. This approach is illustrated by a case study.

Keywords: personal information management systems, aspect modeling, models composition.

1 Introduction

People naturally collect and store information that is relevant to their personal needs. In today's word people have an enormous quantity information on which depends the their daily lives; registration numbers with government services, addresses, telephones and e-mail addresses, banking information, etc. However, research has consistently shown that most of users have difficulties to remember where they placed their personal information and thus have difficulties in retrieving it (Jones & Teevan, 2007). As the quantity of information a person possesses increases, users must develop additional mechanisms for organizing their information space.

Personal computers are often used with Personal Information Management (PIM) systems, as they allow people to collect items of information and store them outside their cognitive system (Malone, 1983). In the last years, users are more likely to interact with many applications and computers, thus causing fragmentation of their information space. Indeed, in order to manage their personal information, users frequently rely on multiple tools such as e-mail managers, agendas and file managers.

M. Grossniklaus and M. Wimmer (Eds.): ICWE 2012 Workshops, LNCS 7703, pp. 26–40, 2012.

The **Fig. 1** illustrates how PIMS can be used to share personal information with other users and applications. When the users interact with services such their banks, online stores, or even other users, the PIMs provide the user a repository, an **information space** where they can store and re-find the information they need, such as their bank accounts, addresses to know where to deliver what gets bought, or contacts or photos they might want to share with their friends. However, fragmentation is just the tip of the iceberg. Users have to remember where their information is stored and also if it corresponds to the correct version and/or required format. Users also lose control of the information after it is shared, which can have serious consequences regarding the privacy and security. That is mostly in the context of the Web because many of the interactions with Web applications involve sharing of users' personal information.

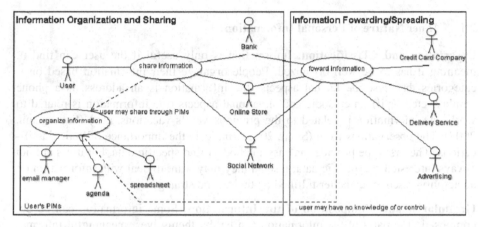

Fig. 1. PIMs and the use of personal information

Though personal information collections are unique to the user and the tasks accomplished with personal information vary, making it difficult to provide a uniform organization of the information space for everyone, most PIMS are concerned by similar aspects of information management such as information granularity, physical storage, disclosure, versioning, etc. Despite the fact these aspects concerns information management system in general, this paper is particularly interested in analyzing how such aspects affect the development of PIMS deployed over the Web.

This work is being developed for the PIMI project (Personal Information Management through Internet). The project already analyzed how users manage information and services and their expectations towards PIMs. (Scapin, 2011) analyses, through a mocked up system, the users' views on personal information management and their desires for flexibility to organize and classify the information, control of how it is shared and re-used.

Our goal on this paper is to try to understand how aspect modeling can help to build PIMS tools that fulfill the users' requirements for managing and sharing personal information. The paper is organized as follows: section 2 presents aspects regarding how users manage information; section 3 provides models for individual aspects and how they can be composed to build PIMS that fulfill different scenarios of use; section 4 describes and ongoing implementation of a PIMs based on our approach.

The implementation took place simultaneously to the modeling and helped to better understand the different aspects. The rest of paper presents related and future work.

2   Aspects Involved with Personal Information Management

In this section introduces some aspects that affect the development of personal information management systems. These aspects are presented accordingly to the inner nature of personal information (section 2.1), the management of the information by the system (section 2.2) and the use made of the information (section 2.3). This section ends with an analysis of how existing tools support these aspects.

2.1   Inner Nature of Personal Information

Description and Classification: Information is only useful if the user can find it, meaning it has to be well organized. People organize their information based on i) categories that describe factual aspects (the information is an address, is a phone number, etc.) or ii) on episodic and situational aspects (the information is related to work, the information is related to the previous year's vacations, etc.) (Sauermann, 2007). The observations from (Sohn, 2011) indicate the importance of both classifications. The first type provides an easy method to find specific data, but users are not always interested on specific data; instead they may want to deal with information on an activity-based level, better fulfilled by the second strategy.

Granularity and Composition of the Information: Some information can be decomposed. The parts of the information can be, by themselves, meaningful information for the user. For example, when a user talks with its bank account manager, the account number probably gets shared. When giving the account information so that someone can transfer money the user shares different information, which is composed of the bank name, the agency number and account number. In the first case, the relevant grain of information is just the 'account number'. In the second situation, the grain is the 'bank account', which contains the 'account number'. The capacity to compose information relates to the its classification, as the user can compose information into groups, the same way folders are used to organize files on the computer.

Versioning: As time passes, information can change and the user has to keep track of the versions. This is an issue that also relates with the granularity of the information. Using the bank account example, the user may have its account transferred to another agency. Considering the bank account as the grain of information, the user still has the same bank account (it still refer to the same bank account in the real world), but its content has changed. By keeping track of versions the user can know who shares the current version and who shares the outdated one.

History of Use: Keeping track of the history of the information is important to help users keep track of how and when information were created, re-used or shared (Jensen, 2010) and who is involved in these actions. Taking the versioning example, there is an important event which is the change of agency. The user knows that on a given day the bank shared new information (the new agency) and the bank account got changed (new version). Knowing this history the user can know, for example, that all bank documents using the old agency refer to before this day.

2.2 How Personal Information Is Handled by the System

The following aspects affect the management of the personal information, but they are related to technical aspects, such as where the information is stored and from where it is accessed, or how it is represented.

Location of the Information: There are several possibilities on where to keep the information. The choice taken affects the information fragmentation:

- Store the information in only one information space (from several available spaces). This space can be the memory of a user's device or Web service. Every time it is necessary to use the information, it is accessed from that space. This option requires previous planning from the user on where to store the information (Sohn, 2011).
- Replicate the information in all of the spaces used by the user. This ensures that the information can be easily accessed. However, this solution may demands frequent synchronization to ensure all spaces have the same version of the information.
- Provide a unified view of the content on all of the spaces, as if there were only one (Dhumbumroong, 2011). The synchronization problem still persists and the solution assumes there are no incompatibilities when communicating with all the spaces.
- Store all the information in a single space. This solution provides one centralized point for storing the information. This space is used by the user and any other parties (users or services) that want to access the user's information. This solution supposes a generic solution capable of dealing with whatever requirement may arise.

Independently of the previous possibilities, parts of the information can be cached by applications, but this is an implementation choice which is not considered.

Versioning: Though versioning was already cited regarding the evolution of the information, it is also a technical aspect. If the user has the information stored replicated through different information spaces it might be difficult for the users to manage which version is stored on which space (Song, 2011). This may lead to problems when sharing an outdated information or overwriting the current version with an old one when trying to synchronize the different spaces.

Information Structure and Format: People can interpret information if they know what it is about and sometimes ignore that the same information can be represented in many ways. However information systems usually require data to conform to predefined schemas (Parent, 2000), as illustrated in **Fig. 2**. The figure shows three forms to represent the bank account; it can be identified by the bank name, agency and account number, it can be identified as IBAN (International Bank Account Number) or through a QR-Code which can encoded both information. The choice for one or the other may be influenced by legacy systems, standards, specific needs, etc.

Platform/Environment: Although each user has an individual organization and information can have multiple formats, the systems the users share their information with may not be that flexible. Systems might require that information follows certain schemas or may have restrictions to some formats.

Fig. 2. Different structures and formats

Sharing and Control of the Shared Information: The sharing aspect involves giving access to specific information to others and knowing how the information is used after it is shared. Frequently when sharing information online it is necessary to accept a use agreement. Agreements are contracts that specify conditions of use, privacy and obligations of all involved parties (Meziane, 2010) and are the only control the user has over the shared information. However, once the user agrees with the contract, the information can be copied, re-shared, or the service can change its use agreement, all without knowledge or consent of the user. It is important, for reasons of privacy, security and trust to be able to revisit those conditions, so that the user can know if the information is being properly used.

2.3   Regarding the Purpose of the Information

Users might have different purposes when sharing personal information with other parties. This is not related to what is done to the information, but instead if the information is stored or not. This includes the following:

Information Is for Immediate Use: There are several services whose workings are not dependent on storing the user's information. Common examples are search engines or online maps; the user provides information as a parameter and receives results. Though the service may store the information, it is not necessary to do so.

Some Information Is Stored for Supporting an Activity: There are services that cannot be immediately executed, or which need to keep a history of the interactions with the user, even though the service is not an information service. This is the case of online shops that need to store personal information such as delivery addresses, credit card numbers, etc. Once the user shares the information with those systems, the direct control over the information is lost, at least partly (i.e.: the user may be able to change the delivery address, but the user has no control over previous orders).

Information Storage Is the Goal of the Service: There are services such as social networks, online file repositories, agendas, etc. whose purpose are store and manage information. Users usually have a personal account and control which information is provided and, if they want, they can remove or edit the information. Many of those services support information sharing (at least with other users of the same systems). But once the information is shared, the user also loses control over it.

2.4   Overview of Some Existing PIMS

This section presents some systems for managing personal information and summarizes how they cope with the different aspects previously mentioned. It does not intend to provide and exhaustive list of tools, only to illustrate the diversity of tools available and the solution they provide to the issues presented. Table 1 list the different issues (1.Location of the information, 2.Platform, 3.Information Structure/Format, 4.Classification, 5.Versioning, 6.History of Use, 7.Sharing and control) and the approaches used by some tools to deal with them.

Table 1. Review of some existing PIMs

	Dropbox	Evernote	KDE (Kontact, Akonadi, Nepomuk)	PIMOnline	DeepaMehta
1	Web or local (information is kept synchronized)	Web	Local / remote servers	Web	Web
2	Browser, desktop, mobile	Browser, desktop, mobile	Desktop	Browser	Browser
3	Files and folders	Notes and images	Depends on the application. Semantic information can be added with RDF.	Calendar, contacts, to-do list, notes	Files, text
4	Folders	Tags	Tags (using Nepomuk) or by type (contacts, notes, calendar)	Folders (for notes). 'personal' or 'business' (for tasks)	Association,/ composition, tags
5	Yes	Yes	No. It depends on the individual PIMs	No	No
6	Timeline of what that has happened in the user's Dropbox	No It acts only as storage	No. It depends on the individual PIMs	No It acts only as storage	No
7	User can share folders with other Dropboxes or read-only urls	Shares the stored information as a link or e-mail	Sharing between applications that implement the Akonadi API	no	Provides a shared workspace. There is no individual information

Dropbox stores the information on the web and can be accessed as a web application or platform specific applications. Despite the timeline, it serves as file storage. It provides limited capabilities for classifying the stored content, organizing files into folders, which may not be adequate for all types of information. Evernote focuses on storing notes for personal re-use, not sharing. The notes are text fragments or images which can be describe with tags. Kontact acts only as an access point to the information managed by desktop applications, but it does not store them; the information can be classified with tags, using RDF triples (through Akonadi). DeepaMehta allows to compose and organize information as needed, but it is intended to manage information from shared projects, not individual information.

These examples show that, although there are tools that address the aspects and related problems presented on this work, the solutions are not all present simultaneously in a single application.

3   Modeling the Aspects

This section presents a series of models that describe the aspects presented in the previous section. Moreover, it describes how individual models can be combined.

3.1   Types of Service

We begin to model the aspects associated to personal information management by identifying the different parties that may come to interact with the user's information.

A 'Party' is anyone or anything that uses the personal information. Though a party could be either a person or a system, when two users interact, they interact through services; they use their email services, their instant message systems, their social networks, etc. 'ConsumerOnly' are the parties that consume the information for immediate use, without persisting it, such as the search engines. A 'Collector' is a party that needs to store the information, and it can be of two types.

The 'InformationAsMean' collector are the ones that collect and stores information because they provide a service that cannot be immediately executed, or which demands to keep a history of past interactions. It is the case of online stores, who store the information to be used during the payment, preparation and shipping operations. And there is also the 'InformationAsEnd', which are the services whose explicit purpose are store and manage information.

Independently of the type, one party may use or store information differently from how it publicly promote its services. For example, even if the user has the option to delete information, the user has no way of knowing if the service actually removes the information or just "hides" it. This type of issue is related to reputation; whether a service can be trusted or not based on its historic of interaction with other users.

3.2   The Sharing and Conditions of Use

As previously described, while some times information is shared without establishing persistent links with the user, there are many situations where information is persisted and associated to the user, even if through the user's account.

On these situations it is very important to keep track of who has access to which information, and under which conditions. Knowing who uses the information is important so that the user knows who to notify when information changes, so everyone is kept up-to-date. It is also important to know how the information is going to be used, including whether or not it may be shared.

Sometimes services rely on third services to operate. For example, some on-line retail stores or auction services serve as proxies between the buyer and the product seller. Sometimes it is not clear to the user if the information given to the online store stays with the store, or if it is shared with the buyers (in case the user is selling) or the sellers (in case the user is buying).

Usually this is settled through contracts (disclaimers, conditions of use, privacy agreement, etc.) the user agrees with when subscribing to the service. The relation between information and how it is used is illustrated in Fig. 3.

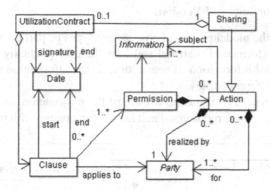

Fig. 3. Shared information and its utilization

Sharing information is an action that involves at least two parties, the one that has the information and the receiver(s). After the information is shared, its use may be governed by certain conditions ('UtilizationContract'). The contract lists which actions can (rights) or should (obligations) be performed by all involved parties, even if the user no longer has direct control over the information.

The conditions may not be the same for every party involved and they are also not restricted to the parties directly involved in the sharing (such as the case of the online store that forwards the user's information to the buyers or sellers).

3.3   Keeping Track of Everything

Though the contracts provide some security to the user by specifying what can be done with the information, users interact with several services on the Web. This means they keep sharing information with different parties, each time under a new contract. Keeping track of this history can be difficult for the user.

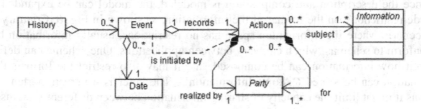

Fig. 4. Information's history of use

The history of use is a sequence of events. When information is shared, it is shared because of an event, such as buying a product on a store or adding a friend in a social network. But events can also relate to other actions, such as updating (e.g.; updating a profile on a social network) or removing information.

Thus, each user has a history regarding its personal information, composed of a series of events. Each event is associated with an action that took place on a certain moment ('Date'). The actions are performed by some party, to other party(ies) (which can be the same performing the action). The user can use any of those elements to recall information; e.g.: the user may remember the date the information was shared.

3.4   Different Formats and Versions

Until this moment the model presented covered the types of parties that might use the information, how information is shared and how the user gradually creates a history of use of its personal information. It was assumed that information can be easily exchanged between different parties.

This part of the model focus not on the use of the information, but on its organization; how it is built, reused, represented and how it can change with time.

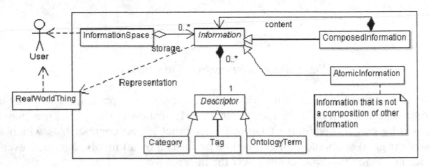

Fig. 5. Information description and composition

Fig. 5 models how users organize their information, considering they can store they information in an information space, without restrictions of form or structure.

One difficult is keeping information organized in such a way the user can find it, so that the information can be reused. The user can re-find information using its description, which can be provided through several means, such as categorization, tagging, semantic annotation using ontology terms, etc. The information can be composed or can be an atomic. Composed information re-uses other information. The atomic information is indivisible, and it can be a literal value, such as a text, or a file.

Once the description and composition is modeled, the model can be expanded to include restrictions on the format of the information, as shown in Fig. 6. Contrary to the scenario where the information space has no restrictions, usually information has to conform to schemas, which can vary between applications. One schema can define or limit how information can be composed, and it may also restrict the formats that information can be stored ('AtomicInformation'). The latter is a very important aspect, as it might limit the capacity of sharing information between different systems.

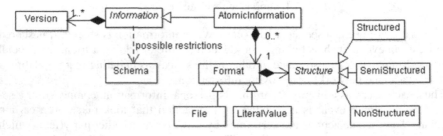

Fig. 6. Versioning and formats

3.5   Model Composition

Once all the aspects have been modeled separately, it is necessary to put them all together and identify where their points of interaction are. Fig. 7 shows a slightly simplified complete model. The painted elements ('Information', 'Action', 'Party' and 'Sharing') are the one through which the different aspects interact.

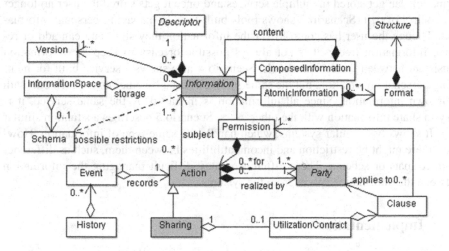

Fig. 7. The whole model and the connection points

The 'Information' is the center of the model, which is clear since the purpose of the model is to model the aspects related to personal information management. The 'Sharing' is a special type of action which allows the user to share and receive information from and with other parties. The history of who use the information and how it is used is a sequence of events that are constructed around the 'Action'.

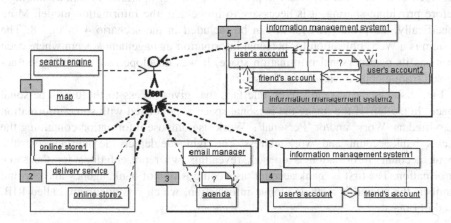

Fig. 8. Diversity of information uses and systems

Fig. 8 shows several scenarios where personal information is used, and how different they can be depending on the different aspects. The scenario 1 shows services such as search engines and map tools that need information from the user to work, but do not store the information, neither they know who is using them. Scenario 2 shows a different type of situation where the services consuming the information need to trace the information to a specific user and also store the information. The same information can get stored in multiple services and once it gets stored the user no longer has control over it. Scenario 3 shows tools built to help managing personal information. Though the user has control over the information they store and can add or remove information freely, it is not always possible or easy to keep the information consistent between the different tools. Scenario 4 also shows a service built for managing personal information, but the same service is used by other users, each one with their own information. Since all information is managed by the same service, it is easy to share information with the other users. Scenario 5 describes a situation similar to 4. It shows two similar systems, which handle the same type of information. However, there might be restriction and incompatibilities between them, such as differences in formats or schema. These differences may difficult managing the information between the information spaces from the systems.

4   Implementation

This section described the development of a prototype application. It is being developed iteratively, in parallel with the modeling of the aspects. It is used during the iterations to verify and adjust the models; for that, we use the bank account scenario, which is touched by all aspects and it is frequently experienced by people, thus it is well known.

So far, our prototype does not cover in details all of the aspects, as not all aspects can be approached in the implementation at the same time. For example, before keeping track of history it is necessary to provide support for operations (such as sharing), before providing sharing, it is necessary to implement the information model. More specifically, the prototype system can be included in the scenario 4 in Fig. 8. The system is a Web application for personal information management system where each user has its own personal information space. It was developed so that it can be accessed from mobile devices' Web browsers.

Fig. 9 shows the system's Web interface that gives access to the user's personal space. In the left of the image the personal space is populated with some information classified as 'Work' and/or 'Personal'. 'Work' is compose information containing the user's 'bank account' and 'work address' The right side depicts the interface after the 'bank account' information is opened, revealing two representations for the same information. The first is 'bank account' as a composition of bank, agency and account number; the second is a single atomic information, which is a document called RIB, used in France.

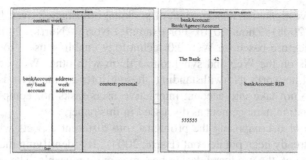

Fig. 9. Implementation of support for classification and composition

The implementation also allows the user to add new information, as shown in Fig. 10. The user gives a name to the information and can describe it further using keywords. The content can be a literal value or a file, which allows the user to store any information, despite of its format.

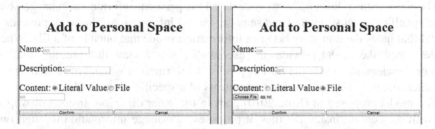

Fig. 10. Implementation of support for multiple formats of information

Finally, Fig. 11 demonstrates the sharing functionality. In the picture the user is sharing the whole content of the personal space. Once the information is shared it appears in the personal space of the other user, however only the original owner can edit it, since the contracts of use have not been implemented yet.

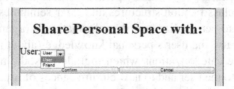

Fig. 11. Implementation of limited sharing

5   Related Work

So far, most of PIMs studies have mostly focused on very large data sets, such has the whole content of a user hard drive, and therefore has mainly concentrated on search/ retrieval issues; with some findings about the great variability in which people search their own information (Jones W. a., 2001). However, in more recent years some authors start to investigate the management of personal information over the Web (Voit, 2009) (Norrie, 2008) (Zhou, 2010). For example, Norrie (Norrie, 2008) proposes a complete architecture based on Web 2.0 technology enabling users to manage their personal records on the Web and synchronize them with other Web applications, in particular social networks. Notwithstanding, these efforts are mainly related to textual flat data and do not take into account interactive users tasks nor complex aspects of personal information management as discussed in this paper.

The benefits of decomposing the problems into different aspects when designing systems have already been pointed out (Barra, 2004) . By identifying the aspects early on the development, the produced design becomes more reusable. The multiple representations for the same information were the first problem researched. The work (Parent, 2000) calls attention on the fact that the same information may adopt different representations depending on the intended use. Though work focus on geographic information systems (e.g.: in a detailed map a city is a composition of polygons and lines, on a smaller scale, the city may turn into a polygon, and on even smaller scale, only a point), the relevant problem is still how to work with multiple representations.

The work from (Dittrich, 2006) is centered on personal information management, more specifically on structured and semi-structured information. The work presents a model that hides the boundary between information inside and outside of a file. When implemented, the model provides the user with a single view that presents folders, files or the elements inside the files as pieces of information which are related one to the other, ignoring if he is viewing the contents of a specific file or folder.

The model proposed in (Kim, 2010) goes in the other direction. Instead of worrying with the content inside the files, it proposes to manage information through two spaces; a concept space and a document space. The documents in the document space are referenced by the 'items', which are instances of the concepts in the concept space. As long as the user describes the files, the information space has no need of knowing their contents. The user can perform keyword searches (assigning tags to the items) or faceted searches (through the concepts).

The PIMO model (Sauermann, 2007) is centered about the user's knowledge. The work argues that one limitation with many personal information management systems is that they burry the classification structures and their semantics in the applications, which makes difficult to personalize how the information is organized. Instead, PIMO proposes a model that use the user's personal knowledge (about people, roles, things, etc.), to create flexible categorizations which include episodic and situational information and can adapt to the user and to new circumstances of use.

Though until this moment most of the efforts were towards the issues with multiple formats, structures and classification of the information, the sharing aspect was also visited. The work on (Meziane, 2010) proposes a dynamic privacy model for web services. The model decomposes the privacy agreement into several elements. The elements cover not only the rights and obligations towards the information, but towards the agreement itself, so that it can be dynamically renegotiated with participation of all parts involved.

6   Conclusion and Future Work

Personal information management is a daunting task as it might be influenced by many requirements raised by either by users that collect information as those users (or systems) that expect to consume information provides by personal information owners. Nonetheless, the identification of software aspects might help to choose features required for building PIMS.

In this paper we have discussed several aspects that might affect the development personal information systems. Whilst most of these aspects are not really new in information system in general, it is quite surprisingly they are barely supported by most of the existing tools, presented in Table 1.

Each aspect identified in this paper has been duly illustrated and modeled by scenarios that describe how they influence personal information management. Moreover, we have illustrated how these aspects can be combined to support different scenarios of PIMS. Such aspects may be considered for composing new applications or envisaging mapping mechanisms on existing tools.

We strongly believe that with the increasing use of Web applications, users will ultimately require more advance PIMS tools for help then to cope with such amount of personal information generated by such interactions. The results presented in this paper are rather preliminary but yet they contribute to understand how models can help to describe aspects related to PIMS and how to integrate them to build PIMS tools.

Future work will include the implementation of all aspects identified in this paper for covering all scenarios, which might include the integration and data exchange of PIMS with existing third party application. We also plan to refine the meta-model composition to integrate more fine-grained interaction of users with their personal data.

Acknowledgments. This work was performed under the French National Research Agency (ANR) project PIMI (Personal Information Management through Internet).

References

Barra, E.: An approach to Aspect Modelling with UML 2.0. In: Aspect-Oriented Modeling Workshop, AOM (2004)

Dhumbumroong, S.: Personal Cloud Filesystem: A distributed unification filesystem for. In: 2011 Eighth International Joint Conference on Computer Science and Software Engineering, JCSSE (2011)

Dittrich, J., Salles, M.: iDM: a unified and versatile data model for personal dataspace management. In: Proceedings of the International Conference on Very Large Data Bases (2006)

Jensen, C., et al.: The life and times of files and information: a study of desktop provenance. In: Proceedings of the 28th International Conference on Human Factors. ACM, New York (2010)

Jones, W.: Keeping found things found on the web. In: Proceedings of the Tenth International Conference on Information. ACM, New York (2001)

Jones, W., Teevan, J.: Personal Information Management. University of Washington Press (2007)

Kim, J., et al.: Building a semantic representation for personal information. In: Proceedings of the 19th ACM International Conference on Information and Knowledge Management. ACM (2010)

Malone, T.W.: How Do People Organize Their Desks?: Implications for the Design of Office. ACM Trans. Inf. Syst., 99–112 (1983)

Meziane, H., Benbernou, S.: A dynamic privacy model for web services. In: Comput. Stand. Interfaces, Elsevier Science Publishers B.V., The Netherlands (2010)

Norrie, M.: PIM Meets Web 2.0. In: Li, Q., Spaccapietra, S., Yu, E., Olivé, A. (eds.) ER 2008. LNCS, vol. 5231, pp. 15–25. Springer, Heidelberg (2008)

Parent, C., et al.: MurMur: Database management of multiple representations. In: AAAI 2000 Workshop on Spatial and Temporal Granularity, Austin, Texas, USA (2000)

Sauermann, L., et al.: Pimo-a framework for representing personal information models. In: Proceedings of I-Semantics (2007)

Scapin, D., et al.: Personal Information Systems: User Views and Information Categorization. In: The Fourth International Conference on Advances in Human-oriented and Personalized Mechanisms, Technologies, and Services, CENTRIC 2011, ThinkMind, Barcelona (2011)

Sohn, T., et al.: Myngle: unifying and filtering web content for unplanned access between Multiple Personal Devices. In: Proceedings of the 13th International Conference on Ubiquitous Computing. ACM, New York (2011)

Song, G., Ling, C.: Users' Attitude and Strategies in Information Management With Multiple Computers. International Journal of Human-Computer Interaction (2011)

Voit, K., et al.: Why personal information management (pim) technologies are not widespread. In: Workshop on Personal Information Management 2009 (2009)

Zhou, D., et al.: Optimizing user interaction for Web-based mobile tasks. In: 19th International Conference on World Wide Web (WWW 2010). ACM, New York (2010)

Model-Driven Development of Social Network Enabled Applications with WebML and Social Primitives

Marco Brambilla[1] and Andrea Mauri[2]

[1] Politecnico di Milano
Dip. di Elettronica e Informazione
P.za L. Da Vinci, Milano, Italy
marco.brambilla@polimi.it
[2] Università di Trento, DISI
Via Sommarive,
Povo, Trento, Italy
andrea.mauri@disi.unitn.it

Abstract. Social technologies are transforming the Web to a place where users actively contribute to content production and opinion making. Social networking requirements are becoming a core part of the needs of modern enterprises too, which need ad-hoc Web platforms that incorporate the right set of social features for their business. This leads to the need to provide facilities and methods for developing such socially enabled applications. In this paper we propose a model-driven approach that is specifically focused on the development of Web applications that exploit social features. In particular, we describe an extension of the WebML notation (a Domain Specific Language designed to model Web applications), comprising a set of modeling concepts that encapsulate the logic of the interaction with the social platforms. Upon this, we define a set of design patterns that respond to the typical needs of enterprises and we show some sample application scenarios.

1 Introduction

Social technologies are transforming the Web to a place where users actively contribute to content production and opinion making [SR+08, TK10]. While the broad public is aware of only a bunch of world-spread applications (including Facebook, Gowalla, Foursquare, LinkedIn, Twitter), social networking requirements are becoming a core part of the needs of modern enterprises, at the B2C (Business-to-Consumer), B2B (Business-to-Business), and B2E (Business-to-Enterprise, i.e., the connection between the company and its own internal organization and workforce) levels.

Several examples of applications exist at B2C level, spanning from brand management and viral marketing to Customer Relationship Management, while at B2E level, enterprises look at social networking tools as possible means for improving their operations thanks to the unstructured interaction they foster among employees [TK10].

M. Grossniklaus and M. Wimmer (Eds.): ICWE 2012 Workshops, LNCS 7703, pp. 41–55, 2012.
© Springer-Verlag Berlin Heidelberg 2012

The growth in the need of specific features within social network and collaboration platforms raised the problem of designing and developing Web applications integrating such a heterogeneous set of services into a single application. The purpose of this is to provide enterprises with ad-hoc Web platforms that incorporate the right set of social features to comply with the specific context of the company.

This leads to the need to provide facilities and methods for developing such socially enabled applications. One option is obviously that of applying traditional developing techniques based on manual coding. However, this solution is quite inappropriate both in terms of efficiency and of effectiveness. Indeed, developing an application integrated with social networking platform with a manual approach implies that the developer must know how each platform works and must rely on different external libraries to interact with the social services. This is time consuming and error prone. On the other hand, existing social enterprise platforms like Salesforce Chatter [SF12] or Tibco Tibbr [Tibco12] now exist, which provide a fixed set of features. Another solution could consist of applying general-purpose model-driven approaches to the problem, possibly specifically focused on web application development [CFB+02, RS+01, KR02]. However, these solutions cannot capture the details of the interaction with the social platforms and therefore still require manual modeling of social network API invocations.

To address these shortcomings, we propose a model-driven approach that is specifically focused on the development of Web applications that exploit social features. In particular, we describe an extension of the WebML notation (a Domain Specific Language designed to model Web applications)[CFB+02], comprising a set of modeling concepts that encapsulate the logic of the interaction with the social platforms. Those modeling concepts provide both cross-social platform capabilities and platformspecific ones and allow seamless integration between the ad-hoc application development and the social networking features. The proposed units can be used within a full-fledged model-driven development cycle that covers all the phases from requirement specification, to high level business need design (with notations based on BPMN or similar) down to application design with WebML and implementation and deployment with automatic code generation techniques. The development method is not part of the contribution of this paper, but can be found in [BFV11].

In this paper we discuss the basic modeling artefacts we define in WebML, the design patterns that can be repeatedly used for solving the typical needs, and then a few sample applications that demonstrate the feasibility and advantages of the approach. Our experiments are run within the MDD tool WebRatio [WR12], a modeling tool that allows automated code generation and fast application deployment starting from BPMN and WebML models.

The paper is organized as follows: Section 2 describes the social components (i.e., WebML units) that model social behaviours; Section 3 describes the design patterns that cover the most common requirements of social applications; Section 4 shows some applications developed with our approach; Section 5 discusses the related work; and finally Section 6 draws the conclusions.

Table 1. Operations that can be performed by the cross-platform social units

Social Login Unit	Login through social network credentials. It supports in a transparent way all the needed handshaking with the platform and allows to get or reuse an authorization token and to get information on the user. The main actions that can be performed are: starts authorization process and produce URL for redirection; define "landing" custom URL name receiving the authorized user back from the social network; and verify the status of a given authorization token.
Social Search Unit	Keyword search over social network contacts. It retrieves a set of people whose profiles match the search criteria.

2   WebML Extension: The Social Units

The first contribution we propose in this paper is an extension to the WebML notation for covering social network integration requirements. WebML [CFB+02] is a visual language for designing data- and service-intensive Web/SOA applications. A WebML model consists of one or more site views, which represent hypertext application used to publish or manipulate data and interact with the back end business logic. A different site views can be defined for each process actor; internally, a site view consists of a set of pages, atomic units of interface, containing units, representing data publishing components. Units are related to each other through links, representing navigational paths and parameter passing rules. Additionally, the WebML application model may comprise the definition of backend operations, parallel and independent threads (which can be activated manually, automatically or based on temporal triggers), Web services, REST APIs and their invocations.

In order to enable the development of social applications using a model-driven approach, we extended the WebML notation by adding a set of units that encapsulate the logic of the interaction with the social platforms. These units are designed as wrappers of the social platform APIs and hiding the underlying complexity from the developer, reducing the cost of designing new applications. The units are divided in three sets: cross-platform units, social platform-specific units, and collaboration platform units.

First we designed the conceptual definition of the units, analyzing the most common functions provided by the social networks, then

we implemented their behavior within the WebRatio tool [BBF10]. This has been obtained by implementing new WebRatio components and model transformation rules that allows automatic code generation from models. The code generated from WebML models is a standard Java application, which can be deployed on any Java application server. Connectivity to the social software is realized by APIs calls to the external platforms, which is the concrete way to implement the Social units.

2.1   Cross-Platform Units

The units belonging to this group can perform operations (enumerated in Table 1) on multiple social networks at a time. These units are thought as conceptual representations of behaviors that are common among all the social networks. The units we implemented up to now provide two basic behaviors: login through social network credentials, and search over the set of contacts in the social network. The social networks we cover with our implementation are: Facebook, Twitter, LinkedIn and Google+. For both units, one can decide to query one or more networks at a time, by choosing the network either at design time or at run time.

Table 2. WebML operations that can be performed by the social platform-specific units

	Operation	Description
Facebook Unit	Verify Token	Verify the status of the authorization token
	Get User Id	Get the id of the current logged user
	Get Friends	Get the list of friends of the logged user
	Post to Wall	Post a message on the logged user's wall
	Post to Friend	Post a message on the wall of a friend of the logged user
	Post Comment	Post a comment to a given post
	Post Note	Post a note
	Create event	Create a event
	Invite to Event	Send an invitation to a friend to participate to an event
	GetPost fromWall	Get the list of posts form the wall of the logged user
	Get Comments	Get the list of comments of a given post
	Upload photo	Upload a photo to the user's Facebook account
	Tag photo	Tag a photo
	Get Groups	Retrieves the list of groups of the logged user
Twitter Unit	Get User Id	Get the id of the current logged user
	Get Friends	Get the list of friends[1] of the current logged user
	Send Message	Send a direct message to a friend
	Tweet	Post a tweet
	Search	Perform a keyword search on Twitter
	Get Tweets List	Get the tweet list of a given user
Linkedin Unit	Keyword Search	Perform a keyword search over the user's connections
	Get connections	Get the first-level connections of the current logged user
	Message	Send a message to a connection
	Get User Id	Get the user id of the logged user

---

[1] We define "friends" in Twitter the people that follow and are followed by the user. This is also the necessary condition for sending direct messages.

2.2   Social Platform-Specific Units

The units belonging to this group encapsulate all the operations specific of one social network, and up to now they implement the set of API functions enumerated in Table 2 The units developed up to now cover the networks of Facebook, Twitter and Linkedin. Each unit allows invoking an operation within a large set of actions available through the API.

2.3   Collaboration Platform Units

The units belonging to this group represent the interaction on services that enhance the collaboration between users. In particular, the units that have been developed so far include interaction with Doodle, Google Docs and Google Calendar and implement the functions enumerated in Table 3. These units do not address social networking, while instead focus on information sharing and collaboration, which are some additional crucial aspects of the Web 2.0 paradigm.

Table 3. WebML operations that allow integration with collaboration platforms

Doodle Unit	Create Poll	Create a poll with the given options
	See Poll Details	See the details of a given poll
	Vote Poll	Select an option of a given poll
	Close Poll	Close a given poll
	Comment Poll	Comment a given poll
Google Calendar Unit	Create Calendar	Creates a calendar
	Create Event	Creates an event on a given calendar
	Get Events	Get the list of events from a calendar satisfying some conditions
Google Docs Unit	Get Documents	Get the list of the documents owned by the user
	Upload Documents	Upload a document to Google Docs

3   Social Design Patterns

In this section we show how the units we developed can be used to implement reusable design patterns that address the typical requirement of Web 2.0 applications. We refer to the needs presented [B12] as a starting point for our analysis and we identify a set of social design patterns with the aim of covering the most common requirements that a social application must fulfill. Notice that the patterns we present are derived from typical usage we registered in the design of various social-enabled applications.

The most important patterns we identify are: Post, Comment, Send Message, Like/ Vote/ Rate, Login, Group Management, Event Management, Content Management, People Search, and Content Search.

Since the different units implement different operations, not all the units can be used to implement a specific pattern. This is either due to a missing feature in the unit conceptualization, or because the social platform doesn't provide a specific feature, or because the platform is not addressing the issue at all. The choice of implementing a feature within a unit is also based on orthogonality reasons. For instance, while it could have been possible to implement a Facebook login function within the Facebook unit, we decided to provide the login only within the cross-platform Login unit. Table 4 shows the mapping between the identified patterns and their implementability within the various units.

The following subsections describe each pattern and show how they can be implemented using the social units. Notice that this section is not meant to show the usage of the units, but instead aims at describe reusable design solutions to the problem of expanding the features of a Web application to the social networking needs. As such, they represent conceptual models that can be easily represented with other alternative notations such as UWE, OOWS, or others.

Table 4. Social Design Pattern vs. Unit type. Y: unit supports the pattern; N: unit does not support the pattern; ND (not defined): the specific platform does not support the pattern.

WebML Units / Patterns	Cross Platform	Facebook	Twitter	Linkedin	Doodle	GDoc	GCalendar
Post	N	Y	Y	N	ND	ND	ND
Comment	N	Y	N	N	Y	ND	ND
Message	N	Y	Y	Y	ND	ND	ND
Like/Vote/Rate	N	N	ND	N	Y	ND	ND
Login	Y	N	N	N	ND	N	N
Group Management	N	Y	ND	N	ND	ND	ND
Event Management	N	Y	ND	N	ND	ND	Y
Content Management	N	Y	N	N	ND	Y	ND
People Search	Y	Y	Y	Y	ND	ND	ND
Content Search	N	N	Y	ND	ND	N	N

3.1   Social Login

This pattern implements the interactions for allowing the login through the credentials of a social platform. For this purpose we use the cross-platform Social Login unit. It implements the Oauth authentication protocol in order to obtain the login response and to get permission to use the service API. The protocol is implemented using the units as shown in Figure 1.

In the *Social Login Sample* page the user see a form (the unit *Social Network*) in which he can choose which social network use to perform the login; then the operational unit *Social Login* redirects the user to the social network authentication page. Eventually the user is brought back through the green OK link. In case of error, the user is redirected to the *Social Login Failed* error page. If the Oauth token is already present and valid the authentication phase is skipped.

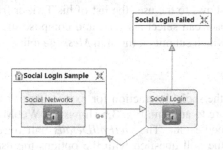

Fig. 1. The *social login* pattern modeled in WebML with the cross-platform Social Login unit

3.2   Post

This pattern covers all the cases in which a message is published to an undefined number of users (e.g., on the Twitter timeline or Facebook wall). Fig. **2**.a shows the WebML diagram describing the implementation of the Post pattern using the Facebook unit. In the *Home* page to the user can enter the post text through the *Write a post* form. Once the form is submitted, the message is posted on the user's wall by the *Post to Wall* operation unit.

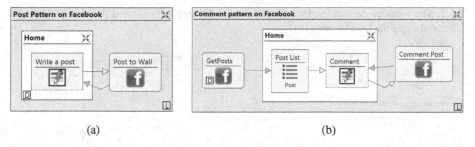

| (a) | (b) |

Fig. 2. The *post* pattern (a) and the *comment* pattern (b) implemented with the Facebook unit

3.3   Comment

This pattern describes the workflow that is executed when a message is published as a comment to another content on a social network. Fig. **2**.b shows the Comment pattern implemented using the Facebook unit. In the *Home* page, the index unit *Post List* presents to the user the list of posts from his Facebook wall, retrieved by the *GetPosts* operation unit. The user can select one post, write his comment in the *Comment* form, and submit and publish it with the *Comment Post* unit.

3.4   Message

This pattern describes the workflow that is executed when a message is sent to a single, identifiable user (e.g., a Twitter / Facebook direct message). Fig. **3**.a shows the implementation of the Message pattern using the Twitter unit. In the *Home* page the index unit *Friend List* shows to the user the list of his Twitter friends retrieved by the *GetFriends* unit. The user select a friend and compose the message through the form *Send a message*, which submits it through *Message* unit

3.5   Like-Vote-Rate

This pattern describes the social interaction for expressing of a preference (liking) or the assignment of a score to an item. Fig. **3**.b shows the WebML design pattern implemented with the Doodle unit. The *GetPollDetails* unit retrieves the details of a given poll and shows the poll question with the options the user can vote using the *Vote* unit.

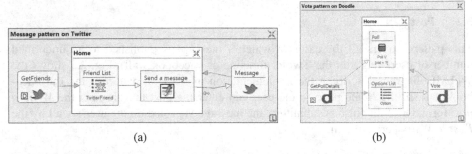

(a)   (b)

Fig. 3. The message pattern implemented using the Twitter units (a) and the vote pattern implemented using the Doodle units (b)

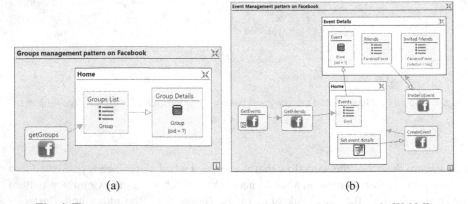

(a)   (b)

Fig. 4. The groups management (a) and event management (b) patterns in WebML

3.6   Group Management

This pattern describes the interaction with the social platform for the management of user groups, for instance retrieving information about the groups a user belong to. Fig. 4. a shows the WebML diagram for groups management using the Facebook units. In the *Home* page the *Group List* index unit shows the list of the groups the user belongs to (retrieved with the *getGroups* unit). By clicking on a specific group, the *Group Details* data unit shows to the user the details of the group.

3.7   Event Management

This pattern   comprehends all the actions that enable the management of social events like meetings, or others.   For example scheduling events, inviting people, and so on. Fig. 4.b shows the WebML diagram describing the event management pattern implemented using the Facebook unit. In the *Home* page the *Events* index unit shows to the user the events retrieved by the *GetEvents* unit. Clicking on an event the user is brought to the *Event Details* page, where he can invite some friends (through the *InviteToEvent* unit) by selecting them from the *Friends* index unit. The *Set event details* form in the *Home* page lets the user create a new event through the *Create event* unit.

3.8   Content Management

This pattern describes the interaction with the social platform in order to manage binary content (i.e., photos or documents). Fig. 5.a shows the WebML content management pattern using the GoogleDocs units. The *Select the file to upload* form in the *Home* page lets the user browse his computer for a file he wants to upload. Then the *UploadFile* unit uploads the file to the user's Google Docs account.

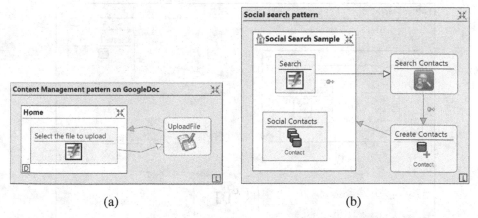

(a)   (b)

Fig. 5. The content management pattern implemented using the GoogleDocs unit (a) and People search pattern implemented using the Cross-platform units (b)

3.9   People Search

This pattern describes the search of contacts in a social network based on text search criteria. Fig. 5.b shows the pattern implemented using the Cross-platform units. In the *Social Search Sample* page the user can insert the keywords to be searched within his social contacts. The *Search Contacts* unit carries out the actual search. The *Create Contacts* unit creates the *Contact* objects in the user session and finally the *Social Contacts* multi-data unit shows the list of the retrieved contacts.

4   Sample Application Scenarios

In this section we show 5 simple applications built using WebML extended with the new social units proposed in this paper and used according to the above patterns.

All these applications are modeled within WebRatio tool, which allows automated code generation and fast deployment of the applications, thanks to the fact that specific code generation rules have been devised for the new units.

4.1   Twitter Keyword Search

This simple application allows the user to perform a keyword-based search over the Twitter timeline. Fig. 6 shows the WebML diagram of this application. In the *Home* page to the user is presented a form (the *Search Form* entry unit) where he can submit a search criterion or ask for more results for the last search.

In the former case the keyword is passed directly to the *Search* unit that performs the search, while in the latter the *getLastTweet* unit returns the id of the last tweet retrieved in the last search that is passed to the *Search* unit as the starting point in the result list, together with the keyword used. In both cases, the retrieved tweets are stored in the user session and then shown in the *Tweets List* index.

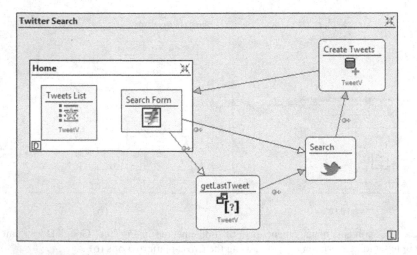

Fig. 6. WebML diagram of the Twitter Keyword Search application

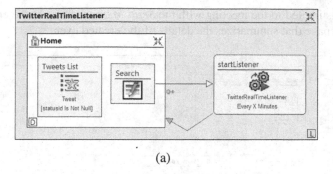

(a)

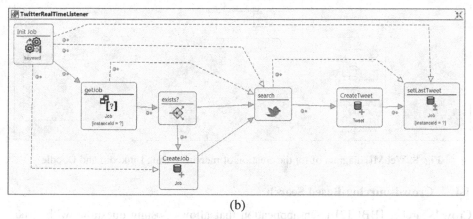

(b)

Fig. 7. WebML diagram of the Twitter real-time listener application (a) and of the WebML *thread* that retrieves the tweets from the timeline every X minutes (b)

4.2   Twitter Real-Time Listener

This application allows the user to follow the stream of tweets that talk about a given topic. Fig. 7 (a) shows the WebML diagram of the application. The user, through the *Search* form, starts a thread that every X minutes gathers the tweets that contain the words specified in the form. Fig. 7 (b) shows the diagram of the thread, which selects the last tweet retrieved in the previous iteration and performs the search over the Twitter timeline starting from the last tweet. Then the tweets are stored in the database and the last tweet is updated. In his *Home* page, the user sees the new tweet list.

4.3   Meeting Setup

This application allows the user to create meeting with his Linkedin contacts, with the possibility of deciding the date of the event with a poll created in Doodle, as shown in Fig. 8. In the page *Search Contacts* the user can search over his Linkedin connection for people to invite to the meeting. Then, in the second page (*Add Time option*), the user can add different date options for the meeting. In the *Define Meeting Details* page, the user configures some aspects of the meeting (topic, description, location). Finally a poll is created on Doodle with the *Create Poll* unit, and a message is sent to the contacts invited to the meeting with the *Send Message* unit. At the end to the user is shown a page that summarizes the details of the created event.

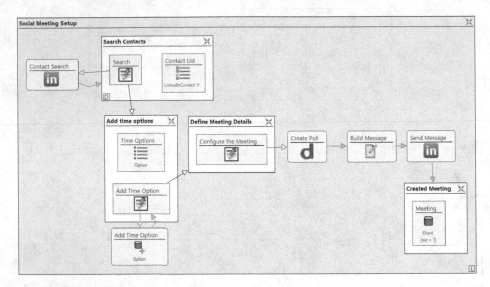

Fig. 8. WebML diagram of for the creation of meetings using Linkedin and Doodle

4.4   Crowdsourcing-Based Search

CrowdSearcher [BBC12] is an application that allows posting questions with structured objects over different social networks. Fig. 9 shows the WebML diagram of the query creation phase, in which the user creates the query to be posted on the social networks, by defining a textual question, creating a schema and adding a list of structured object. In the *Responder Selection* page, the user must select among his friends the recipient of his question.

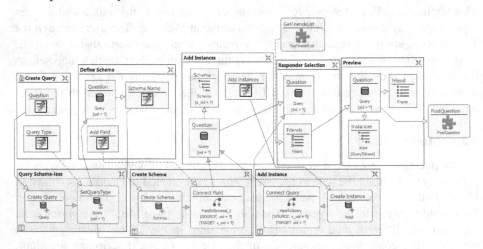

Fig. 9. WebML diagram of the query creation phase of CrowdSearcher

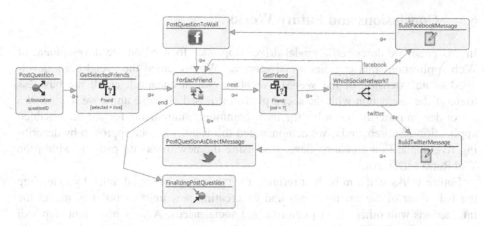

Fig. 10. WebML diagram of the module that post the question on various social networks

The friend list is retrieved at run time by the *GetFriendList* module, which selects the friends of the logged user in each social network. This module is not shown here for space reasons; the reader can easily figure out the general behavior of the module, which is inspired to the People Search design pattern presented in Section 3.9. After selecting the recipients, the query is posted on different social networks by the *Post-Question* module (whose WebML diagram is depicted in Fig. 10).

The module receives as input the id of the query and the authorization level required by the user (public or private question), then for each selected friends, depending on the social network he belongs to, it either sends a private message on Twitter or posts it on the Facebook wall.

5 Related Works

This paper applies MDD techniques to a specific domain of Web applications, namely Social-networking enabled applications. Other Web engineering approaches have tackled these problems. Among the various Web engineering methods, we can mention OOWS as one of the most complete approaches with respect to requirement specification and social interaction coverage [VP+09]: the method proposed there provides a set of design patterns, covering also social aspects and also a mapping to an executable model.

Some works already tried to collect and classify design patterns for social web applications. Among them, we mention [FT+10], collecting WebML design patterns describing the most used social interactions within online platforms. The paper [B12] presents a requirements-engineering driven approach to customized social network development. Other preceding works focused on pattern-based development [KR02] [RS+01] and have been inspirational for this work too.

6   Conclusions and Future Works

In this paper we described a model driven approach focused on the development of Web applications that exploits social services. We presented the social units developed as an extension of the WebML notation, which encapsulates all the business logic of the interaction with the social platform. Based on these units, we identified a set of design patterns that solve the most common requirements for socially enabled applications. Subsequently, we demonstrated the validity of our approach by describing five application scenarios developed using the new units and patterns within the WebRatio MDD tool.

Future works will aim both at refining the current set of social units, by extending the behaviour of the existing units and by creating new units in order to model the interactions with other social platforms and social needs. A very important step will be to factorize the API calls that are currently spread all over the set of the network-specific units into a set of appropriate cross-social network units, in order to group functions that share the same semantic.

Acknowledgements. This research is partially supported the BPM4People project, funded by the 7th Framework Programme of the European Commission. We thank all the project contributors for their efforts and useful discussions.

References

[BBC12] Bozzon, A., Brambilla, M., Ceri, S.: Answering search queries with Crowd-Searcher. In: Proc. WWW Conference 2012, Lyon, France, pp. 1009–1018 (2012)

[CFB+02] Ceri, S., Fraternali, P., Bongio, A., Brambilla, M., Comai, S., Matera, M.: Designing Data-intensive Web Applications. Morgan Kaufmann (2002)

[B12] Brambilla, M.: From requirements to implementation of ad-hoc social Web applications: an empirical pattern-based approach. IET Software (in print, 2012)

[BBF10] Brambilla, M., Butti, S., Fraternali, P.: Business Process Modeling and Quick Prototyping with WebRatio BPM. In: Proc. of BPM Demonstration Track 2010, Hoboken, USA, September 14-16, vol. 615. CEUR-WS.org (2010), http://ceur-ws.org/Vol-615

[BFV11] Brambilla, M., Fraternali, P., Vaca, C.: BPMN and Design Patterns for Engineering Social BPM Solutions. In: Daniel, F., Barkaoui, K., Dustdar, S. (eds.) BPM Workshops 2011, Part I. LNBIP, vol. 99, pp. 219–230. Springer, Heidelberg (2012)

[FT+10] Fraternali, P., Tisi, M., Silva, M., Frattini, L.: Building Community-Based Web Applications With a Model-Driven Approach and Design Pattern. In: Murugesan, S. (ed.) Handbook of Research on Web 2.0, 3.0, and X.0: Technologies, Business, and Social Applications. IGI Global (2010)

[F10] Fuchs, C.: Social Software and Web 2.0: Their Sociological Foundations and Implications. In: Murugesan, S. (ed.) Handbook of Research on Web 2.0, 3.0, and X.0: Technologies, Business, and Social Applications, pp. 763–789. IGI Global (2010)

[KR02] Koch, N., Rossi, G.: Patterns for adaptive web applications. In: Proc. 7th European Conference on Pattern Languages of Programs (2002)

[RS+01] Rossi, G., Schwabe, D., Danculovic, J., Miaton, L.: Patterns for Personalized Web Applications. In: Proc. of EuroPlop, pp. 423–436 (2001)

[SF12] Salesforce Chatter,
http://www.salesforce.com/chatter/whatischatter/
[SR+08] Subrahmanyama, K., Reich, S.M., Waechter, N., Espinoza, G.: Online and offline
social networks: Use of social networking sites by emerging adults. Journal of Applied Developmental Psychology 29(6), 420–433 (2008)
[Tibco12] Tibco Tibbr, http://www.tibbr.com/
[VP+09] Valverde, F., Panach, I., Aquino, N., Pastor, O.: Dealing with Abstract Interaction
Modelling in an MDE Development Process: a Pattern-based Approach. In: New Trends on
Human-Computer Interaction. Springer, London (2009)
[TK10] Yang, T.A., Kim, D.J.: A Comparative Analysis of Online Social Networking Sites and
Their Business Models. In: Murugesan, S. (ed.) Handbook of Research on Web 2.0, 3.0, and
X.0: Technologies, Business, and Social Applications, pp. 662–672 (2010)
[WR12] WebRatio, http://www.webratio.com/

Model Driven Extraction of the Navigational Concern of Legacy Web Applications*

Roberto Rodríguez-Echeverría, José M. Conejero, Pedro J. Clemente,
Víctor M. Pavón, and Fernando Sánchez-Figueroa

University of Extremadura (Spain),
Quercus Software Engineering Group
{rre,chemacm,pjclemente,vpavonru,fernando}@unex.es
http://quercusseg.unex.es

Abstract. Nowadays, there is a current trend in software industry to modernize traditional Web Applications (WAs) to Rich Internet Applications (RIAs). RIAs improve the user experience by combining the lightweight distribution architecture of the Web with the interface interactivity and computation power of desktop applications. In this context, Model Driven Web Engineering (MDWE) approaches have been extended with new modeling primitives to obtain the benefits provided by RIA features. However, during the last decade, widespread language-specific web frameworks have supported actual web system development. In this paper we present a model driven modernization process to obtain RIAs from legacy web systems based on such frameworks. model driven techniques reduce complexity and improve reusability of the process, making the development more systematic and less error prone. Being navigational information of upmost importance for the modernization process of a web application, the paper is focused on presenting the model driven extraction of such concern from the legacy system artifact, presenting the extraction tools and process.

Keywords: Model-driven Engineering, Re-engineering, Web Applications, RIA.

1 Introduction

Rich Internet Applications (RIAs) have emerged as the most promising platform for Web 2.0 development combining the lightweight distribution architecture of the web with the interface interactivity and computation power of desktop applications [11]. To take advantages of these new capabilities, there is a current trend in the industry to perform a modernization of their legacy WA to produce RIA counterparts. This trend is, even, more evident with the transition to the

* Work funded by Spanish Contract MIGRARIA - TIN2011-27340 at Ministerio de Ciencia e Innovación and Gobierno de Extremadura (GR-10129) and European Regional Development Fund (ERDF).

M. Grossniklaus and M. Wimmer (Eds.): ICWE 2012 Workshops, LNCS 7703, pp. 56–70, 2012.

forthcoming HTML5 that implements natively most of these features gaining momentum.

In this context, MDWE approaches [14] have been extended with new modeling primitives to obtain the benefits provided by RIA features [7][10][17]. This way, introducing RIA features in legacy WA developed using models becomes a feasible task as it has been shown in [15][13]. However, during the last decade, widespread language-specific Web frameworks (e.g. Struts[1]) have supported the actual developments of these WAs, neglecting the benefits provided by model driven approaches. These frameworks are often tied to the programming-language level, making maintenance and modernization processes a difficult task. Traditionally, these modernization processes have been performed in an ad-hoc manner, resulting in very expensive and error-prone projects.

This work is part of a larger research project, called MIGRARIA, where a systematic and semi-automatic process to modernize legacy non-model-based data-driven WAs into RIAs has been defined. The process is based on model driven reengineering techniques used to mainly obtain (i) a new RIA front end to interact with the legacy system and (ii) a server-side connection layer to allow this interaction. The modernization process outlined before comprises a series of complex challenges so we try to provide the engineer with a systematic method and a partially automated toolkit.

In this paper we focus on the extraction of the navigational information from the legacy system artifacts (source code, pages, configuration files, etc.). First, we identify and locate the navigational information scattered over the WA artifacts. Then, we provide the engineer with the tool and method to generate model representations of such information. And finally we detailed the final representation we have devised to specify the navigation flows of the WA in an integrated and homogeneous way. The Struts web framework is clearly widespread through the web industry. So there exists a wide range of web applications, some of them publicly available, that may come to an interesting source of case studies. That is the rationale behind the selection of such framework for this work..

The rest of the paper is structured as follows. Section 2 presents an overview of the MIGRARIA project. In Section 3 an illustrative example is depicted. Section 4 introduces our approach to extract navigational models from a Struts-based legacy WA. In Section 5 we provide the results obtained in a study case for validation. The related work is discussed in Section 6. Finally, main conclusions and future work are outlined in Section 7.

2   MIGRARIA Project Overview

In this section, a general overview of the MIGRARIA project is introduced to provide the proper context to the work presented in this paper. One of the leading ideas of this project is to use model driven techniques and tools to deal with the complexity of extraction and interpretation processes [12]. As figure 1 presents, our approach is fundamentally organized in two different stages: (1)generating

---

[1] http://struts.apache.org/

58   R. Rodríguez-Echeverría et al.

of a conceptual representation of the legacy WA; and (2). generating the RIA
front-end and its infrastructure . Three information extraction plans have been
defined, marked as 1-A, 1-B and 2-B, and one restructuring process, 2-A. Our
purpose is to obtain information from three complementary views of the same
system: (1) the dynamic runtime view at client-side; (2) the static view of the
system source code at server-side; (3) and the dynamic view of user interaction
trace from server-side runtime log.

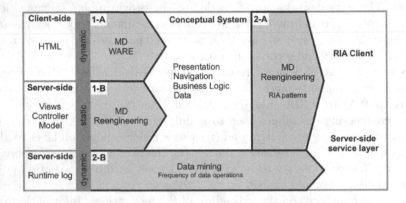

Fig. 1. MIGRARIA overview

Regarding action plan 1-A, we apply Web Application Reverse Engineering
(WARE) techniques [9] to perform dynamic analysis mimicking the user interaction with the WA. And representations of different concerns of a WA are
generated, such as its navigation map or its inferred data model.

Concerning action plan 1-B, we apply model driven reengineering methods
to perform static analysis of all the different sources available at server side ,
such as: the source code of the views and the controllers, database schemas,
configuration files. Again our purpose is to generate a conceptual representation
of the legacy system by producing models of its conceptual layers.

Then, approaches 1-A and 1-B share a common objective but they follow
different strategies. Our aim is to get two complementary conceptual representations of the same legacy WA. Both of them will be mixed, in a later stage,
to get a more precise representation, decreasing ambiguity and knowledge loss
derived from information extraction and interpretation activities.

On the other side, action plan 2-B consists of the application of data mining
techniques to extract the user interaction trace from the server log files. In this
case, we use the statistical information retrieved to derive a proposal of the RIA
Client UI composition, because a compelling RIA Client UI composition cannot
be derived right from a mere mapping of the navigation and presentation layers
of the WA obtained at the fist stage.

Finally, the second stage of our approach is mainly realized by action plan 2-A.
We apply model driven techniques to restructure and to evolve the conceptual

models of the WA into conceptual models of its RIA counterpart. In [13] we introduced an approach based on model weaving and RIA patterns.

3   Illustrative Example

The Agenda[2] system is one of the case studies used within the MIGRARIA project. Agenda is an example of data-driven WA since the web layer of the system mainly consists of a CRUD client that interacts with the underlying information system. Several frameworks and Java stack technologies for WAs have been used in the development of the system, as Struts for the web layer.

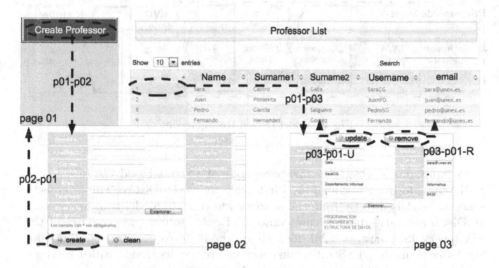

Fig. 2. Pages and flows of the illustrative example

Figure 2 shows the professor management process and includes all the CRUD operations related to the professor data entity resulting in different navigational flows departing and arriving to *page01*. This part of the system is representative enough to be an example of the most common navigational flows used in this system. Observe in the figure that the page containing the list of professors (Display action) is marked as *page01*, the professor sign in page (Creation action) is marked as *page02* and the removing and updating page (Remove and Update actions) as *page03*. We have also identified the navigational flows between these pages in order to be referenced in subsequent sections. The example contains 5 different navigational flows identified as: *p01-p02* flow (*page01 Create Professor* link), *p02-p01* flow *(Page02 create* button), *p01-p03* flow (*page01* list item links), *p03-p01-U* flow (*page03* update button), and *p03-p01-R* flow (*page03* remove button).

---

[2] http://www.unex.es/eweb/migraria/cs/agenda

4 The Approach

The main goal of this work consists of the extraction of navigational models from WAs developed with MVC-based web frameworks. As shown in section 2, for the first stage of our approach, information is extracted from a legacy WA by two different means: (1) applying WARE techniques, and (2) reengineering the original WA. In this work we focus on the latter, so figure 3 describes the main steps of our model driven reengineering process (labelled 1-B at figure 1). As previously shown, for practical purposes, Struts 1.X[3] has been selected as the reference web framework for this work.

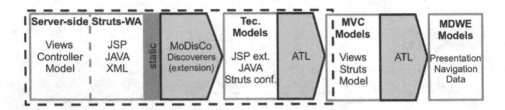

Fig. 3. Model Driven Reengineering

As input, our process takes the source code of a Struts-based WA (JSP, Java, XML) to perform a static analysis. First of all, we use MoDisCo [2] discoverers to generate models directly from the source code (text-to-model transformation). MoDisCo gives us a model representation of every source code resource of the WA (every JSP, Java, or XML file). However, MoDisco discoverer outputs not Struts-aware models, i.e Struts main concepts are not first level entities. So those models are complete but too complex to derive navigational models from them. In this work we have adapted MoDisco to create Struts-aware models from our legacy application. We then use these models to produce a representation of the WA on a higher level of abstraction conformed to our MVC (Struts) metamodel. This transformation is specified by the definition of ATL Rules. On this stage, our main concern is to get an accurate specification of the navigational aspect of the WA. With that purpose, we build a MVC (Struts) model that collects all the interaction flows (and the elements involved) defined on the web layer, generating a comprehensive view of the navigational concern.

Following, the main elements and activities involved in the first section of our process are detailed, surrounded by a dashed line at figure 3.

4.1 Locating Navigation Information

In this work, we are only interested in the information related to the navigational concern of the WA (page linking and data transferring). In MVC web

---

[3] http://struts.apache.org/1.x/

frameworks, the navigational information is scattered throughout the views and the controller specification so that the encapsulation of this information into a software artifact (model) is also a contribution of our work. The Struts architecture is derived from a combination of the Front Controller and Intercepting Filter patterns. Struts provides a single controller that governs the application events, while filters catch and process incoming and outgoing events to ensure that each of the MVC components receive exactly the information they need. The framework also provides custom tags for communication between these layers.

To define the views, Struts provides four different taglibs created by applying the JSP extension mechanism[4]: bean, html, logic and nested. Table 1 shows a summary of the main tags that provide information regarding the navigational concern,useful for our extraction process. Basically, we are interested in those tags that define server requests and their parameters. In HTML, these requests are mainly represented by form submissions and requests performed by means of hyperlinks (*anchor* tag). Struts defines its own JSP tags to generate dynamically this type of HTML elements. These tags are defined within the HTML taglib and they generate HTML 4.01 or XHTML compliant outputs in Struts.

Table 1. Information extraction summary

Taglib	Tag	Relevant information
html	form	Requested Action (ActionMapping)
		Optional attributes for form bean
	common form tags	Request parameters (name)
		Name attribute: form bean name
		Property att.: field name and bean property name
	link	4 different types: forward, href, action and page
		1 request parameter, attributes: paramID, paramName, paramProperty, paramScope
		Multiple request parameters, attributes on a Map: name, property and scope
logic	redirect	3 different types: forward, href and page
		Attributes for parameter specification as html:link
	forward	Attribute name: global ActionForward

Regarding the Controller component (MVC pattern), Struts provides three main components to define it: (1) ActionForm classes to manage and encapsulate data serialization and validation; (2) Action classes to handle each logical request that may be received by the WA; and (3) ActionMappings to relate each logical request to its corresponding handler. The two formers are defined in JAVA whilst the latter is defined by using XML (conformed to the struts-config DTD). In Struts 1.X, the ActionsMappings database is a key element for defining navigation in the system. Each ActionMapping allows the developer to relate a set of requests with the action (or actions) that handles them, including

---

[4] http://java.sun.com/j2ee/tutorial/1_3-fcs/doc/JSPTags.html

all the information needed to deal with these requests (ActionForms as request parameters, forwards as replies to the request, etc). On the other hand, Actions contain the code that: (1) populates the data for the views; (2) handles the operations to modify the model; and (3) directs the control flow (navigation), providing a particular view as reply to the request or passing the control to a different action (forwards).

Regarding the model, Struts does not explicitly provide any related element. For the system state maintenance, a Data Access Framework is usually used in order to keep the code independent of the persistence actions: separate the business logic from the role that Action classes play.

In order to make the information extraction process systematic, we have defined a set of base navigation flows that categorize the ways that Struts deals with requests. These cases will drive the definition of the information extraction queries. Table 2 presents the different base types we have observed in our case study.

Table 2. Application base flow cases

Base case	Request	Parameters			Forwards	
		0	1	N	Page	Action
Link to a page	html:link				X	
Link to an action	html:link	X	X	X	X	X
	logic:redirect					
Form submit	html:form			X	X	X

As may be observed in Table 2, each base case is characterized by the tuple (request, parameters, forward), so we actually get 9 different cases. In a Struts-based WA, these cases does not usually appears isolated, instead the same action often handles different requests that may generate different navigation flows. Thus, we may also find two main types of actions (situations): the ones that define only one navigation flow and those that define multiple flows. It is worth noting we only consider navigation flows derived from different request (i.e., with different request parameters). We are not considering exceptional situations, such as error navigation flows, because we want to extract regular navigation flows and to avoid unnecessary complexity.

Figure 4 shows a whole example of a navigation flow specification in Struts. As may be observed, the view specifies the details of a request by using the *html:link* tag (request tuple (link to action, 1 parameter, JSP)). The mapping between this request and the action handler is specified in the configuration file by defining an ActionMapping. Finally, the execute method of the action handles the request and provides a reply. In this case, based on the request parameters, the action will reply an OK forward and the view defined in *professordetail.jsp* which presents the details of the selected professor. As the example denotes, it is common practice to write Actions that both navigate to a page and handle forms submitted from that page. Its general form is to hard code the mapping decision, depending on the value of a request parameter, inside the execute method of the Action and to use a single ActionMapping in *struts-config.xml* to configure it [6].

```
<logic:iterate id="professor" name="professorList">              JSP
<tr class="gradeA">
    <td>
        <html:link action="professorDetail" paramId="id" paramName="professor" paramProperty="id">
            <bean:write name="professor" property="id"/>
        </html:link>
```

```
<action path="/professordetail"                                 config
        type="com.university.professor.ProfessorDetail"
        name="professorForm"
        scope="request">
        <forward name="ok" path="/WEB-INF/jsp/professor/professordetail.jsp" />
        <forward name="list" path="/professorlist.do" />
</action>
```

```
if((af.getUpdate()==null)&&(id!=null))                          action
        forward="ok";
else{
    if(af.getUpdate()!=null)
        forward="list";
}
```

Fig. 4. Navigation flow specification in Struts

Navigation Paths in the Case Study. Regarding our running example, Table 3 shows the information to be extracted from the ActionMappings and their relationships with the navigational flows described in Section 3. As the example denotes, two of the three ActionMappings considered follow the anti-pattern aforementioned: a single action both navigates to a page and handles forms submitted from that page. Both, createProfessor and *ProfessorDetail* respond in a different way to the same request with different parameters. On the other hand, if the request does not contain data (page01 as source) they forward to page02 and page03 respectively, whilst forward and returns to page01 if the form contains data, processing previously the operation with the data contained in the form. ActionMapping *ProfessorDetail* may be considered a special type of this pattern: one action responds to three different requests (multiple submit handling). The first ActionMapping is related with the request of the action that generates page01 (the source of this request is out of the scope of the example considered).

4.2   From Struts Code to Struts-Aware Models

On one hand, a Struts-based WA is basically conformed by JavaServer pages (HTML extended with Struts taglibs, XML), the FrontController configuration

Table 3. Navigation information in the ActionMapping instances considered

Page	Page Name	Request	Parameters	Action	Forward	Nav. Path
		link to action	No	ProfessorList	Page: P01	
01	ProfessorList	link to action	No	CreateProfessor	Page: P02	p01-p02
	ProfessorList	link to action	Request: OID	ProfessorDetail	Page: P03	p01-p03
02	CreateProfessor	form	form bean: professorForm (submit: create)	CreateProfessor	Action: listProfessor (P01)	p02-p01
03	ProfessorDetail	form	form bean: professorForm (submit: update)	ProfessorDetail	Action: listProfessor (P01)	p03-p01U
	ProfessorDetail	form	form bean: professorForm (submit: delete)	ProfessorDetail	Action: listProfessor (P01)	p03-p01R

file (XML), Actions and ActionForms (Java code). So there are three different kinds of information sources: (X)HTML, XML (DTD Struts config) and java code.

On the other hand, MoDisco provides the modernization engineer with discoverers to extract models from common java web artifacts as JavaServer pages, XML and WA configuration files (*web.xml*). However, those discoverers present some limitations when processing WAs developed with web frameworks, because they are conceived from a technological base and not from a concrete framework point of view. That approach leads to more complex transformation scenarios due to the lost of the semantics related to the web framework. So we propose an extension to MoDisco to support the extraction of models closer to Struts concepts. Such extension may be approached by two different means: (1) defining new discoverers; (2) defining transformations to refine the output of MoDisco regular discoverers.

Concerning the MoDisco discoverer for JSP, it defines a JSP metamodel as an extension of the XML metamodel that covers the concepts defined in the JSTL (JSP Standard Action Eclass). Any other tag defined by the JSP custom taglib support, as Struts taglibs, is extracted as generic JSP Action elements losing its structure and semantics. In order to get a more precise representation of Struts-specific tags we have defined a new metamodel to define every Struts tag as an extension of MoDisco JSP metamodel. Figure 5 shows an excerpt of our Struts taglibs metamodel (the root EClass is JSP Action at JSP metamodel, not shown). We also provide the corresponding transformation rules to refine the JSP models obtained with MoDisco into our Struts taglib models. So, in this case, the second MoDisco extension approach has been followed.

To extract the model representing the information of the Struts configuration file we have followed the first extension approach previously proposed: the definition of a new discoverer. The development of this discoverer is based on the Web Application discoverer that processes *web.xml* files. Basically, it is conformed by two main steps: metamodel generation and model extraction. In this case, by

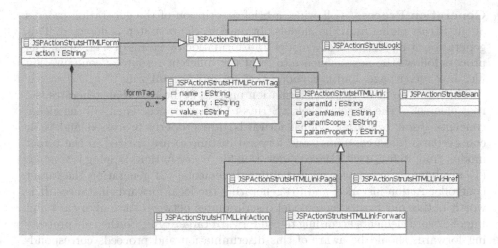

Fig. 5. Struts taglib metamodel excerpt

means of Eclipse EMF functionality the Struts configuration metamodel (Struts-conf, for short) is automatically generated from the XML Schema Definition of the Struts configuration file. So we may easily generate a Struts-conf metamodel for every version of this schema (actually 4 different versions for Struts 1.X). Once the Struts-conf metamodel is available, the extraction process is straightforward because EMF functionality permits to serialize a XML file to a XMI file conforming to the resulting metamodel, i.e. a model representing the original XML file.

Finally, regarding the java code artifacts, no extension is currently proposed because its suitability (or necessity) is under study right now. So, in this case, our process consumes the model artifacts produced by the Java MoDisco discoverer.

4.3   Modeling Navigational Information

To provide a comprehensive view of the navigational information extracted from the legacy system, an Ecore metamodel has been defined, named the Struts metamodel[5] (not detailed in this work). This metamodel allows specifying the elements of the Struts framework but also their relationships in order to define the different navigational flows of the legacy WA. As aforementioned, in a Struts-based WA, the ActionMapping database plays a key role to relate all the elements involved in a navigation flow. So we have tried to maintain Struts semantics by considering ActionMapping as the main concept of the metamodel. That way we try to simplify the automatic generation process of models conformed to our Struts metamodel, collecting just useful information (navigational concern, in this work) for its later processing.

---

[5] http://www.unex.es/eweb/migraria/cs/agenda

Generation Process. Following, a brief description of the generation process of the Struts model from the models obtained in the first step is depicted. This generation is implemented as a model transformation by means of ATL rules. The process follows the next sequence to treat the different resources: configuration file, JavaServer pages and java code (Actions and ActionForms).

The entry point of the transformation process is the rule that generates the root element of the target model: a Struts EClass instance. Then, all the global concepts (form beans and global forwards) are properly processed and their counterparts (data containers and forward instances) are created in the target model. And, to finish with the configuration file, every ActionMapping is treated: (1) resolving its references with the global elements; (2) generating the target controller Action instance; and (3) generating the local forwards instances. It is worth noting our Struts metamodel discriminates between ActionForward and PageForward elements according to the forward target type. So the rule processing forwards should be aware of this discrimination and proceeds correspondingly, i.e. selecting the appropriate EClass and filling its references properly.

Once the configuration file has been processed, we query the JSP model to extract the information of the requests contained in every page (*html:form* and *html:link* instances). Then, every request instance of the target model is related to the ActionMapping instance according to its *path* attribute. And the request parameters are specified by means of parameters instances.

Finally, the Java code is processed. Actually, the *Action* processing rule is invoked from the *ActionMapping* rule, so the different portions of the java code model are processed on demand. The relevant information to extract from an *Action* is the correct identification of the navigation flows that treats. In concrete, we are interested on identifying the input (request parameter set conforming the conditional expression granting access to a concrete control flow) and output (returned forward) of every navigational flow. That way, the corresponding references between request, action and forward instances can be established in the target model.

Struts Model of the Illustrative Example. Taking as a base our Struts metamodel, figure 6 shows the final model obtained for the driving example (*p01-p02* flow). This way, it can be seen in a single view all the elements of the model belonging to the definition of a navigation flow. For example, in the *p01-p02* navigation flow, we have:

- Origin: the page *page01* and the request *request01* contained in this page.
- Mapping: the *ActionMapping AM_RegisterProfessor* which is related to the action *CreateProfessor* by means of the action attribute.
- Target (response): the action *CreateProfessor* for the request *request01* follows the forward *PageForward01* that returns the page *page02* as response.

The flow *p01-p02* has not an explicit parameter passing between both pages. So, the entity *request01* is not related with any *RequestParameters* or *Form* instances, that act as data containers in the metamodel. The opposite situation is represented by the flow *p02-p01* where there is a data transferring (represented

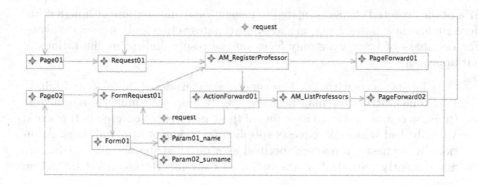

Fig. 6. Struts Model

by the entities *Form01* and *Param0X_X*) related to the operation of creating a new register in the database. Moreover, *p02-p01* flow involves an action chain: *AM_RegisterProfessor* action forwards to *AM_ListProfessors* action that finally forwards to *page01*.

It can be observed how all the navigation flows are represented in a homogeneous way, easing their querying and extraction. Moreover, all the elements implied in a navigation flow are reflected in a single model. This way, we can obtain a representation of the navigation layer of the legacy WA following one of the existing MDWE approaches (not shown in this work). Additionally, *Page* and *Action* instances include a reference to its corresponding element instances on the Struts-aware models generated in the previous step. So direct access is granted to relevant information for other concerns, such as page composition structure.

5 Evaluation

In order to evaluate our approach, we have followed a simple comparison strategy between two different versions of the Struts models for our case study: (1) one built manually by an engineer; and (2) one generated automatically by our process.

Regarding comparison results, table 4 presents some of the main results we have obtained. As shown, our approach generates automatically more than the

Table 4. Evaluation results

	Pages	Link Reqs	Form Reqs	Action Flows	Action Forwards	Page Forward
Manual	50	36	13	99	23	76
Automatic	50	30	13	119	29	90
total diff	0	-6	0	+20	+6	+14
% diff	0%	-16,67%	0	+20,20%	+26,09%	+18,42%

97% of the expected elements related to navigational information, although it underestimates link-based requests and overestimates action and forward elements. For the shake of brevity we only focus on the results indicating limitations of our approach:

- Only link requests with 0 or 1 parameter are considered (h:link-0 and h:link-1 columns). Struts use map beans to specify links with multiple parameters (h:link-n column). Actual decoding of these maps is not covered in this work.
- We only deal with link requests specified by means of html:link tags. Additionally, request parameters specified as a query string within an URL are not currently parsed. Just the action is conveniently identified for action mapping.
- Forward instances differentiation is evaluated by the equality of the values of their path attributes. Some forward instances with different path values may be considered as duplicates because the actual forwarded pages are clones located at different paths.

6   Related Work

Web Application information extraction has been performed by reverse engineering techniques [9]. Although those approaches obtain similar results to those presented herein, we consider they follow the alternative strategy identified as 1-A plan in MIGRARIA overview.

Although our intention is to follow the guidelines proposed by Architecture Driven Modernization (ADM) [16] , we have declined to use Knowledge Discovery Metamodel (KDM) because of its complexity and lack of a comprehensive definition for user interface representation. In that sense, MoDisco [2] is a generic, extensible and open source approach for software modernization that makes an intensive use of MDD principles and techniques which could be used as base to implement ADM. Our work presents a specialization of the framework defined by MoDisco to be applied in concrete modernization scenarios from Struts-based legacy WAs into RIAs.

Framework-Specific Modeling Language (FSML) [1] is a DSL to support the development of framework-based applications. The framework models are expressed using FSMLs that capture the framework abstractions as language concepts. FSML has been applied successfully to migrate a WA from Struts to JavaServer Faces. But it is a migration proposal defined at a low-level of abstraction and, though interesting, meanwhile we are interested on generating a conceptual representation of the navigational concern of a legacy WA in order to propose a modernization approach. Moreover, the migration of the views (JSPs) is not considered in that approach.

In [3] and [4] the authors introduce a process to extract models from Struts systems. In [4], the authors use two different DSLs to generate the models from the system based on source code conformed to a grammar and not well-formed source code, respectively. Based on these models, they define several model transformations that generate a JavaServer Faces version of the system. In [3] the authors complete the work by adding an intermediate layer where KDM is used to represent the models of the system. Note that the goals of this work and ours are slightly different. The former proposes a migration of a legacy system based on a web framework to a system based on a different framework whilst our work presents a modernization approach to a RIA. The Struts metamodel presented in [4] covers the representation of the configuration file and the code related to the actions. This metamodel is on a level with the models we generate by means of our extended version of MoDisco. In our case, we propose a discoverer able to treat any version of the Struts 1.X configuration file and define a new metamodel to represent the Struts taglibs (JSP definition). Moreover we define a conceptual Struts metamodel that yields on a higher level of abstraction and provide us with a integrated view of the navigation concern of the legacy WA.

7   Conclusions and Future Work

This work outlines MIGRARIA project, an approach for systematic WA-to-RIA model driven modernization, whose main goal is to generate a RIA client and its infrastructure. In this paper, we have specially focused on extracting navigational models from Struts-based Web Applications.

By means of a running example (excerpt of a case study) we have detailed the main activities (locate, represent, transform) and artifacts (code, metamodel, model, transformation rules) related to the extraction process. The process is driven by different model artifacts that allows to define a systematic and reusable process. We have specified our own set of Struts metamodel (Struts taglibs, Struts-config and Struts metamodel) to define intermediate navigation models that remain independent of any MDWE approach. Those intermediate models may be projected to the selected MDWE approach by means of model transformations. So the methods and tools of a concrete MDWE approach may leverage our modernization process.

As main lines for future work on navigation extraction we consider the following: (1) eliminating most of the current limitations of the approach; (2) refining and validating the approach with a larger set of case studies; (3) extending the approach to support uniformly a set of MVC-based web frameworks; (4) complementing the approach with WARE strategies; and (5) defining a comprehensive tool chain to assist the whole extraction process.

References

1. Antkiewicz, M., Czarnecki, K.: Framework-Specific Modeling Languages; Examples and Algorithms. Technical Report 2007, Electrical & Computer Engineering. University of Waterloo, Waterloo (2007)
2. Bruneliere, H., Cabot, J., Jouault, F.: MoDisco: A Generic and Extensible Framework for Model Driven Reverse Engineering. In: IEEE/ACM International Conference on Automated Software Engineering, pp. 1–2 (2010)

3. Cánovas Izquierdo, J.L., Molina, J.G.: A Domain Specific Language for Extracting Models in Software Modernization. In: Paige, R.F., Hartman, A., Rensink, A. (eds.) ECMDA-FA 2009. LNCS, vol. 5562, pp. 82–97. Springer, Heidelberg (2009)
4. Cánovas Izquierdo, J.L., Sánchez-Ramón, Ó., Sánchez-Cuadrado, J., García-Molina, J.: DSLs para la extracción de modelos en modernización. Actas de los Talleres de las Jornadas de Ingeniería del Software y Bases de Datos 2, 1–10 (2008)
5. Di Lucca, A.G., Distante, D., Bernardi, M.L.: Recovering Conceptual Models from Web Applications. In: Pierce, R., Stanrney, J. (eds.) Proceedings of the 24th Annual ACM International Conference on Design of Communication, SIGDOC 2006, pp. 113–120. ACM Press (2006)
6. Dudney, B., Lehr, J.: Jakarta Pitfalls: Time-Saving Solutions for Struts, Ant, JUnit, and Cactus (Java Open Source Library). Wiley (2003)
7. Fraternali, P., Comai, S., Bozzon, A., Carughi, G.T.: Engineering rich internet applications with a model-driven approach. ACM Transactions on the Web 4(2), 1–47 (2010)
8. Mesbah, A., van Deursen, A.: Migrating Multi-page Web Applications to Single-page AJAX Interfaces. In: 11th European Conference on Software Maintenance and Reengineering, CSMR 2007, pp. 181–190 (March 2007)
9. Patel, R., Coenen, F., Martin, R., Archer, L.: Reverse Engineering of Web Applications: A Technical Review. Technical Report. University of Liverpool Department of Computer Science, Liverpool (July 2007)
10. Pérez, S., Díaz, O., Meliá, S., Gómez, J.: Facing Interaction-Rich RIAs: The Orchestration Model. In: 2008 Eighth International Conference on Web Engineering, pp. 24–37 (July 2008)
11. Preciado, J.C., Linaje, M., Sanchez, F., Comai, S.: Necessity of methodologies to model Rich Internet Applications. In: Seventh IEEE International Symposium on Web Site Evolution (2005)
12. Rodríguez-Echeverría, R., Conejero, J.M., Clemente, P.J., Preciado, J.C., Sánchez-Figueroa, F.: Modernization of Legacy Web Applications into Rich Internet Applications. In: Harth, A., Koch, N. (eds.) ICWE 2011. LNCS, vol. 7059, pp. 236–250. Springer, Heidelberg (2012)
13. Rodríguez-Echeverría, R., Conejero, J.M., Linaje, M., Preciado, J.C., Sánchez-Figueroa, F.: Re-engineering Legacy Web Applications into Rich Internet Applications. In: Benatallah, B., Casati, F., Kappel, G., Rossi, G. (eds.) ICWE 2010. LNCS, vol. 6189, pp. 189–203. Springer, Heidelberg (2010)
14. Rossi, G., Pastor, O., Schwabe, D., Olsina, L.: Web Engineering: Modelling and Implementing Web Applications (Human-Computer Interaction Series) (October 2007)
15. Rossi, G., Urbieta, M., Ginzburg, J., Distante, D., Garrido, A.: Refactoring to Rich Internet Applications. A Model-Driven Approach. In: 2008 Eighth International Conference on Web Engineering, pp. 1–12 (July 2008)
16. Ulrich, W.: Modernization Standards Roadmap, pp. 46–64 (2010)
17. Valverde, F., Pastor, O.: Facing the Technological Challenges of Web 2.0: A RIA Model-Driven Engineering Approach. In: Vossen, G., Long, D.D.E., Yu, J.X. (eds.) WISE 2009. LNCS, vol. 5802, pp. 131–144. Springer, Heidelberg (2009)

Model-Driven Testing for Web Applications Using Abstract State Machines

Francesco Bolis[1], Angelo Gargantini[1], Marco Guarnieri[1],
Eros Magri[1], and Lorenzo Musto[2,*]

[1] Dip. di Ing. dell'Informazione e Metodi Matematici, Università di Bergamo, Italy
{francesco.bolis,angelo.gargantini,marco.guarnieri,eros.magri}@unibg.it
[2] Optics Division Alcatel-Lucent, Vimercate, Italy
lorenzo.musto@alcatel-lucent.com

Abstract. The increasing diffusion and importance of Web Applications has led to strict requirements in terms of continuity of the service, because their unavailability can lead to severe economic losses. Techniques to assure the quality of these applications are thus needed in order to identify in advance possible faults. Model-driven approaches to the testing of Web Applications can provide developers with a way of checking the conformance of the actual Web Application with respect to the model built from the requirements. These approaches can be used to automatically generate from the model a set of test cases satisfying certain coverage criteria, and thus can be integrated in a classical test driven development process. In this paper we present an automated technique for Web Application testing using a model-driven approach. We present a way of modeling Web Applications by Abstract State Machines (ASMs), and a process for generating automatically from the model a concrete test suite that is executed on the Web Application under test in order to check the conformance between the application and the model.

1 Introduction

The wide diffusion of Internet combined with mobile technologies has produced a significant growth in the demand of Web Applications with an increasing request for efficient techniques tailored for their validation [8]. Researchers and practitioners are still trying to find viable approaches in order to validate Web Applications. A possible approach is to apply Model-driven or model-based testing (MBT)[16] to Web Applications. Since software testing is a costly and time-consuming activity, specification-based (or model-based) testing permits to considerably reduce the testing costs. MBT consists in building an abstract model of a Web Application and using the model instead of the code to derive tests (including the oracles) and to define adequacy of the testing effort with respect to the requirements. The model of the Web Application does not need to include all the details of the implementation, but it should be precise enough to guarantee that the test cases represent actual use scenarios of the Web Application.

---

* This work has been partially supported by the project Ricerca Applicata per il Territorio - Berg. II - Regione Lombardia and Alcatel-Lucent Spa.

M. Grossniklaus and M. Wimmer (Eds.): ICWE 2012 Workshops, LNCS 7703, pp. 71–78, 2012.
© Springer-Verlag Berlin Heidelberg 2012

Having an abstract model that represents a Web Application is no longer an unrealistic hypothesis for three reasons. Firstly, several model-driven techniques for the development of Web Applications have been developed in the last decade [12] and thus by using these techniques models are easily available as a result of the development process. Secondly, techniques for extracting abstract models from existing Web Applications have been developed [2] and have been already used in several approaches to Web Application testing [1]. Thirdly, designers often manually build an abstract model from the requirements and this model is used to check whether the Web Application satisfies the requirements.

MBT can be integrated in an agile development process [14], by helping the developers to automatically derive tests and execute them. Our approach, that belongs to the third alternative presented before, assumes that initially the designer develops a model of the Web Application (in a model-driven classical view), derives some tests cases from it, and executes these tests against an empty implementation (in a test-driven development - TDD). He/she then implements the Web Application and automatically runs the tests until they pass. Any change in the code that does not require a modification of the model is checked again by the original test cases. Some modifications of the code may cause a failure of the tests because the model must be updated. In this case, the designer does not update the test cases (differently from a classical agile development) but he/she modifies the model and extracts the test cases again.

MBT can be used also in the other two scenarios presented above: (a) if the Web Application is developed by using a model-driven technique, our approach can be applied to check the correctness of the model-to-code transformations; (b) if the model is automatically built from the application, then our approach can be used to generate test suites for regression testing.

This development process works better than the classical TDD if maintaining the model, deriving the abstract test cases, and transforming them in concrete test cases is easier than maintaining the test suite. To this aim, the following features of the proposed process are critical: (1) the model must be written in a notation powerful enough to express any behavior of the Web Application, and at the same time abstract enough to ease the process of model definition; (2) it must be possible to automatically analyze and execute the models in order to find faults in them and to gain confidence that they capture the intended behavior of the application; (3) the test generation process must be automatized; (4) the concretization of the abstract tests must be automatized and the resulting tests must be automatically executed.

In this paper we propose a model-based approach to Web Application testing that uses sequential nets of ASMs and satisfies all the features listed above. Section 2 presents some background about ASMs, whereas in Section 3 we present our model based approach including a technique to model Web Applications by ASMs and how to generate and execute tests for Web Applications. In Section 4 we present an example of our approach. Section 5 presents the related work, whereas in Section 6 we draw some conclusions and present future work.

2 Background

Abstract State Machines. ASMs, whose complete presentation can be found in [5], are an extension of Finite State Machines (FSM), where unstructured control states are replaced by states with arbitrary complex data. The *states* of an ASM are multi-sorted first-order structures, i.e. domains of objects with functions and predicates defined on them. ASM states are modified by *transition relations* specified by "rules" describing the modification of the function interpretations from one state to the next one. There is a limited but powerful set of *rule constructors* that allow to express guarded actions (if-then), simultaneous parallel actions (par) or sequential actions (seq).

An ASM state is a set of *locations*, namely pairs (*function-name, list-of-parameter-values*). Locations represent the abstract ASM concept of basic object containers (memory units). Location *updates* represent the basic units of state change and they are given as assignments, each of the form $loc := v$, where loc is a location and v its new value.

Functions may be *static* (never change during any run of the machine) or *dynamic* (may change as a consequence of agent actions or *updates*). Dynamic functions are distinguished between *monitored* (only read by the machine and modified by the environment), and *controlled* (read and written by the machine).

A *computation* of an ASM is a finite or infinite sequence $s_0, s_1, \ldots, s_n, \ldots$ of states of the machine, where s_0 is an initial state and each s_{n+1} is obtained from s_n by firing the (unique) *main rule* which represents the starting point of the computation. An ASM can have more than one *initial state*. Listing 1 reports a fragment of the ASM specification of a Web Application.

```
asm index
import Pages
signature: // Declarations
    enum domain States = { EMPTY | PASSWORD | USERNAME | USERPASSW }
    enum domain Events = { SUBMIT_SUBMIT | RESET_RESET | TEXT_USERNAME |
    TEXT_PASSWORD | TEXTDEL_USERNAME | TEXTDEL_PASSWORD | LINK_PREV }
    dynamic controlled currentPage : Pages
    dynamic controlled currentState : States
    dynamic monitored event : Events
definitions: // Definitions
    macro rule r_Reset =
        event = RESET_RESET then
            if currentState != EMPTY then
                currentState := EMPTY
        endif
    macro rule r_UsernameText = ...
    ...
    main rule r_Index =
        if currentPage = INDEX then
        par
            r_Reset[]
            r_UsernameText[]
        ...
        endpar endif
default init initial_state : // Initial values
    function currentState = EMPTY
    function currentPage = INDEX
```

Listing 1. AsmetaL code of Index page

The ASM methodology has been successfully applied in different fields [5] as: definition of programming and modeling languages, modeling e-commerce and web services, design and analysis of protocols, architectural design, and verification of compilation schemes and compiler back-ends.

The ASMETA toolset [4] supports designers and developers of ASMs. They can assist the user in developing specifications and proving model correctness by checking state invariants and temporal logic properties. A number of tools helps the designer also during the validation phase by means of a model reviewer, a simulator, and a scenario-based validator. Among the ASMETA tools, ATGT is the test generation tool.

Model-based testing for ASMs. By using ASMs in MBT, we assume that a *test sequence* or *test* is a finite sequence of states, whose first element is an initial state, and each state follows the previous by applying the transition rules.

Several coverage criteria have been defined for ASMs [9]. For instance, one basic criterion is the *rule coverage* which requires that, for every rule r_i, there exists at least one state in a test sequence in which r_i fires and there exists at least a state in a test sequence in which r_i does not fire.

Starting from the definition of coverage criteria, several approaches have been defined in order to build test suites. ATGT uses a technique based on the capability of the model checker SPIN [11] to produce counterexamples [10]. A recent work [3] in this area, improves considerably the scalabilty of the approach and extends the concept of ASM to *sequential nets* of ASMs.

3   Model-Based Testing for Web Application by ASM

Assuming the existence of an abstract model of the Web Application, we can use model-based techniques in order to compute an adequate test suite for the Web Application under test (AUT) in order to check whether it conforms to the model or not. We have chosen to use ASMs to represent the model because they are a good compromise between abstraction and expressive power. For instance, they are more flexible than FSMs, and they can also handle shared variables that can represent session data, which are vital for testing dynamic Web Applications.

Figure 1 shows the testing process we have devised. It takes as inputs the abstract model and the AUT. By giving the ASM model as input to the ATGT tool, we generate a set of tests according to several coverage criteria, for instance a basic criterion is the *Rule Coverage* whereas a more advanced one is the *Modified Condition Decision Coverage* [9]. The ATGT tool produces as output the Abstract Test Suite (ATS) which is a high level representation of the resulting test sequence.

Since we are testing Web Applications, we have chosen to represent our test suites in terms of the interactions that a user can do with the AUT, and thus, in order to model concrete tests and to automate their execution, we have chosen to use Sahi[1], a *capture and replay tool* that lets users express test cases using scripts

---

[1] Sahi Web Automation and Testing Tool - http://sahi.co.in/

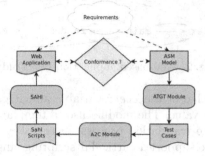

Fig. 1. Testing Process

and then it executes them. A translation is needed in order to map the ATS to a concrete set of Sahi scripts that can be executed on the Web Application under test, further details on the translation process are given below.

Then we execute the generated concrete test suite using the Sahi runner. Using the oracles automatically inserted in the scripts we can check whether the application under test conforms with the model or not.

Modeling Web Applications by using ASMs. We have defined an approach that builds an ASM model for each page in the Web Application, and then the entire Web Application is represented by a net of ASMs. To be more precise, in order to avoid the problem of the combinatorial explosion in the number of states of the ASM, we have used the technique based on hierarchical decomposition presented in [3] that introduces the *sequential nets* of ASMs. The modeling of one web page is done in the following way:

1. We define a shared domain, called *Pages*, that contains a value for each page in the application and a controlled variable *currentPage* of domain *Pages*.

2. We define a domain called *States*, local to each page, that contains an adequate number of states in order to represent the behavior of the page. We define a controlled variable *currentState* of domain *States*.

3. For each input element *e* in the web page and for each event associated with *e*, we define a constant in the *Events* enumerative domain. Each constant identifier reflects the kind and name of the event and the input element. We define a monitored variable *event* of domain *Events*. The kinds of the input elements are: (a) links, (b) buttons, (c) submit buttons, (d) reset buttons, (e) text fields and text areas, (f) password fields, (g) file dialogs, (h) checkboxes, (i) radio buttons, and (j) select lists.

4. For each input element *e* we write a rule that handles the events associated with *e* by either updating the current state of the page or executing the transition to another page, represented by another ASM.

A2C: Translating Abstract Tests to Concrete Tests The A2C module is a general purpose translator from an abstract test sequence into a concrete script in a selected scripting language. The application scans the abstract test sequence in

Fig. 2. Web-based application case study

order to extract the value of the *event* variable and it generates the concrete script according to this value. The module uses a template in order to describe the rules that guide the translation process; in this way if we want to extend the A2C tool in order to support a particular scripting language we only have to define a new template file. For instance, the Sahi transformation rule for a click event is as follows:

SUBMIT(name) ::= « _click(_submit("*name*"));»

4   Case Study

As a case study we have chosen a simple PHP Web Application, already presented in [13], that is composed by six different pages:

index.php is the login and initial page that requires to the user the username and the password in order to access to the other pages. It contains a *Reset* button and a *Submit* button that opens up the **main.php** page.

error_b.php is an error page opened up if any information in **index.php** is missing or wrong.

main.php contains several input elements, such as a link, a file dialog that can be activated by clicking on the *Browse* button, a textbox, a checkbox and the button *Submit* that activates the **random.php** page.

error_a.php is an error page opened if any field in **main.php** is missing.

random.php contains two link, one to **index.php** and the other one to **main.php**, a drop-down menu, radio buttons and a *Submit* button that activates the **end.php** page.

end.php contains a link to **index.php** or the option of closing the browser.

By following the process presented in Section 3, we have modeled each page using an ASM and then we have built a sequential net of ASMs, which is shown in Figure 2. Using the technique presented in [3] allowed us to avoid the explosion in the number of states in the model.

Once we have defined the model, we have used it in order to generate the test cases, which have been translated in Sahi scripts. Listing 2 shows a snippet of an ATS generated by *ATGT* from the ASM presented in Listing 2, whereas Listing 3 shows the corresponding Sahi scripts generated by the *A2C* tool.

ATGT has generated 212 test cases that achieved a 100% coverage of the PHP source code. We have used *XDebug*[2] and *PHP-Coverage*[3] in order to compute the coverage achieved by the test suite.

---

[2] XDebug, Debugger and Profiler Tool for PHP - http://xdebug.org/
[3] PHPCoverage, code coverage tool for PHP -
http://phpcoverage.sourceforge.net/

```
[ currentState=EMPTY
  currentPage=INDEX
  event=TEXT_USERNAME ]
[ currentState=USERNAME
  event=TEXT_PASSWORD ]
[ currentState=USERPASSW
  event=SUBMIT_SUBMIT ]
[ currentState=EMPTY
  currentPage=MAIN ]
```

```
_navigateTo("index.php");

_setValue(_textbox("username"),"admin");

_setValue(_textbox("password"),"admin");

_click(_submit("submit"));

_assertEqual("main.php",top.location.href);
```

Listing 2. ATS Example   **Listing 3.** CTS Example

5 Related Work

An approach quite similar to ours is the one presented by Andrews et al. [2]. They developed *FSMWeb*, a tool that can be used to test Web Applications. They model the Web Application by a hierarchy of FSMs, where a FSM represents either a logical web page, i.e. the model of a subsystem of the AUT, or a top level FSM, i.e. an aggregate of logical pages. In our opinion modeling Web Applications with ASMs offers a higher degree of expressiveness w.r.t. the FSMs. They propose also a way of automating the definition of the model from the Web Application under test. However, their tool does not implement this feature and thus they are tied to a manual implementation of the model as in our approach.

Deutsch at al. [7] present an approach that models data-driven Web Applications by means of ASM^+ models, which represents the transitions between pages, determined by the input provided to the application. Our approach can be applied to a wider range of Web Applications, i.e. actually it works with any Web Application for which exists an ASM model. In our opinion handling the testing of events by linear or branching-time temporal logics leads to complex models that can made the integration with agile development too hard, although it can discover more subtle errors. Another advantage of our approach is that we can use all the features provided by the ASMETA tool set, including a simulator, a model checker and a model advisor.

Tonella and Ricca [15] propose a technique to automatically generate and execute test cases starting from a UML model of the Web Application. Their approach requires a manual intervention in several phases, i.e. in the UML modeling phase and in the test refinement phase (their tool requires that the user fills in the input values in each URL), whereas our approach requires the intervention of the user only in the model definition phase. This is an advantage primarily because if we are in a situation in which the model already exists, the testing process can be executed without any intervention from the user.

6 Conclusion and Future Work

We have presented our ongoing work on using MBT for Web Application in an Agile context. Our approach provides the designers with an expressive but abstract language, an automatic generator of tests and a translator to concrete tests, and an automatic executor of the tests over the AUT.

A crucial activity in the application of our approach, is building an abstract model of the AUT. We plan to provide some help during this phase by generating automatically part of the ASM model from the AUT. We also plan to extend our approach with a model-to-model transformation tool which takes as input WebML [6] models, i.e. only Navigation and Composition models, and translates them into ASMs. Given the fact that WebML is a well-known Web application modeling language, its use could ease the definition of ASMs.

We also plan to study how our approach behaves on a real Web Application, i.e. the web interface ZIC (Zero-Installation Craft) integrated in some of the Alcatel-Lucent devices.

References

1. Alalfi, M., Cordy, J., Dean, T.: Modelling methods for web application verification and testing: state of the art. Softw. Test Verif. Reliab. 19(4) (2009)
2. Andrews, A., Offutt, J., Alexander, R.: Testing web applications by modeling with FSMs. Software and Systems Modeling 4, 326–345 (2005)
3. Arcaini, P., Bolis, F., Gargantini, A.: Test Generation for Sequential Nets of Abstract State Machines. In: Derrick, J., Fitzgerald, J., Gnesi, S., Khurshid, S., Leuschel, M., Reeves, S., Riccobene, E. (eds.) ABZ 2012. LNCS, vol. 7316, pp. 36–50. Springer, Heidelberg (2012)
4. Arcaini, P., Gargantini, A., Riccobene, E., Scandurra, P.: A model-driven process for engineering a toolset for a formal method. Softw., Pract. Exper. 41(2), 155–166 (2011)
5. Börger, E., Stärk, R.: Abstract State Machines: A Method for High-Level System Design and Analysis. Springer (2003)
6. Ceri, S., Fraternali, P., Bongio, A.: Web modeling language (WebML): a modeling language for designing web sites (2000)
7. Deutsch, A., Sui, L., Vianu, V.: Specification and verification of data-driven web applications. J. Comput. Syst. Sci. 73(3) (2007)
8. Di Lucca, G.A., Fasolino, A.R.: Testing web-based applications: The state of the art and future trends. Information and Software Technology 48(12) (2006)
9. Gargantini, A., Riccobene, E.: ASM-Based Testing: Coverage Criteria and Automatic Test Sequence Generation. Journal of Universal Computer Science (2001)
10. Gargantini, A., Riccobene, E., Rinzivillo, S.: Using Spin to Generate Tests from ASM Specifications. In: Börger, E., Gargantini, A., Riccobene, E. (eds.) ASM 2003. LNCS, vol. 2589, pp. 263–277. Springer, Heidelberg (2003)
11. Holzmann, G.: Spin model checker, the: primer and reference manual. Addison-Wesley (2003)
12. Manolescu, I., Brambilla, M., Ceri, S., Comai, S., Fraternali, P.: Model-driven design and deployment of service-enabled web applications. ACM Trans. Internet Technol. 5(3) (2005)
13. Memon, A., Akinmade, O.: Automated Model-Based Testing of Web Applications. In: Google Test Automation Conference 2008 (2008)
14. Puolitaival, O.: Adapting model-based testing to agile context. VTT (2008)
15. Ricca, F., Tonella, P.: Analysis and testing of web applications. In: Proc. of ICSE. IEEE (2001)
16. Utting, M., Legeard, B.: Practical Model-Based Testing: A Tools Approach. Morgan-Kaufmann (2006)

Understanding Web Augmentation

Oscar Díaz

ONEKIN Research Group, University of the Basque Country (UPV/EHU),
San Sebastián, Spain
oscar.diaz@ehu.es

Introduction

The increasing volume of content and actions on the web, combined with the growing number of "digital natives", anticipate a growing desire of more sophisticated ways of controlling the Web experience. Webies 2.0 do no longer take the web as it is but imagine fancy ways of customizing the web for their own purposes. So far, mashups are the forerunner exponent of this tendency where consumers (companies and laymen alike) come up with new applications by synergistically combining third-party resources. This presentation moves the focus to another approach: *"Web Augmentation"* (WA). Rather than creating a new application, WA builds on top of the rendering of an existing website. In some sense, WA is to the Web what Augmented Reality is to the physical world: layering relevant content/layout/navigation over the existing Web to customize the user experience. Unlike mashups, the purpose for WA is not so much coming up with a new application, but framing the new development within the Web experience of an existing website. Since this is achieved by third parties in a non-intrusive way, WA is a client-side technology: extensive use of *JavaScript (JS)* using browser weavers (e.g. *Greasemonkey*) or plugs-in. Rationales for WA include:

- addressing long-tail requirements. Minority usage patterns might not be worth considering in the general release of a website but even so, be catered for as plugs-in to be deployed in an individual basis. An example is *A Bit Better Remember-The-Milk (RTM)* [3]. This plug-in improves the navigation experience of the *RTM* website through a side navigation bar that speeds up specific ways to access to-do tasks. The most of users will be satisfy by the RTM website but this does not prevent long-tail demands from being served by augmenting the RTM website,
- affordance. A company might increase the affordance of its services by transparently embedding its offerings as parts of someone else's website. An example is the *Skype* add-on, [4] a plug-in that turns any phone number found in a web page into a button that launches *Skype* to call that number. The security company AVG provides another example. Its plugin *LinkScanner* [2] scans search results from *Google, Yahoo!* or *Bing*, and places a safety rating next to each recovered link that informs about the trustworthiness of the site,

M. Grossniklaus and M. Wimmer (Eds.): ICWE 2012 Workshops, LNCS 7703, pp. 79–80, 2012.
© Springer-Verlag Berlin Heidelberg 2012

– end-user customization. Skilful users might also adapt their frequently-visited websites to their specific needs. *BookBurro* [1] is a case in point. This is a plug-in for price comparison at Amazon. *BookBurro*'s developer is a frequent *Amazon* buyer that likes to check other online bookshops before the purchase. From this perspective, WA departs from more traditional personalization scenarios where the website itself either caters for the adaptation (i.e. Web Personalization) or provides the means for register users to configure their Web experience (i.e. Web Customization).

We anticipate a quick eclosion of these "augmentations" as Web users demand more sophisticated ways of controlling the Web experience. As an evidence of this impulse, a repositoy for augmentation scripts, *www.userscripts.org,* holds over 85,000 scripts. Despite these figures, WA is still an art without a clear definition of its aim, good practices or development guidelines.

The presentation advocates for a more rigurous WA development by proposing (1) a set of good practices, (2) an architectural pattern for WA, and (3), a case for an agile approach to WA development. A non-trivial Wikipedia augmentation is used as a running example. In so doing, we hope to pave the way towards empowering users and organization alike with principles and methodologies that make the Web a truly customizable space.

Acknowledgements. Thanks are due to Cristobal Arellano who participates in the birth of these ideas. This work is co-supported by the Spanish Ministry of Education, and the European Social Fund under contract TIN2011-23839 *(Scriptongue)*.

References

1. Andrews, B.: Book Burro (2010),
   https://addons.mozilla.org/addon/book-burro/
2. AVG: AVG LinkScanner - How it Works (2010),
   http://linkscanner.avg.com/ww.sals-how-it-works.html
3. Paprotsky, A.: A Bit Better RTM (2009),
   https://addons.mozilla.org/addon/a-bit-better-rtm/
4. Skype: Skype button in Internet Explorer or Firefox toolbar (2005),
   http://www.skype.com/intl/en/support/user-guides/toolbar?lang=en

UML2 Profile and Model-Driven Approach for Supporting System Integration and Adaptation of Web Data Mashups

Patrick Gaubatz and Uwe Zdun

Faculty of Computer Science
University of Vienna, Vienna, Austria
{firstname.lastname}@univie.ac.at

Abstract. From a system integration perspective, Web data mashups used in larger architectures often need to be integrated with other system components, such as services, business processes, and so on. Often a change in one of these components requires changes in many of the dependent components. Similarly, an analysis of some system properties requires knowledge about other system parts than just the mashup. Such features could be implemented using the model-driven development (MDD) approach, but existing MDD approaches for mashups concentrate on modeling and execution only. To remedy this problem, we propose a generic approach based on a UML2 profile which can easily be extended to model other system parts or integrated with other existing models. It is the foundation for generating or interpreting mashup code in existing languages as well as other system parts using the MDD approach and performing system adaptation or analysis tasks based on models in a standard modeling language.

1 Introduction

Web mashups are used to combine data from different Web documents and services to create new functionality. Web data mashups concentrate on extracting and transforming data from such Web data sources and offer them as a service. Different domain-specific languages (DSLs) that are tailored specifically to facilitate the development of Web mashups (see e.g. [1–4]), model-driven approaches for Web mashups and Web data integration [5,6], and extensions of existing behavioral modeling languages like BPEL [7,8] have been proposed to model Web mashups.

Most approaches today concentrate on mashup modeling and execution. From a system integration perspective, they offer two means for system integration: (1) they integrate data from Web documents and services and (2) they offer their results either as Web documents or services. The larger system integration or architectural context is usually not supported any further by current approaches. For instance, Web data mashups may be used to integrate data from various internal and external information systems. Changes (e.g. of the service interface) in any of these information systems might require adaptations of the dependent Web data mashups.

The model-driven development approach (see e.g. [9]) offers a convenient way to address this problem. Via a model-driven generator, we can generate different components

M. Grossniklaus and M. Wimmer (Eds.): ICWE 2012 Workshops, LNCS 7703, pp. 81–92, 2012.

from models and re-generate the code upon changes in the models. Via a model-driven interpreter we could even support model-based runtime (on-the-fly) adaptation of the mashups. Finally, the model-driven approach could be used to generate other representations of the models. For instance, we could generate a Petri Net or automata representations of the complete process and mashup behavior to analyses aspects like deadlocks or life-locks in the entire model.

From a modeling perspective, mashups are similar to areas like behavioral software modeling (see e.g. [10]) and business process modeling or workflows (see e.g. [11]). In essence, mashups can be seen as behavioral composition models similar to UML activity diagrams [12] or microflows [13] (a microflow is a short-running, non-persistent workflow [13]), with specific functionality such as extracting data from Web pages, invoking services, and combining the data retrieved from Web pages and services using scripts. Some modeling approaches that extend existing behavioral modeling languages like BPEL have been proposed [7, 8], but BPEL is designed for long-running, transactional business processes (macroflows) rather than short-running microflows.

In this paper, we propose a UML profile for mashup modeling that is based on a core package describing basic microflows as an extension of UML activity diagrams. Mashup-specific functions are added in an extension package. In this package we semi-formally modeled some of the most common mashup functionalities. The profile is designed so that it can be extended with more specific mashup functions that are provided by mashup approaches. The core contribution of this paper is a semi-formal profile for core mashup functionality as an extension of the UML2 meta-model. As a proof-of-concept we have also implemented a model-driven interpreter for the mashup profile. To explain the generalizability of our mashup modeling profile and show that it can serve as a unified modeling approach for many existing mashup approaches, we also discuss how our approach can be used in model-driven code generators to cover other existing mashup approaches.

2   Problem Description

Current Web data modeling approaches do not consider Web data mashups in a larger architectural context. For instance, the mashup may be used inside of a business process, and both mashup and process must be monitored. Figure 1 shows the architectural overview of this example scenario. In this simple architecture example, we must integrate the business process, the mashup, the used services, and the used Web sites, and provide monitoring rules for all these components as well as their deployment configurations. If we perform changes, all these artifacts might need to be changed. Keeping them consistent during development and maintenance is tedious and error-prone.

The model-driven development approach helps to overcome this problem. Unfortunately, using the model-driven approach with mashups is difficult as they are often described in proprietary modeling or script languages and there is no unified modeling approach for them that enables us to use model-driven development approaches together with mashup approaches. Standard modeling languages that provide convenient ways to model other system parts as well like the UML are usually not used (e.g. service interfaces can be modeled as extensions of class diagrams). Furthermore, the existing model-driven mashup approaches (e.g. [5, 6]) focus on specific aspects (like user

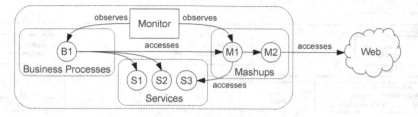

Fig. 1. Architectural Overview of a System Integration Scenario

interface layer integration) and offer only limited support for the integration of mashups in larger architectural contexts.

3   UML2 Profile for Modeling Web Data Mashups as Microflows

In order to model Web data mashups, different primitives, such as service invocations, transformation of data, and output generation in a mashup must be modeled and interconnected. To model such primitives we chose the profile extension mechanism of UML2 because there are already existing UML2 meta-classes that are semantically a close match to the characteristics of a Web data mashup. In particular, a mashup can be seen as a series of activities that perform data transformations. From the perspective of behavioral modeling, a mashup can be seen as a special purpose *microflow*: The term microflow refers to a short running, rather technical process model [13][1]. A typical way to model microflows are UML2 activity diagrams, which we will extend using a UML2 profile for modeling mashups as microflows.

This is done by semi-formally extending semantics of the respective UML2 meta-classes (rather than having to define completely new meta-classes). A profile is still valid, standard UML2. That is, it can be used in existing UML2 tools, instead of having to offer proprietary ones which are rarely used in practice. We use the Object Constraint Language (OCL) to define the necessary constraints for the defined stereotypes to precisely specify their semantics. OCL constraints are the primary mechanism for traversing UML2 models and specifying precise semantics on stereotypes.

Below, each primitive is precisely specified in the context of the UML2 meta-model using OCL constraints. This is a very important step for the practical applicability of our concepts: Without an unambiguous definition of the primitives, they cannot be used (interchangeably) in UML2 tools and model-driven generators. That is, our main reason for using the UML2 – a potential broad tool support – could otherwise not be supported.

3.1   Modeling Microflows

As a Web data mashup can be seen as a microflow, we decided to found our profile for Web data mashups on a meta-model extension for microflows. More precisely, we are proposing a meta-model for scripting language-based microflows in the context of service composition and service-based data integration.

---

[1] Microflows can be contrasted to macroflows which describe long-running, rather business-oriented process [13].

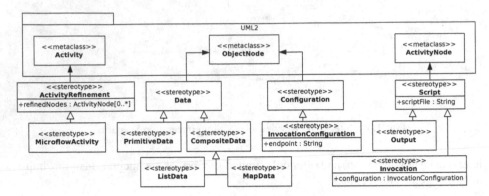

Fig. 2. The Microflow Meta-Model

Figure 2 depicts the UML2 class diagram of the microflow meta-model. The *MicroflowActivity* stereotype allows us to denote an UML2 activity to be a microflow. It also allows us to make the model subject to model constraints. For example, we defined an OCL constraint (see Listing 1) specifying that an instance of a microflow must have exactly one *InitialNode* – a requirement needed to allow the execution of microflows.

```
context MicroflowActivity
  inv: self.baseActitiy.node->select(oclIsTypeOf(InitialNode))->size() = 1
context Script inv: self.scriptFile->notEmpty()
context InvocationConfiguration inv: self.endpoint->notEmpty()
context Invocation inv: self.configuration->notEmpty()
context Output inv: self.baseActivityNode.incoming->exists(in |
  Data.allInstances()->exists(data |
    in.source.oclIsTypeOf(ObjectNode) and in.source = data.baseObjectNode))
```

Listing 1. OCL Constraints for the Microflow Model

Microflows of Web data mashups read, write, transform, process, analyze, annotate, group, ... data. Consequently, our meta-model defines a *Data* stereotype. In our approach, instances of *Data* are called data objects. *Data* can either be *PrimitiveData* (e.g. strings, numbers, or boolean values) or complex *CompositeData*. The latter can either be *ListData* (i.e. arrays) or *MapData* (i.e. key/value-pairs). These two complex data structures allow us to accommodate and map (at least) the two most widely used data formats in the Web context: XML and its variations (e.g. HTML) as well as JSON.

Having introduced data objects, we have yet to define means to get them into/out of a microflow. An *Output* returns data and/or a result (e.g. an XML document) back to the executor of the microflow (e.g. a Web application). An *Invocation* is used to retrieve data to be processed from a service (e.g. a RESTful Web service).

A *Script* acts as a "placeholder" for implementation-level code. This way arbitrary extensions from existing mashup implementation languages can be integrated – allowing us to model mashups in a generalizable fashion, but still being able to incorporate the specialized features of different mashup languages via code generation. That is, the model-driven interpreter or generator will take the code in the script files and insert it at the dedicated points into the generated or interpreted code. For this reason, *Script* serves both as the meta-model's primary extension point and as a "fallback" activity. Although the meta-model is extensible, in practice there will always be situations, where no "suitable" modeling-construct is available. In such cases, the developer can either extend the meta-model (i.e. introduce a new modeling-construct) or he/she directly attaches implementation-level code.

The main purpose of the *ActitivyRefinement* stereotype is to allow a *MicroflowActivity* to refine a concrete *ActivityNode*. For example, a *MicroflowActivity* (A1) might contain an *ActivityNode* – with the name N1 – to be refined. A second, *MicroflowActivity* (A2) might then use the tag `refinedNodes` to indicate, that it refines the node N1 (from A1). As we will see in Section 5, this mechanism can not only be used to refine *MicroflowActivities* but also to integrate our meta-model with other meta-models.

3.2 Modeling Web Data Mashups

Based on the rather generic microflow meta-model introduced in the previous section, we will now present a model extension aiming to cover the most basic set of invocation activities related to Web mashups (i.e. "plain" HTTP and SOAP). Note, that the resulting model is far from "complete" and mainly tries to give the reader an idea of our meta-model's extension mechanism (see Section 4 for further details).

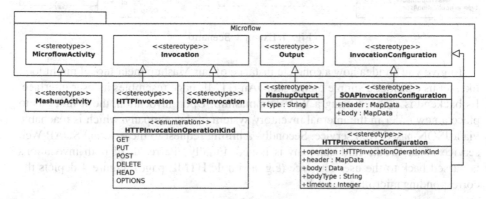

Fig. 3. The Mashup Meta-Model

Figure 3 illustrates the Mashup meta-model in its UML2 class diagram representation. *Invocation* is derived twice: *HTTPInvocation* and *SOAPInvocation*. The former is used to model a plain HTTP request (e.g. to retrieve a resource from a RESTful service or to post data to a JSON-based Web service). The stereotype *SOAPInvocation* indicates an invocation of a SOAP Web service. Finally, *MashupOutput* is derived from *Output*. The mandatory `type` tag is used to specify the MIME type of the data to be returned.

```
context HTTPInvocationConfiguration
  inv:  self.operation->notEmpty()
  inv:  self.operation = POST or self.operation = PUT
          implies self.body->notEmpty()
  inv:  self.body->notEmpty() implies self.bodyType->notEmpty()
context HTTPInvocation
  inv:  self.configuration.oclIsKindOf(HTTPInvocationConfiguration)
context SOAPInvocationConfiguration inv:  self.body->notEmpty()
context SOAPInvocation
  inv:  self.configuration.oclIsKindOf(SOAPInvocationConfiguration)
  inv:  self.type->notEmpty()
context MashupOutput inv:  self.type->notEmpty()
```

Listing 2. OCL Constraints for the Mashup Model

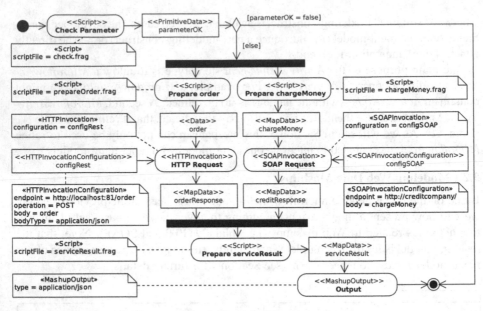

Fig. 4. Example Scenario

To give you an idea how a concrete instance of our Mashup meta-model might look like, let us consider a simple online shop. An HTML page resembles its user interface. Its backend is realized using a Web data mashup. Upon invocation, the it first has to place a new order in the internal inventory system of the company, which is reachable via a JSON-based Web service. Secondly, a billing request to the external SOAP Web service of an Credit card company is issued. Finally, the result of both invocations is passed back to the user interface (e.g. a simple HTML page). Figure 4 depicts the corresponding microflow model.

4   Exploring the Generalizability of the UML2 Profile

A generic and unified modeling approach implies, that – thanks to its generalizability – it is possible to accommodate models from similar approaches. This is achieved by mapping the model abstractions of one approach to the ones of the other. As this

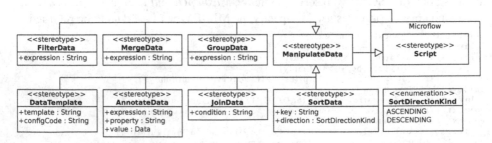

Fig. 5. EMML Extensions to the Mashup Meta-Model

is not always possible (e.g. because there is simply no matching modeling construct available), a generic modeling approach should provide an extension mechanism.

```
context ManipulateData
  inv: self.baseActivityNode.incoming—>exists(in |
          Data.allInstances()—>exists(data |in.source.oclIsTypeOf(ObjectNode)
              and in.source = data.baseObjectNode))
context AnnotateData
  inv: self.expression—>notEmpty()
  inv: self.property—>notEmpty()
  inv: self.value—>notEmpty()
context FilterData inv: self.expression—>notEmpty()
context GroupData inv: self.expression—>notEmpty()
context JoinData
  inv: self.condition—>notEmpty()
  inv: self.baseActivityNode.incoming—>forAll(in |
          Data.allInstances()—>select(data | in.source.oclIsTypeOf(ObjectNode)
              and in.source = data.baseObjectNode)—>size() > 1
context MergeData
  inv: self.expression—>notEmpty()
  inv: self.baseActivityNode.incoming—>forAll(in |
          Data.allInstances()—>select(data | in.source.oclIsTypeOf(ObjectNode)
              and in.source = data.baseObjectNode)—>size() > 1
context SortData inv: self.key—>notEmpty()
```

Listing 3. OCL Constraints for the EMML Mashup Model Extension

To explore the generalizability of our modeling approach we tried to map the concepts and model abstractions of the Enterprise Mashup Markup Language (EMML) [4]. EMML is an XML-based standard that supports the specification of processing flows for Web mashups in a platform- and vendor-independent manner. Table 1 contains a list of EMML statements (taken from the reference [4]) and shows how each statement can be mapped to our UML2 profile. In Table 1a we can see, that many statements (e.g. control flow-related) can directly be mapped to plain UML2 (e.g. <if>).

For a large part of the domain-specific statements (e.g. <mashup>) this is also the case. To cover the remaining, we had to extend our model. Figure 5 shows, that we have extended the *Script* stereotype – the primary extension point of our model – to introduce 8 new stereotypes. Listing 3 shows the corresponding OCL constraints (e.g. *JoinData* needs at least two incoming activity edges originating *Data* objects) and Table 1b shows how they are mapped to EMML. The remaining statements are listed in Table 1c. We considered them either to be "generic" in a sense that they are not very specific for the

Table 1. Mapping of EMML language elements to UML2

(a) Plain UML2

EMML	UML2
<input>	ActivityParameterNode
<variables>	ObjectNode / ObjectFlow
<include>	
<macro>	Activity
<macros>	
<if>	
<for>	
<foreach>	DecisionNode
<break>	
<while>	
<parallel>	ForkNode / JoinNode
<sequence>	ControlFlow

(b) UML2 Stereotypes

EMML	UML2
<mashup>	MashupActivity
<directinvoke>	Invocation
<invoke>	
<annotate>	AnnotateData
<filter>	FilterData
<group>	GroupData
<join>	JoinData
<merge>	MergeData
<sort>	SortData
<xslt>	DataTemplate
<output>	Output

(c) Script Fallbacks

EMML	UML2
<script>	
<select>	
<appendresult>	
<assert>	
<assign>	Script
<constructor>	
<template>	
<display>	
<datasource>	
<sql*>	

domain of "data mashups" (e.g. <constructor>) or to mainly exist for debugging purpose (e.g. <assert>). Hence, we used the *Script* "fallback" to cover them.

As we could show, our modeling approach provides a model-driven abstraction that can be used to model the essence of mashups expressed in languages like EMML in a technology-independent way that supports implementing features for model-driven generation of system integration code, analysis, or adaptation based on the abstract models. EMML code could be generated from our models and Section 7 will show that it is feasible to implement a model-driven interpreter that can execute instances of our meta-model on-the-fly.

5   Integration of the UML2 Profile with Existing Models

Different meta-models can be integrated via a common meta-meta-model, like MOF for UML2. That is, every single meta-model to be integrated has to be defined using the same meta-meta-model. The profile definition mechanism of UML2 provides straightforward means to define meta-models. As a standard modeling language, lots of different UML2 profiles and UML2-derived meta-models have been proposed. Hence, basing model integration on the common UML2 meta-model allows for an straightforward integration with other UML2-based meta-models.

Using an extension of our illustrative example, we will demonstrate the model integration capabilities of our mashup meta-model via the standard UML2 extension mechanisms. As mentioned before, mashups may very likely be used in larger architectures. For instance, our example mashup from Section 3.2 may be used by a macroflow [13], a long-running, interruptible process flow which depicts the business-oriented process perspective (e.g. a business process).

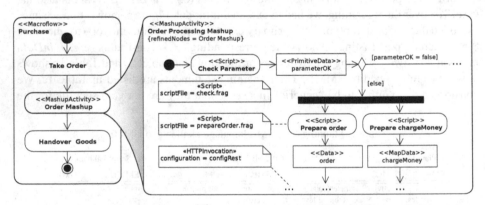

Fig. 6. Integrating the Mashup Model with a Macroflow Model

Suppose that the company from our example scenario (see Section 4) also provides a physical "brick and mortar" store. The left side of Figure 6 depicts a very simplistic and high-level macroflow model of the whole buying process. The first as well as the last activities have to be conducted by a human (i.e. the shop assistant). That is, after taking the order, the original mashup model (from Section 4) shall be used to process it. Hence, we insert an activity node (*Order Mashup*) to be refined. Using the *ActivityRefinement* stereotype and the `refinedNodes` tag, we can then specify that our order processing mashup refines the mentioned activity node in the macroflow model.

This way of integrating different compatible meta-models using a tagged value introduced in the mashup profile (i.e., `refinedNodes`) is one way of model integration – in this case with other activity models. Other types of UML2 models can easily be integrated in the same way. Another option is named-based matching. For instance, the object nodes in our mashup models can easily be matched by name with the corresponding classifiers in class or component models that describe them in detail. Class models can also be used to describe the service interfaces used in a mashup.

A model-driven generator or interpreter can then use the linking tagged values or names to navigate both models and generate code for different system artifacts. The big benefit of our UML2 profile is that mashups can easily be integrated with models in other types of models and that UML2 already provides a wide variety of models that can be used to describe all kinds of other artifacts relevant for mashups.

6 Implementing a Model-Driven Tool Chain

The presented UML2 meta-models have been developed and specified using a textual DSL. Frag [14, 15], a tailorable language, specifically designed for the task of defining DSLs, provides the syntactic foundation of this DSL. Among other things, Frag supports the tailoring of its object system and the extension with new language elements. Hence, it provides a good basis for defining a UML2-based textual DSL because it is easy to tailor Frag to support the definition of the UML2 meta-classes. Frag automatically provides us with a syntax for defining application models using the UML2 meta-classes. In addition Frag also provides a constraint language similar to OCL as well as a model validator. Using the model validator we can easily check a models conformance to its meta-models as well as its model constraints.

```
# define a new stereotype
FMF:: Stereotype create MashupOutput \
  -superclasses Microflow:: Output \
  -attributes { type String }
# define a new model constraint
MashupOutput addInvariant [notEmpty [self type]]
```
Listing 4. Frag DSL example

Note, that the textual syntax of the DSL is mainly intended to be used internally in the model validator, as a common syntax for model integration, and for debugging purposes. The developers should mainly work with UML2 and OCL tools to define the models and constraints. The main contribution of our prototypical tool chain is to validate and demonstrate that a model validation support following our concepts is feasible and can be implemented with moderate effort from scratch.

7 Implementing a Model-Driven Interpreter

As a proof-of-concept, we have also implemented a basic model-driven interpreter, that is able to execute instances of our mashup meta-model on-the-fly. Using the Frag language, and mainly due to its realization of the transitive mixins concept [15], it could be implemented in roughly 450 lines of code. Mixins allow us (among other things) to add methods to classes dynamically at runtime.

```
# create executor classes
FMF::Class create MashupActivityExecutor —method execute args { ... }
FMF::Class create ScriptExecutor —method execute args { ... }
# add mixins
Mashup::MashupActivity mixins MashupActivityExecutor
Microflow::Script mixins ScriptExecutor
```

Listing 5. Defining Mixin Classes

Thus, the basic idea of our model execution-approach is to use mixins to extend our (Frag-specified) meta-model with additional execution functionality. For instance, Listing 5 shows how we define two mixin classes (`MashupActivityExecutor` and `ScriptExecutor`), both implementing the method `execute`. For every defined stereotype a corresponding executor mixin – containing the execution-logic – is needed. For instance, the execution-logic of the `MashupActivityExecutor` is to execute the model's initial node. The initial node's execution logic is to traverse its outgoing activity edge and execute the next activity node. In Listing 5 we can see, that the previously defined mixin classes are then directly attached to the classes of the meta-model (e.g. `Microflow::Script`).

```
# define a model instance
UML2::Activity create A1
Mashup::MashupActivity create M1 —baseActivity A1
# execute the model instance
M1 execute
```

Listing 6. Executing a *MashupActivity*

Having the mixin classes attached, it is then possible to directly execute any instance of our meta-model. Listing 6 depicts both the instantiation of the meta-model as well as the execution of the newly created instance via the `execute` method.

8   Related Work

A considerable amount of work has been done on the design and development of DSLs that are tailored specifically to facilitate the development of Web mashups (see e.g. [1–3]). In particular, the idea of seeing Web mashups as compositions of Web services and Web data leads to the design of numerous service composition languages. For instance, the Bite language [7] has been proposed as a simplified variant of the Web Services Business Process Execution Language (WS-BPEL) [16], a current standard technology for business process execution in the context of Web services. Like our approach this approach uses a behavioral model as the foundation of a mashup model. But BPEL is designed for long-running, transactional business processes (macroflows) and contains many language elements not useful for mashup composition, whereas our approach offers a model focused on the short-running microflows typically required for mashup composition tasks. Rosenberg et al. [8] demonstrate the applicability of Bite to model RESTful Web services and collaborative workflows.

Our model-based approach does not compete with the already existing languages and approaches. But rather it provides a model-driven abstraction that can be used to model the essence of mashups expressed in these languages. This has been demonstrated in Section 4 for the Enterprise Mashup Markup Language [4], a standard proposed by the Open Mashup Alliance. In contrast to our approach, the existing modeling approaches are not based on a standard modeling language that provides convenient ways to model other system parts as well like the UML2 (e.g. in UML2 service interfaces can be modeled as extensions of UML2 class diagrams). Our approach can be used to augment those other mashup modeling languages with links to UML2 models for other system parts via the standard UML2 extension mechanisms.

Model-driven development in the context of Web mashups and Web data integration is nothing new and numerous approaches have been presented before. For example, Daniel et al. present mashArt [5], a model-driven approach to UI and service composition on the Web, consisting of component model for mashup components as well as an event- and flow-based service composition model. A meta-model for context-aware component-based mashup applications is presented by Pietschmann et al. [6]. The model provides means to describe all necessary application aspects on a platform-independent level, such as its components, control and data flow, layout, as well as context-aware behavior. Koch et al. present UWE [17], a model-driven approach for Web application development. The proposed UML2 profile aims to cover the entire development life cycle of Web systems and therefore clearly surpasses the scope of our own meta-model. Similarly, Kapitsaki et al. [18] also suggest a UML2 profile for modeling Web applications using UML2 class and state transition diagrams. A conceptual modeling approach to business service mashup development is presented in [19]. Bozzon et al. demonstrate the feasibility of modeling Web mashups as Business Processes using BPMN (Business Process Management Notation). In summary, these approaches attach great importance to the integration of the data and the user interface layer – which is the main focus of the meta-models of these approaches.

In contrast to these approaches, our approach tries to be as generic as possible and focus on the microflow abstraction needed to support features for model-driven generation of system integration code, analysis, or adaptation. Thus, our meta-model constitutes the bare minimum needed to model the microflows of Web mashups. Also, our main focus lies in the Web data integration and service composition aspect of Web mashups. In future extension of our model we plan to extend it to also support the user interface layer integration.

9   Conclusion and Future Work

In this paper we introduced an UML2 profile for semi-formally modeling the essence of Web data mashups based on activity diagrams and formal constraints in the OCL. We divided our meta-model into an abstract microflow layer and a mashup specific layer. We were able to show the applicability of our approach in a prototype implementation, realizing a mashup DSL and a model-driven interpreter. We showed the generalizability of our approach by mapping it to a standard mashup language, the EMML. We argued and showed how other UML2 diagrams can be integrated with our approach. Hence, the UML2 profile together with the model-driven approach help to make the mashup approach usable in a system integration context, in which the mashups and other dependent components must be changed together. The approach can potentially be used to better support the adaptation and analysis of mashups – especially together with other system components. As future work we plan to apply our approach in for these tasks.

References

1. Maximilien, E.M., Ranabahu, A., Gomadam, K.: An Online Platform for Web APIs and Service Mashups. IEEE Internet Computing 12(5), 32–43 (2008)
2. Vallejos, J., Huang, J., Costanza, P., De Meuter, W., D'Hondt, T.: A programming language approach for context-aware mashups. In: Proceedings of the 3rd and 4th International Workshop on Web APIs and Services Mashups, Mashups 2009/2010, pp. 4:1–4:5. ACM, New York (2010)
3. Sabbouh, M., Higginson, J., Semy, S., Gagne, D.: Web mashup scripting language. In: Proceedings of the 16th International Conference on World Wide Web, WWW 2007, pp. 1305–1306. ACM, New York (2007)
4. Open Mashup Alliance: Enterprise Mashup Markup Language, http://www.openmashup.org/omadocs/v1.0/
5. Daniel, F., Casati, F., Benatallah, B., Shan, M.-C.: Hosted Universal Composition: Models, Languages and Infrastructure in mashArt. In: Laender, A.H.F., Castano, S., Dayal, U., Casati, F., de Oliveira, J.P.M. (eds.) ER 2009. LNCS, vol. 5829, pp. 428–443. Springer, Heidelberg (2009)
6. Pietschmann, S., Tietz, V., Reimann, J., Liebing, C., Pohle, M., Meißner, K.: A metamodel for context-aware component-based mashup applications. In: Proceedings of the 12th International Conference on Information Integration and Web-based Applications & Services, iiWAS 2010, pp. 413–420. ACM, New York (2010)
7. Curbera, F., Duftler, M., Khalaf, R., Lovell, D.: Bite: Workflow Composition for the Web. In: Krämer, B.J., Lin, K.-J., Narasimhan, P. (eds.) ICSOC 2007. LNCS, vol. 4749, pp. 94–106. Springer, Heidelberg (2007)
8. Rosenberg, F., Curbera, F., Duftler, M.J., Khalaf, R.: Composing RESTful Services and Collaborative Workflows: A Lightweight Approach. IEEE Internet Computing 12(5), 24–31 (2008)
9. Mellor, S.J., Clark, A.N., Futagami, T.: Guest Editors' Introduction: Model-Driven Development. IEEE Software 20, 14–18 (2003)
10. Bock, C.: Unified Behavior Models. Journal of OO-Programming 12(5), 65–68 (1999)
11. Aguilar-Savén, R.S.: Business process modelling: Review and framework. International Journal of Production Economics 90(2), 129–149 (2004)
12. Object Management Group: UML 2.4.1 Superstructure, http://www.omg.org/spec/UML/2.4.1
13. Hentrich, C., Zdun, U.: Process-Driven SOA - Proven Patterns for Business-IT Alignment. CRC Press, Taylor and Francis, Boca Raton (2012)
14. Zdun, U.: Frag, http://frag.sf.net/
15. Zdun, U.: Tailorable language for behavioral composition and configuration of software components. Comput. Lang. Syst. Struct. 32(1), 56–82 (2006)
16. OASIS: Web Services Business Process Execution Language, http://docs.oasis-open.org/wsbpel/2.0/wsbpel-v2.0.pdf
17. Koch, N., Knapp, A., Zhang, G., Baumeister, H.: Uml-Based Web Engineering. In: Rossi, G., Pastor, O., Schwabe, D., Olsina, L. (eds.) Web Engineering: Modelling and Implementing Web Applications. Human–Computer Interaction Series, pp. 157–191. Springer, London (2008)
18. Kapitsaki, G.M., Kateros, D.A., Pappas, C.A., Tselikas, N.D., Venieris, I.S.: Model-driven development of composite web applications. In: Proceedings of the 10th International Conference on Information Integration and Web-based Applications & Services, iiWAS 2008, pp. 399–402. ACM, New York (2008)
19. Bozzon, A., Brambilla, M., Facca, F.M., Carughu, G.T.: A Conceptual Modeling Approach to Business Service Mashup Development. In: Proceedings of the 2009 IEEE International Conference on Web Services, ICWS 2009, pp. 751–758. IEEE Computer Society, Washington, DC (2009)

Extending Web Standards-Based Widgets towards Inter-Widget Communication

Olexiy Chudnovskyy, Sebastian Müller, and Martin Gaedke

Chemnitz University of Technology
{olexiy.chudnovskyy,martin.gaedke}@cs.tu-chemnitz.de,
sebastian.mueller@s2011.tu-chemnitz.de

Abstract. In the last decade user interface mashups have gained much interest both in academia and in industry. Their development paradigm enables end users to develop applications without dealing with complexities of the underlying technologies by using so-called widgets. However, user interface mashups haven't reached their full potential yet. Widgets are currently implemented in an isolated manner hindering seamless user-mashup interaction due to the need of manual state synchronization between widgets. Even though mashup run-time environments often enable inter-widget communication, current widget implementations surprisingly make use of it seldom. In this paper, we present a generic approach to semi-automatically extend widgets with dedicated inter-widget communication functionality. Thus, facilitating many cumbersome tasks of the end users when combining different widgets to a single application.

1 Introduction

In the last decade plenty of data sources, Web services and user interfaces have been published on the Web, which led to new development paradigms focusing on reuse and composition [1]. One very promising approach in this context are user-interface mashups (UI mashups), which have the goal to enable end-users to develop their own solutions by simply combining functionalities at the user-interface level [2]. In contrast to data and service mashups, which require understanding of basic programming techniques, UI mashups support end-user development techniques like visual composition, immediate feedback, recommendation etc.

The building blocks for composition of UI mashups are widgets, which have the goal to hide the complexity of utilized data sources and Web services from end-users. UI mashup environments additionally provide messaging facilities, so that widgets can communicate their internal state among each other, allowing different widgets to act like one, and as a result improve the overall user experience [3]. For example, a widget, whose goal is to display a weather forecast for a given day, may adapt its display to a date chosen in a calendar widget. A map widget can adapt its focus to a new location, if it gets notified about the user's choice of a contact in the address book widget.

M. Grossniklaus and M. Wimmer (Eds.): ICWE 2012 Workshops, LNCS 7703, pp. 93–96, 2012.

Unfortunately, almost none of the currently available widgets on the Web support this inter-widget communication (IWC). In this paper, we present our approach to tackle the aforementioned problems. We show how stand-alone widgets can be extended towards a particular IWC technology. The rest of the paper is structured as following. Section 2 gives some background of inter-widget communication. In section 3 we present our framework to observe and extend existing widgets towards IWC-enabled ones. Finally, Section 4 concludes the paper and gives an outlook of our further research.

2   Background on Inter-Widget Communication

Inter-widget communication is a widely adopted aid both to improve user experience in UI mashups and to enable seamless execution of widget-based workflows. It is based on message transfer between isolated contexts, which can occur either in a centrally controlled manner (so called *orchestrated model*), decentralized self-organized manner (so called *choreographed model*) or decentralized inhibited manner (so called *hybrid model*) [4]. In our approach, we focus on the *choreographed* IWC model, where interactions between widgets are not centrally defined but occur in a distributed manner depending on events taking place inside the widgets. Either a user or a widget can raise a message to be emitted. It contains both type of the event occurred (e.g. city selection has changed) and further information about the event (e.g. the current city selection is "Chemnitz, Germany"). In the choreographed model the message is published on a dedicated event bus provided by the UI mashup environment. Other widgets may subscribe to a particular event type, so that they get notified when the corresponding message is published. The message is then passed to a widget-internal callback-routine, so that widgets can react to the event appropriately. We believe that though the choreographed IWC model requires syntactical and semantic compatibility between emitted messages, it is still best suited for end user development. As such, user don't need to explicitly configure the inter-widget communication and can re-use the IWC-functionality among different deployments.

3   Extending Widgets with IWC-Functionality

The extension of widgets is performed by deploying and modifying the corresponding widget packages in a dedicated "widget extension environment" (Figure 1). The extension environment performs a learning process, during which it collects data about the widget behavior and then extends the widgets with modules required for inter-widget communication. Some of the injected modules are responsible for publishing events to the global event bus; whereas the other ones subscribe to those events and replay certain actions if the events occur. During the learning process user can also specify how the event messages look like. To establish interoperability between sending and receiving widgets it is required to use the same vocabulary while describing outgoing and incoming messages of both widgets.

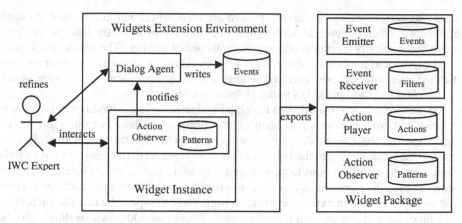

Fig. 1. Widget Extension Environment

The first step of the learning process foresees an extension of widgets towards emitting messages on internal state changes.

For this purpose a dedicated widget observer module is automatically embedded into the widget source code. The main goal of the module is to observe actions taking place in the widget and to detect pre-defined patterns from a given knowledge base. In the current implementation the observation is taking place by attaching dedicated event handlers to HTML input elements and accumulating data until some pattern is recognized (e.g. text input and subsequent form submission). After a pattern has been detected, the observer instructs the learning environment to clarify the performed action. A dedicated dialog with captured data is presented to the user, so that she can refine the semantics of the actions and annotate the corresponding parameters (Figure 2).

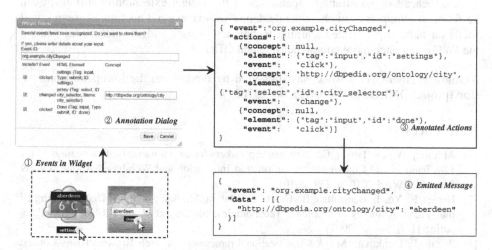

Fig. 2. Refining events to be emitted

The approach assumes that the user is familiar with concepts from choreographed IWC and can enrich the captured data with sufficient semantics. The refined event data and corresponding occurrence pattern are then stored within a dedicated events repository. When the user decides to finish the training process, the learning environment automatically injects another module, the event emitter. The widget package is then exported as a new extended widget version. At run-time the action observer notifies the event emitter about detected actions, which converts them into the semantically enriched form and publishes to the global event bus.

As the second step towards IWC-enabled widgets, we inject modules being able to receive and process events published on the global event bus. For this purpose, we again use the observer module for recording user actions within the widget. In contrast to the prior approach, the recorded data is not used to define messages to be published, but to specify actions to be replayed if certain external events occur. Users can stop the recording process at any time and parameterize the recorded actions according to expected data in external events. To trigger and to repeat the recorded actions at run-time, the widgets extension environment injects two additional modules into the widget package – an event receiver and an action player. The event receiver module takes messages of the pre-defined type from the global event bus and passes them to the action player, which replays actions recorded during the learning process.

4   Conclusions and Outlook

In this paper we presented our approach to extend widgets towards IWC-enabled ones. We believe, this possibility will significantly improve the user experience within user interface mashups and will enable seamless workflow execution without need of manual state synchronization between involved components. We implemented our approach based on the W3C widget specification and Apache Wookie widget container, which was extended in order to support required observation and module injection features.

A screencast demonstrating capabilities of the widget extension environment can be found at http://vsr.cs.tu-chemnitz.de/demo/iwc-extension. Our future research will focus on more sophisticated learning techniques of user-widget interaction, making the IWC experience more comprehensive and efficient.

Acknowledgment. This work was supported by funds from the European Commission (project OMELETTE, contract no. 257635).

References

[1] Al Sarraj, W., De Troyer, O.: Web mashup makers for casual users. In: Proceedings of the 12th International Conference on Information Integration and Web-based Applications & Services, iiWAS 2010, p. 239 (2010)
[2] Daniel, F., Yu, J., Benatallah, B., Casati, F., Matera, M., Saint-Paul, R.: Understanding UI Integration: A Survey of Problems, Technologies, and Opportunities. IEEE Internet Computing 11(3), 59–66 (2007)
[3] Zuzak, I., Ivankovic, M.: A Classification Framework for Web Browser Cross-Context Communication. CoRR, vol. abs/1108.4 (2011)
[4] Wilson, S., Daniel, F., Jugel, U., Soi, S.: Orchestrated User Interface Mashups Using W3C Widgets. In: Harth, A., Koch, N. (eds.) ICWE 2011 Workshops. LNCS, vol. 7059, pp. 49–61. Springer, Heidelberg (2012)

A Mashup Construction Approach for Cooperation of Mobile Devices

Korawit Prutsachainimmit, Prach Chaisatien, and Takehiro Tokuda

Department of Computer Science, Tokyo Institute of Technology
Meguro, Tokyo 152-8552, Japan
{korawit,prach,tokuda}@tt.cs.titech.ac.jp

Abstract. The purpose of this paper is to present a description based mashup approach for integration of mobile applications, Web services, and Web applications in order to realize cooperation of mobile devices. We define a description language called C-MAIDL for describing logic of mashup. We use a mashup generator for generating mashup applications from the description. We aim to allow composition of existing mobile applications, extracted information from Web pages and RESTful Web services. We use a mashup execution environment to automate cooperation among devices. Finally, we demonstrate that our approach allows users to create mobile mashup applications dealing with cooperation of devices easily and efficiently.

Keywords: Mobile Mashup, Cooperation Mashup, Description Language.

1   Introduction

Mobile mashup is a new tool for mobile application development. It is a combination of Web resources and mobile Internet for enriching mobile services and enhancing user experiences [1]. Mobile mashup takes advantages of mobile devices' capabilities. Data from mobile sensors such as camera and GPS can be integrated with existing Web resources. Mobile applications such as map-based applications or barcode scanner applications can be an important component in mashup. With these advantages, mashup approaches were proposed to allow users to compose mashup applications for mobile environment. However, existing approaches share a common characteristic where they are targeted on mashup for single device. Existing approaches still lack attention to enable mashup for multiple mobile devices.

Recently, trend of mobile application usage is constantly changing from individual use to collaborative use. Collaborative applications such as groupware or social applications are adapted to the mobile platform. Similarly, mashup development for cooperation of mobile devices is now taken into account. With the collaboration of the devices, information from the devices can be shared and integrated with other mashup components to produce new variety of mashup output.

Mashup with cooperation of mobile devices has clear benefits for mobile computing. Multiple mobile devices can participate in a mashup to exchange

M. Grossniklaus and M. Wimmer (Eds.): ICWE 2012 Workshops, LNCS 7703, pp. 97–108, 2012.

information and share mashup result. A simple example is the location-based mashup. A mashup application may request location data from multiple mobile devices and use it to compute the middle coordinate among devices. Then, the middle coordinate can be given to mashup APIs to find the best nearest restaurant or choosing the lowest car rental service around the location. Finally, the selected place can be shared to all participating devices. Hence, mashup with cooperation of mobile devices can be considered as an essential research topic in mobile mashup.

In our previous work [2], we have presented a mobile mashup approach for end-users by using a description language and a mashup generator. We also have presented Tethered Web service (TeWS) to support cooperative mobile application. However, the previous work still has limitations, especially on the cooperation of devices. Thus, this research aims to improve efficiency and extend functionalities of our previous work. In this paper, we present a description based mashup approach dealing with cooperation of mobile devices. Our approach is designed for flow-based mashup where each mashup component is sequentially executed. We aim to allow the integration of mobile applications, Web applications, and Web services with cooperation information from multiple mobile devices. We propose a description language for describing mashup and use a mashup generator to leverage mashup composition effort. We develop a mashup execution environment to automate cooperation tasks among devices.

2   Related Work

Different mobile mashup solutions have been proposed to assist end-users in composing mashup for mobile environment. Mashup editors such as Yahoo Pipes [3] and Intel MashMaker [4] are capable to provide mobile mashup via mobile Web browsers. However, with these tools, we cannot integrate data from devices' sensors into mashup. TELAR mashup platform [5] presents a way to combine mobile devices' features such as GPS with existing Web resources. Kaltofen et al. presents an end-users' mobile mashup for cross-platform deployment [6]. The proposed solutions share a common characteristic where they focus on mashup development for single device. They also have limited capabilities to develop mashup for cooperation of multiple devices.

In our previous study [2], we have proposed a mobile mashup generator system for cooperative applications of different mobile devices. Our work aims to deliver the mashup development for end-users by using a description language and a mashup generator. We have applied a mobile Web server and TeWS to allow cooperation of mobile devices. However, our previous work still has limitations. To compose a cooperation mashup, manual programming effort is still required. The participating devices have to maintain a connection with other devices during the mashup process. In addition, mobile applications on client devices cannot be integrated into mashup.

In existing mashup approaches, cooperation of mobile devices is not explicitly proposed. Therefore, this research aims to find an efficient mashup approach which enables cooperation of mobile devices. Our goals are to reduce the limitations and extend the functionalities of our proposed approach to create a more powerful mashup construction system.

3   Mashup Approach

The general concept of our approach is using a description language for mashup construction. We define an XML-based description language called C-MAIDL (Cooperation - Mobile Application Interface Description Language). C-MAIDL allows mashup composers to specify mashup components and details of their integration. Our approach is designed for flow-based integration where mashup components will be executed in sequence. The mashup components can be Web applications, Web services and mobile applications. To build a mashup application, a mashup composer creates a mashup description file by using C-MAIDL. Then, the file will be used as an input for our mashup generator to generate the mashup application. Our approach aims to support mashup on single device and cooperation mashup on multiple devices. To enable cooperation of devices, we use a mashup execution environment to exchange data among participating devices.

3.1   C-MAIDL

C-MAIDL is an XML-based description language which is designed for describing mashup applications. It provides ways to describe detail and data flow of mashup components which will be used in a mashup application. The components can be arranged as a workflow according to logic of mashup composers. The composers then configure each component's parameters. Results from the components in upper hierarchical order can be used in the lower ordered component. Finally, the composers configure the output component and export the abstracted model to a C-MAIDL description file.

   C-MAIDL is an extension of our proposed mashup description language called MAIDL. The general concept of MAIDL is to provide data flows between mashup components for its execution and output. The components consist of Web Application Component (WA), Web Service Component (WS), Mobile Application Component (MA) and Arithmetic Component (AR). By configuring those components, mashup composers can extract parts of Web pages, consuming Web services, invoke existing mobile applications and perform arithmetic operations between outputs of components. However, MAIDL still has limitations about cooperation of multiple devices. Manual programming effort is required to create cooperative applications. Therefore, C-MAIDL is extended from MAIDL to support cooperation tasks by adding new components to the existing language definition. Additional mashup components, Cooperation Component and Output Component, are added to expand functionalities. Thus, C-MAIDL's mashup components consist of:

1. *Web Application Component (WA).* Web applications are applicable to our integration. This component is used for extracting a part of a Web page or querying through an HTML form. Mashup composers are provided with a Web extraction

assistant tool [7] to indicate part of required information on a Web page. The description of this component will be generated to JavaScript code and executed in the runtime environment on a mobile device.

2. **Web Service Component (WS).** This component is used for consuming a REST Web service by specifying a URL and query expressions (such as XPath or JSON). The target Web service will be invoked to extract a whole or a part of the result.

3. **Mobile Application Component (MA).** A mobile application can be used as a mashup component. This component allows the application which implemented Intent and Service [8] messaging protocol to be integrated in mashup.

4. **Arithmetic Component (AR).** This component provides pre-defined mathematical operations between results from one or more components. The operation includes addition, subtraction, division, multiplication, summation, comparison, and GPS distance calculation.

5. **Cooperation Component (CC).** This component will be used for cooperation of multiple devices. Required information from participating devices can be described in this component. The description of this component will be generated to code for communicating with the mashup execution environment to exchange information with other devices.

6. **Output Component (OC).** Output of mashup application can be defined by using this component. Mashup composers can select to show the mashup result as points on the map view or display as a Web page in the Web view.

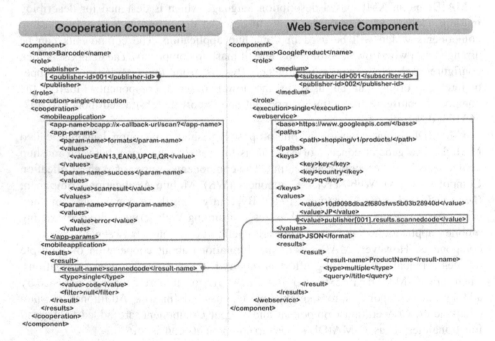

Fig. 1. Samples of C-MAIDL description

To illustrate C-MAIDL, the description of Cooperation Component and Web Service Component are shown in Figure 1. The Cooperation Component is configured as a publisher to provide data to other components. A target mobile application and its launching parameters are specified to activate the barcode scanning on the participating devices. Output data from this Cooperation Component is defined, i.e. in this case, the "scannedcode", to be referred by the other components. The Web Service Component is configured as a subscriber and publisher. As a subscriber, this Web Service Component uses the scanned barcodes from the Cooperation Component as an input of a Web Service API. As a publisher, the result from the Web service execution will be available to the other components.

3.2   Mashup Construction Process

The mashup construction process is shown in Figure 2. To compose a mashup application, a mashup composer creates an abstract model of mashup by using C-MAIDL. The composer composes a C-MAIDL description file to transform the abstract model into mashup description. The description file will be used as an input of the mashup generator to generate Java source code. This generated code will be compiled into a mobile application which can be deployed on a target device. The mashup application can be used as an ordinary mobile application.

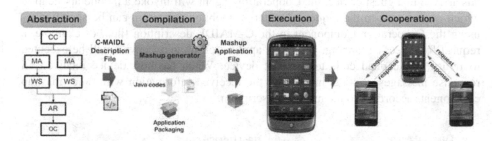

Fig. 2. Mashup Construction Process

According to the mashup generator, this tool takes a C-MAIDL description file as an input to generate a mobile mashup application. First, the generator extracts component's description from the C-MAIDL, and then generates Java source code corresponding to the specification. Next, all the source code will be manually compiled into an Android's package file (apk). Then, the package file will be manually installed to the target device by using Android Debug Bridge (adb). After the generated mashup application is installed and invoked by a mashup user, the flow which is defined in C-MAIDL description will be executed. The connection between participating devices will be established upon needs of cooperation information. The mechanism of requests and responses are automatically handled by our mashup execution environment.

3.3   Mashup Execution Environment

To achieve mashup for cooperation of devices, participating devices need a capability to communicate with each others for exchanging mashup required information. We use a mashup execution environment to automate this task. Our mashup execution environment allows the devices to exchange information by using custom mobile applications called *Cooperation Agent* and *Cooperation Center*.

In our mashup execution environment, we have categorized the participating devices into two types which are *Guest Device (Guest)* and *Host Device (Host)*. The guest device is a mobile device which provides device's information to be used in mashup applications. The host device is a mobile device which executes mashup applications by using information from the guest devices. The Cooperation Agent and Cooperation Center will work together to enable information sharing between guests and a host. The Cooperation Agent will be installed on the guest devices to provide device's information for mashup. The Cooperation Center will be installed on the host device to collect required information from guests. Overview of our mashup execution environment is shown in Figure 3.

With our mashup execution environment, mobile applications on guest devices can be integrated into mashup. When a mashup application needs information from guest devices, it will interact with the Cooperation Center. The Cooperation Center provides programming interfaces for sending request messages to all guests. When a request has arrived to a guest device, the Cooperation Agent will invoke a mobile application which corresponds to the request. The target mobile application can be specified by using the Cooperation Component in the C-MAIDL description file. For example, a request for barcode scanning, a barcode application on guest device will be executed to return the scanned code to the host device. When the host device received all response messages, it starts integrating the received information with other mashup components according to the mashup description.

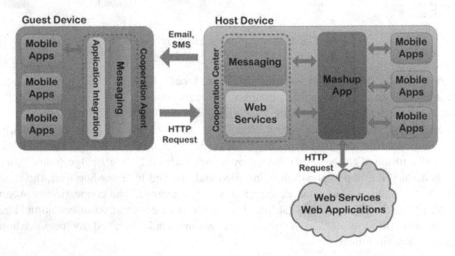

Fig. 3. Overview of Mashup Execution Environment

An important function which enables the cooperation of mobile devices is about sending and receiving information among different devices. An efficient messaging system must be taken into carefully consideration. Our approach presents a messaging system for exchanging cooperation information between mobile devices. This research uses two different mobile platforms to find an effective approach for the messaging system. Google's Android device was implemented as the host device while iOS devices were implemented as guest devices. The Android phone was selected to be the host device because it has a flexible mobile operating system. Using special purpose mobile software is possible, especially the mobile Web server. We apply functionalities of i-Jetty [9] mobile Web server in our messaging system. It is used as a container of Web service APIs to enable communication between different mobile platforms. RESTful Web services and JSON were adapted for better performance [10].

To enable cooperation between an Andriod and iOS devices, we found that there is an important limitation on iOS platform. The iOS platform does not allow a custom mobile application to run as a background process. With this limitation, the capability of communication software which requires listening to incoming request is limited. From this reason, our messaging system applies different techniques for request and response activities to overcome the limitation.

Request Message. For collecting cooperation information from guest devices, the Cooperation Center on the host device creates and sends request messages to all guest devices. The messages will be sent via a standard messaging protocol such as SMS or Email. The Cooperation Agent on guest devices will receive the messages and reply the requested information. However, according to the iOS limitation, the Cooperation Agent has to be an active mobile application to reply the request messages to the host device. To activate the Cooperation Agent we use a technique called URL Scheme Mapping [11]. The custom URL scheme (e.g. cma://) can be registered to the iOS device for invoking a particular mobile application. When a URL with registered scheme was touched by a user, the corresponding application will be brought to active context of the iOS device. In our system, the messages that are sent to guests are included with a registered URL Scheme and additional parameters. Guest device's users can invoke the URL from the received messages. Then, the Cooperation Agent is brought up to extracts query parts of the URL and determines which information is requested. User interfaces of the Cooperation Agent will ask for confirmation before replying the request. An example of request URL is shown in Figure 4-A.

A. *An example of Request for Location (URL Scheme)*

```
cma://host/cooperation/request?mid=cm001&gid=cma@me.com&cmd=gps&lat=[lat]&lng=[lng]
```

B. *An example of Location Response (HTTP)*

```
http://host/cooperation/request?mid=cm001&gid=cma@me.com&cmd=gps&lat=36.1551&lng=15
```

Fig. 4. Examples of Request and Response URL

Response Message. To return a requested data to a host device, the Cooperation Agent will determine the required resources by extracting parameters from the URL in the received message. When the URL was decoded, Cooperation Agent will invoke the target mobile application to acquire the requested information. For example, a request for barcode scanning, the Cooperation Agent will invoke a barcode scanner application and get the result after user has finished scanning. The integration of existing mobile applications is done by using *x-callback-url* specification [12]. The x-callback-url for the iOS platform is aimed to standardize the inter-application communication. However, only several numbers of iOS applications are now supporting the x-callback-url specification. Therefore, we developed testing applications conform to the x-callback-url specification to demonstrate how to enable inter-application integration in the iOS platform. To send the data back to the host device, the Cooperation Agent builds a reply HTTP request by adapting from the original requested URL, and then submits to Web service APIs on the host device. The Web services APIs are implemented with Java Servlet on i-Jetty mobile Web server. An example of response URL is shown in Figure 4-B.

4   Implementation

In order to demonstrate capabilities of our mashup construction approach, we have implemented sample mobile mashup scenarios. In this paper, we present two cooperation mashup sample called *Shopping Assistance* and *Meeting Point*. We have also discussed various aspects of our approach in this section.

To enable host's functionalities, some software is required. The Cooperation Center and i-Jetty mobile Web server must be installed on the host device. For guest devices, Cooperation Agent must be installed to accommodate connectivity among devices. In addition, to demonstrate mobile application integration on guest devices, custom mobile applications (e.g. GPS Locator and Barcode Scanner) have been installed to the guest devices.

4.1   Cooperation Mashup Scenarios

Shopping Assistance: Camera and Data Integration Mashup. This sample scenario simulates a shopping situation in a department store for 3 or more users. Goal of this mashup is to help users to compare prices of products on a local store with online stores, and then create a summary list of selected products. An Android device works as a host device. Two iOS devices coordinate with the host as guests. The guest devices will scan barcodes of selected products and send it to the host device. The host device then executes the mashup by using the collected barcodes to get information of selected products.

Mashup model and screenshots of the mashup application show in Figure 5. In this mashup, a host device sends a request for a barcode to all guest devices. The guest devices read a barcode of selected product and submit it to the host device. The barcode is given to Google's Search API for Shopping [13] to find available online stores and prices. The arithmetic component filters and extracts the lowest price. The price is converted into the designed currency with Exchange Rate API [14]. Selected products from each guest is processed and combined into a list. Finally, the list of products and comparable prices is shared among all devices.

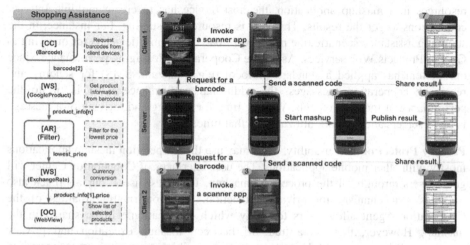

Fig. 5. Mashup Model and Screenshots of Shopping Assistance

Meeting Point: Geolocation Mashup. This mashup scenario aims to find the best ranked restaurant located near the middle point between each device's locations. Geolocation of 3 devices are used as an input to find the middle point. The middle point from arithmetic calculation is used to find the nearest train station via Google Place API Web services [15]. The best nearest restaurant around the selected train station was discovered by Gourmet Navigator API [16]. Finally, detail of the meeting point is shared among all devices by using map views.

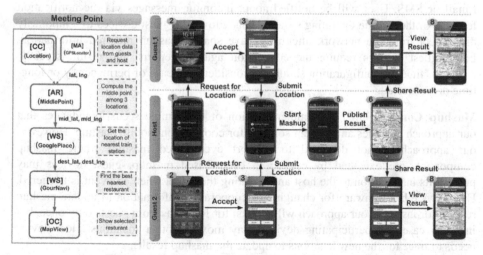

Fig. 6. Mashup Model and Screenshots of Meeting Point

4.2   Discussion

Performance. From the sample scenario, we have noticed that the major performance factors of the cooperation mashup application depend on performance of consuming Web resources and performance of the messaging system. By using multiple Web resources in a mashup application, the host device has to create multiple Internet connections to get the results. This task is resource-consuming. For instance, in the shopping assistance scenario, the major workload of the host device is for querying to Google Products Web services. As for the Cooperation Messaging performance, since our system has applied a standard protocol (e.g. Mail and SMS) for sending and receiving cooperation messages, the additional performance issue is up to the performance of theses protocols. Waiting time for sending and arriving of a message is up to servers and network utilization at that time.

Privacy Protection. For usability, users may use the cooperation mashup applications mostly with other mobile applications. The user interfaces of Cooperation Center will guide users through all the process of mashup. For guest users, our approach also provides a mechanism for privacy protection. The confirmation dialogs of the Cooperation Agent allow users to verify which information will be shared in the mashup. However, there is a trade-off between mashup execution and privacy protection. When we apply the privacy protection which required users to interact in sharing mashup information, the capability of automatic mashup execution will be disabled. User interaction is required through all process of the mashup.

Messaging System. With cooperation messaging, we assumed that participating devices are connected by using global IP addresses. Guests and host require Internet connection to consume Web resources and connect to each others. In some case, problem of losing network connection may interrupt the mashup execution. However, our messaging system leverages the failure of this case by using asynchronous manner. A host and guest devices will wait for the messages similar to waiting for an Email or SMS. User will be notified about incoming messages via the notification features of the mobile operating system. This allows the guest devices to temporarily disconnect from the network after they have shared mashup required information. Later, guest devices require the connection again when mashup result is ready. Anyway, timeout configuration should be considered in case of permanently or long-time disconnected.

Mashup Composition. The implementation of the sample scenario indicates that our approach provides an efficient solution for cooperation mobile mashup. However, our approach is not designed to support event-based mashup where mashup components are executed by events. In event-based mashup, guest devices may publish its information to the host and updating their data when an event is triggered. Host device has to aware for changing of cooperation information to update mashup result. For instance, our approach will request for locations from guests only once, but in some case, the participating devices may move to other locations. Host device needs to trace for the new locations to update the mashup results.

Scope of Integration. According to the integration of mashup components, our system is able to create mashup applications which integrate various types of mashup components. However, we found that some specific type of resources cannot be included in our mashup composition, e.g., Java Applet, Flash Object, authentication required Web services, especially, mobile applications that are not implemented with application integration mechanism. In general, a mobile application is created for a specific purpose. They may not provide the mechanism to collaborate with other applications. Thus, this kind of mobile applications cannot be used in our system.

Mobile Platform. As for the host device, in this research, we implemented host's functionality only on Andriod device. Since our messaging system uses Web services, the target platform must be able to function as a Web server and Web services container. We found that Andriod devices are suited to be the host device because several mobile Web servers are available. However, if there is a new mobile device platform which can be used as the Web service container, it may be applied as a host device for our approach. For guest devices, the participating devices have to install the Cooperation Agent that we have provided for both Android and iOS platform. We can expand coverage of mobile platforms by developing Cooperation Agent software for additional mobile operating system.

5   Conclusion and Future Work

This paper has presented a mashup construction approach that enables composition of cooperation mobile mashup. The mashup created by our approach targeted for multiple mobile devices working together for cooperation. We proposed a description language called C-MAIDL, which enables defining mashup logic and collaboration behavior. The mashup generator is implemented as a fast-paced mashup development tools aiding end-user's mashup composition. We have presented the mashup execution environment that is used to automate cooperation of devices. We have demonstrated our system applicability for cooperation mobile mashup with the sample scenario.

Our future research is targeted towards designing, implementing, and evaluating a novel mashup construction approach for cooperation of mobile devices. We want to enable event-based mashup where mashup components are executed by events. We also aim at easing the mashup composition by using a GUI mashup designer tool to create and deploy the mashup applications. Furthermore, user's evaluation should be conducted.

References

1. Jin, L., Song, M., Song, J.: Mobile Mashup architecture solution, direction and proposal. In: 2010 IEEE 2nd Symposium on Web Society, SWS (2010)
2. Chaisatien, P., Prutsachainimmit, K., Tokuda, T.: Mobile Mashup Generator System for Cooperative Applications of Different Mobile Devices. In: Auer, S., Díaz, O., Papadopoulos, G.A. (eds.) ICWE 2011. LNCS, vol. 6757, pp. 182–197. Springer, Heidelberg (2011)

3. Yahoo Pipes, Inc. (2008), http://pipes.yahoo.com/
4. Intel Corp.: Mash maker (2007), http://mashmaker.intel.com/web/
5. Brodt, A., Nicklas, D., Sathish, S., Mitschang, B.: Context-Aware Mashups for Mobile Devices. In: Bailey, J., Maier, D., Schewe, K.-D., Thalheim, B., Wang, X.S. (eds.) WISE 2008. LNCS, vol. 5175, pp. 280–291. Springer, Heidelberg (2008)
6. Kaltofen, S., Milrad, M., Kurti, A.: A Cross-Platform Software System to Create and Deploy Mobile Mashups. In: Benatallah, B., Casati, F., Kappel, G., Rossi, G. (eds.) ICWE 2010. LNCS, vol. 6189, pp. 518–521. Springer, Heidelberg (2010)
7. Guo, J., Chaisatien, P., Han, H., Noro, T., Tokuda, T.: Partial Information Extraction Approach to Lightweight Integration on the Web. In: Daniel, F., Facca, F.M. (eds.) ICWE 2010. LNCS, vol. 6385, pp. 372–383. Springer, Heidelberg (2010)
8. Android Developers, http://developer.android.com/index.html
9. i-Jetty, http://code.google.com/p/i-jetty/
10. Tsai, C.-L., Chen, H.-W., Huang, J.-L., Hu, C.-L.: Transmission reduction between mobile phone applications and RESTful APIs. In: Proceedings of the 2011 ACM Symposium on Applied Computing (SAC 2011) (2011)
11. iOS Dev Center,
https://developer.apple.com/devcenter/ios/index.action
12. x-callback-url, http://x-callback-url.com/
13. Search API for Shopping,
http://code.google.com/apis/shopping/search/
14. Exchange Rate API, http://www.exchangerate-api.com/
15. Google Place API Web Services,
http://code.google.com/apis/maps/places/
16. Gourmet Navigator API, http://api.gnavi.co.jp/api/manual.html

EnglishMash: Usability Design for a Natural Mashup Composition Environment

Saeed Aghaee and Cesare Pautasso

Faculty of Informatics, University of Lugano (USI), Switzerland
first.last@usi.ch

Abstract. The design of mashup tools combines elements from end-user development and software composition in the context of the Web. The challenge for mashup tool designers is to provide end-users with suitable abstractions, programming models and tool support for easily composing mashups out of existing Web services and Web data sources. In this paper we describe the design of a natural mashup composition environment based on the EnglishMash controlled natural language. The environment proactively supports users as they are learning the syntax of the EnglishMash language with features such as auto-completion, immediate feedback, live preview of the mashup execution and component discovery and selection based on natural language descriptions.

Keywords: Mashups, end-user development, natural language programming.

1 Introduction

Designing effective tools to facilitate mashup programming has become a key strategy to empower non-programmers to harness the potential of the programmable Web [1,2]. However, the main challenge that lies ahead in designing such tools consists of addressing the trade-off between expressive power against the assumed end-user skills [3,4]. In this paper, we present the usability and user interface design intended for the development environment supporting the EnglishMash mashup composition language, a tool that uses a restricted form of natural language (English) for mashup composition. To do so, we follow a use-case driven approach that starts by eliciting use cases from a case scenario and then maps each use case to a detailed model of the system's user interface [5].

One of the difficulties of applying natural language programming techniques lies in the need for end-users to discover and learn the constraints of the language syntax. Clearly, one cannot expect users to type arbitrary correct English sentences in the tool and effortlessly obtain a running mashup. Thus, the natural mashup composition language needs to be supported by the corresponding mashup composition environment, which is the primary focus of this paper. The highly interactive environment gives immediate feedback to users both in terms of correcting their mistakes but also showing them a live preview of the effect of their writing on the mashup output. Since basic sentences of the EnglishMash

M. Grossniklaus and M. Wimmer (Eds.): ICWE 2012 Workshops, LNCS 7703, pp. 109–120, 2012.

language are built out of component descriptions also expressed using natural language, we show how component discovery and selection can be seamlessly embedded into the lifecycle of the natural mashup composition tool.

The rest of this paper is composed as follows. In the next section, we give a brief introduction on the EnglishMash language. In section 3, we explain the barriers of EnglishMash in detail. In section 4, we extract and model the use cases of EnglishMash and provide its corresponding use case diagram. Next, we present the user interface modeling in Section 5. We discuss the related work in Section 6, followed by conclusion in Section 7.

2   EnglishMash: A Natural Language-Based Mashup Tool

EnglishMash is a mashup tool based on a controlled natural language— a subset of a natural language (e.g., English) restricted in terms of vocabulary and grammar. In terms of expressiveness, it supports various programming techniques such as conditional branches, event handling and iteration all expressed using very compact natural language grammar and syntax. For instance, the following Natural Language Mashup Description (NLMD) describes a mashup composing the Twitter search functionality (`https://dev.twitter.com/docs/api/1/get/search`) with the Google Maps widget (`https://developers.google.com/maps/`) as well as a HTML table widget.

``When the map is clicked, do as follows. Display a marker at
the location, and search for tweets at the location. Finally, show
the tweets on the table.''

Mashup Components in EnglishMash are also described in natural language. The Natural Language Component Descriptions (NLCDs) of abstract components allow to use the components in an NLMD by providing patterns of making clauses and sentences that together form an NLMD. For instance, the NLCD ``search tweets at [coordinate: longitude, latitude]'' associated with the Twitter search component is used to construct the clause ``search tweets for the location''. The Twitter NLCD contains a placeholder for the required input parameters of the component (i.e., "longitude", "latitude") which, in the NLMD, is replaced with an object referring to the output parameter of the Google Maps widget ``the map is clicked''.

The given NLMD along with a *component library and layout model* capturing the missing composition metadata including user interface design, and the list of the abstract components used by the NLMD, are passed to the EnglishMash compiler to generate its corresponding executable form. The runtime uses model transformation techniques to transform the input models to an executable form runnable by JOpera—a rapid visual service and mashup composition tool [6]. The detailed explanation of EnglishMash compiler and language, however, is out of the scope of this paper. For this paper, we only focus on the user interface and usability aspects of the EnglishMash natural mashup composition environment.

3   EnglishMash: Barriers and Required Skills

We divide EnglishMash users into two main groups: *NLMD authors*, who are those users interested in creating mashups without getting involved in programming tasks (e.g. non-programmers), and *component developers*, who are expert users (e.g., programmers) willing to develop useful components to be composed by NLMD authors. The focus of this paper is only on the NLMD authors, and therefore, the usability design proposed in this paper emphasizes the needs of users of this group.

Mashup programming is a challenging task that involves many advanced technical skills and knowledge, ranging from configuring the invocation mechanism of distributed mashup components to knowing how to program with Web scripting languages. On the one hand, this technical knowledge is abstracted from EnglishMash by hiding it inside its reusable component library. On the other hand, every tool or system requires certain skills to be mastered by its users and EnglishMash is no exception. Therefore, in order for NLMD authors to create mashups with EnglishMash, they will be required to acquire the following basic knowledge and skills:

Components capabilities. Before creating a mashup, the users must be aware of which components are subject to be mixed by the mashup, as well as what functionality is offered by each of these components. The required level of knowledge is remarkably shallow to the extent of being able to articulate the natural language-based description of the components. For instance, knowing that "**Google Maps** can **display** markers in a given **location**" is enough for a user to be able to compose the "Google Maps" component. This is made feasible by our component meta-model [7], which abstracts the complexity of the underlying invocation mechanisms of mashup components, including (but not limited to) their access methods (e.g., REST, JavaScript, SOAP, etc.), their input/output data types, and whether the components provide data, services, or user interface widgets.

Components vs. Composition. We assume that mashup components have been abstracted, described, and made available as a library to EnglishMash users by the component providers and not necessarily by the users themselves. The EnglishMash can thus be considered as an abstract composition language, which can be used to construct executable mashups once it is used in conjunction with the corresponding library of reusable components, which are described both at an abstract level with natural language and at a concrete level with executable code.

Algorithmic thinking. EnglishMash requires its users to have basic problem solving skills. These skills are needed for orchestrating the components of a mashup by describing how the mashup is supposed to work. Whereas this requires users to think algorithmically, as we are going to see, interesting non-trivial mashups can be already obtained with a small number of mashup components and simple descriptions.

Syntax. The biggest barrier imposed by EnglishMash is, indeed, the need to learn its core syntax rules. Even if the English language is used as a basis for the Mashup composition language, i.e., every EnglishMash sentence is a correct English sentence, users must learn how to restrict their English sentences so that they can be executed by the EnglishMash tool. To do so, EnglishMash includes general composition syntax rules, which are used to define the structure of a mashup. Within this structure, users make references to component descriptions, which impose additional syntax rules contributing to increase the quantity of syntax rules, and consequently raise barriers to the learning process. However, the learning curve is a gentle slope, as the syntax associated with the component descriptions needs to be fully understood only if the components are selected to be included in the mashup.

As described by Nardi [8], end-users such as NLMD authors are not naive users, and they certainly have the ability, willingness and courage to learn, provided that the learning effort is worth the added value the mashup brings for them. Accordingly, the main requirement is to shorten the learning curve of EnglishMash as much as possible through the design of a usable user interface.

4   Use Case Modeling

As shown in the use case diagram of Figure 1, when starting to build a mashup using EnglishMash, a user should first have a goal in mind that reflects his/her situational needs. Let it be: ''I want a mashup to show tweets around a given location''. Having a goal in mind helps the user to elicit the needed mashup components, being, in this example, "Twitter" and "Google Maps". Together with a powerful search engine provided by EnglishMash, the user then searches for the solicited components matching or approximating the given terms. For example, the user may search for the keyword "map" in the component library, which returns a number of mapping components which have been registered with the system. Afterward, the user chooses among the search results and adds the selected components to the stack, which indicates the list of components which are used in the mashup. If the search returns no results, then the user either creates the missing components, or ask other more expert users to do so.

Once the required components are available and selected, the user proceeds with the development of the target mashup. This use case is broken down into the following smaller use cases that should be supported simultaneously: (1) developing the logic of the mashup using NLMD, (2) designing the user interface of the mashup, (4) previewing the results of the execution of the mashup as it is being developed, (3) getting immediate feedback of syntax or runtime errors, (4) receiving NLMD writing aids in terms of auto-completion with drop-down menus containing suggestions.

The component discovery and composition use cases are clearly intertwined, since while developing a mashup, the user should be able to search for and add additional components to be composed within the target mashup, even if the mashup has already been partially described. For example, after adding the

"Google Maps" component to the stack, the user can start typing the mashup description, which should refer to the natural language description of the component. Typing the first few characters of show into the description will trigger another component lookup, based on the entered string. The tool will automatically proposed to complete the description with the show a map. text. Clicking on the auto-completion suggestion will 1) enter the completed natural language description of the component; 2) trigger a rebuild of the mashup, which will be executed and the results (i.e., the map widget centered around a default location) will be shown in the output live preview area.

The user may then proceed to define how to interact with the mashup widget. Typing a new sentence beginning with When will provide a list of auto-completion possibilities, including "When the map is clicked", "When the map is zoomed", "When the map center is moved". These correspond to events made available by the map widget component previouls added to the stack. After selecting the appropriate event, the user can continue typing to specify what should happen in the mashup when the event occurs.

Finally, the user should be able to deploy the mashup in production and share it with others. Even after a mashup has been published, it still remains modifiable and can be adjusted, redeployed and republished at any time.

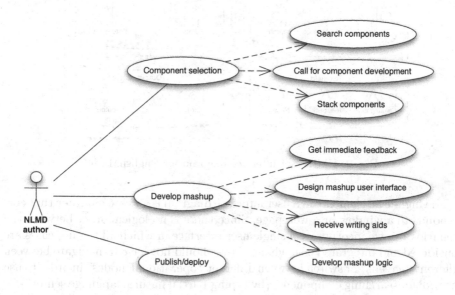

Fig. 1. Use case diagram for semi-automatic mashup platforms

5   User Interface Modeling

To model the user interface corresponding to the previous use cases, we used the UML*i* (http://trust.utep.edu/umli/) modeling language. UML*i* is a UML extension to support user interface modeling. To this end, it introduces user interface diagram used to model the graphical elements of an interface, and extends the UML activity diagram to model the interaction between users and the target user interface.

The use cases elicited in the previous step (Figure 1) drive and inform the user interface modeling by providing various context-of-use scenarios. These scenarios, in turn, help to extract the target user interface elements and produce the user interface diagram as well as to model the user interaction with these graphical elements using the extended activity diagram. According to the EnglishMash uses cases, the following context-of-use scenarios can be identified: (1) searching components, (2) selecting components, (3) NLMD authoring, (4) mashup user interface design, (5) live mashup execution, and (6) publishing and deploying mashups.

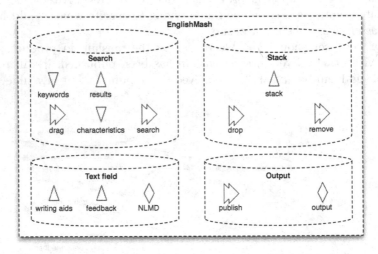

Fig. 2. UMLi user interface diagram for EnglishMash

The high-level elements in a user interface diagram is a *FreeContainer* that corresponds to a window or a web page. Since there is no logical order between the scenarios 1-5, we incorporate a single user interface in which all the use cases are considered and integrated as a whole. Users should not have to navigate between different "screens" or switch between different "operational modes" in order to use the tool for searching components (by typing partial natural language sentences), composing components (by editing and refining the natural language description), and by observing the results which are immediately available. Likewise, we use a What-you-see-is-what-you-get (WYSIWYG) approach to design the mashup user interface and deal with widget placement and layout issues.

A FreeContainer is structured in *Containers*. As it is shown in the user interface diagram (Figure 2), the main FreeContainer ("EnglishMash") consists of four Containers associated to the context-of-use scenarios. These are "search", handling the component discovery scenario; "stack", supporting the component

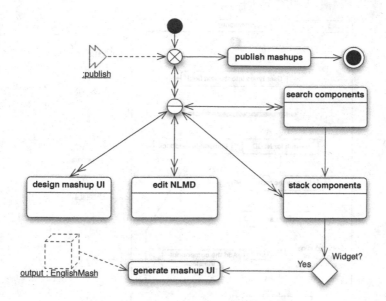

Fig. 3. UML*i* main activity diagram of the EnglishMash tool user interface

selection scenario; "text field", enabling the NLMD editing scenario; and "output", handling both the user interface design and the live execution preview scenarios. In the latter case, two scenarios are merged into a single container to simplify the design of the mashup user interface, which is tightly connected with the result of the mashup execution as described in the "input mashup text" container.

Within each Container, UML*i* allows to distinguish with specific graphical elements the user interface controls responsible for (1) sending visual feedback to users (e.g., "syntax checker"), (2) receiving information from users (e.g., "keywords"), (3) simultaneously sending and receiving information (e.g., "NLMD"), and (4) modeling user interface events (e.g., "drop").

To fully model the EnglishMash user interface requires also describing its interactions with users, we do so through UML*i* activity diagrams. Figure 3 illustrates the main activity diagram modeling the interaction with the English-Mash user interface. It contains six activities, out of which four are composite ("design mashup UI", "edit NLMD", "stack components", and "search components"). The main activity diagram starts by a loop that executes one or none of these composite activities at a time. Inside the loop, the activities "design mashup UI" and "edit NLMD" are both followed by the immediate execution of the "generate mashup UI', which involves the regeneration and synchronization of the output mashup (live execution preview). Also, the live execution preview activity is activated ever time the "stack components" state results in removing or adding a widget (i.e., components with user interface) to the stack. The loop stops when the user publishes the mashup by triggering the "publish" graphical element (e.g., clicking a button).

116   S. Aghaee and C. Pautasso

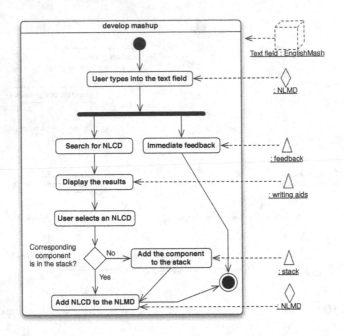

Fig. 4. The UML*i* activity diagram for the "edit NLMD" activity

The composite activities are depicted in Figures 4, 5, 6, and 7. According to the "search component" activity, user begin their search by entering some keywords. If the keywords produce no result, then the user can call for the development of his/her solicited components by describing their characteristics using natural language. The component description will be added to the library but until a matching component implementation is registered, the component will not be executable. In the "stack components" composite activity, in turn, users can either remove a component or add a new one by dropping a result from the search results to the stack.

In the "edit NLMD" activity diagram, as the user types into the "NLMD" graphical element, immediate feedback (syntax and runtime errors) as well as writing aids (auto-completion) will be provided. In the latter case, the partial text input by the user is used by EnglishMash to search the component library for components having a matching NLCD. The results are displayed to the users in a drop-down menu. After choosing among the results, if the selected NLCD does not already belong to the components in the stack, its corresponding component will be added to the stack. Finally, the "designing mashup UI" state involves resizing or relocating widgets in the mashup user interface.

A snapshot of the concrete EnglishMash user interface based on the mentioned models is illustrated in Figure 8. To implement the user interface, we used client side-technologies such as HTML5, CSS3, and JavaScript augmented with the JQuery user interface libraries (http://jqueryui.com/)

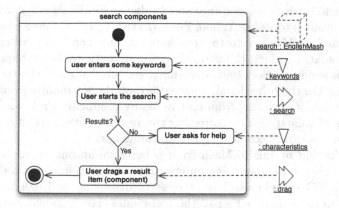

Fig. 5. The UML*i* activity diagram representing the "search components" activity

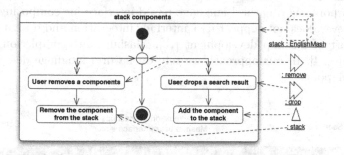

Fig. 6. The UML*i* activity diagram corresponding to the "stack components" activity

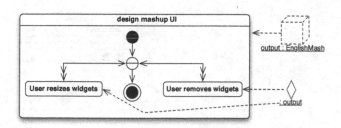

Fig. 7. The UML*i* activity diagram that illustrates the "design mashup UI" activity

6   Related Work

Mashup tools can be generally classified into automatic and semi-automatic [9]. Automatic tools do not necessitate the involvement of users, whereas semi-automatic tools aim at empowering users to quickly build their desired mashups through providing utmost assistance and guidance. EnglishMash along with the majority of mashup tools like Yahoo! Pipes (http://pipes.yahoo.com/), Dash-Mash [10], and JackBe Presto (http://www.jackbe.com/), are all categorized as semi-automatic. In fact, the users of semi-automatic tools are required to go through a learning process that, depending on the design of the tool, can be short or long. On the other hand, automatic tools do not require prior learning, but run the risk of deviating from user needs by producing irrelevant mashups. The process of validating and correcting the resulting mashups (if provided by the tool) can, in turn, become a time-consuming task [8].

The distinction of EnglishMash from other semi-automatic tools lie in its novel interaction technique, being an effective combination of natural language and WYSIWYG techniques. This, therefore, distinguishes EnglishMash from other mashup tools using either of the techniques. For instance, ServFace [11] is a tool relying on WYSIWYG technique. The shortcoming of the tool is in modeling all the required composition techniques (e.g., branches and loops) on the user ointerface level. Regarding natural language, Natural Mashup [12] is a tool incorporating a natural language-based interface for composing mashups which however does not support user interface integration and design which are integral part of mashup development [13]. Mashup auto-completion has been proposed in [14]. In our approach we rely on natural language descriptions of mashup components.

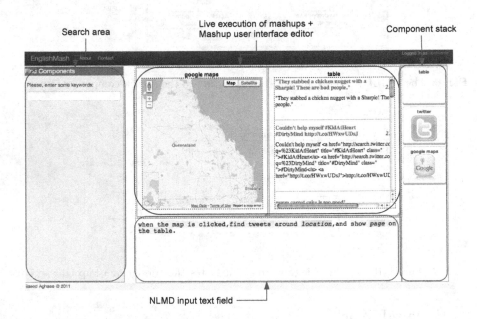

Fig. 8. The Web-based composition environment for EnglishMash

7   Conclusion

Designing a usable interface for a mashup tool plays an important role in addressing the trade-off between maximizing its expressive power and ensuring that it presents users with a gently-sloped learning curve. In this paper, we used a use-case driven approach to design a composition environment for English-Mash, a mashup tool that relies on a novel approach that lies at the intersection of model-driven development and natural language processing. The tool makes use of the EnglishMash mashup composition language that conforms to a restricted form of natural language (English). The high level of abstraction offered by the language eliminates the need for expressing technical details, and consequently makes the executable description of the mashup very similar to its natural language description. The tool supports the users in learning the constrained syntax of the language by means of immediate feedback, both in terms of informing users about syntax and semantic errors, but also by providing a live preview of the mashup execution results. Users typying the description of the mashup are supported by auto-completion features which are closely tied to the component discovery and selection features of the tool.

The paper describes first a set of common use case scenarios for the tool and then presents a detailed model of the user interface of the EnglishMash environment. To do so, we used UML*i*, which is an extension to UML to support user interface modeling, and produced both a user interface diagram, specifying the constituent abstract graphical elements of the user interface, and its corresponding activity diagrams representing the interactions between the user interface and users. Finally, we implemented the user interface using client-side technologies (e.g., JavaScript, HTML5, and CSS3) after creating a mapping between the abstract graphical elements and the concrete elements corresponding to HTML tags, attributes, and events.

We are currently undergoing an internal evaluation of the tool with a small user community made of non-programmers (e.g., High School students). We plan to publish the tool on the Web after its preliminary evaluation has been concluded together with a library of example mashups and reusable component descriptions.

Acknowledgements. The work presented in this paper has been supported by the Swiss National Science Foundation with the SOSOA project (SINERGIA grant nr. CRSI22_127386).

References

1. Benslimane, D., Dustdar, S., Sheth, A.: Services mashups: The new generation of web applications. IEEE Internet Computing 12, 13–15 (2008)
2. Daniel, F., Yu, J., Benatallah, B., Casati, F., Matera, M., Saint-Paul, R.: Understanding ui integration: A survey of problems, technologies, and opportunities. IEEE Internet Computing 11, 59–66 (2007)

3. Bozzon, A., Brambilla, M., Facca, F.M., Carughu, G.T.: A conceptual modeling approach to business service mashup development. In: Proc. of ICWS 2009, pp. 751–758. IEEE Computer Society (2009)
4. Cao, J., Riche, Y., Wiedenbeck, S., Burnett, M., Grigoreanu, V.: End-user mashup programming: through the design lens. In: Proc. of the CHI 2010, pp. 1009–1018 (2010)
5. Lif, M.: User-interface modelling: adding usability to use cases. Int. J. Hum.-Comput. Stud. 50, 243–262 (1999)
6. Pautasso, C., Alonso, G.: The JOpera visual composition language. Journal of Visual Languages and Computing 16, 119–152 (2005)
7. Aghaee, S., Pautasso, C.: The mashup component description language. In: Proc. of iiWAS 2011 (2011)
8. Nardi, B.A.: A small matter of programming: perspectives on end user computing. MIT Press, Cambridge (1993)
9. Fischer, T., Bakalov, F., Nauerz, A.: An overview of current approaches to mashup generation. In: Proc. of WM 2009, pp. 254–259 (2009)
10. Cappiello, C., Matera, M., Picozzi, M., Sprega, G., Barbagallo, D., Francalanci, C.: DashMash: A Mashup Environment for End User Development. In: Auer, S., Díaz, O., Papadopoulos, G.A. (eds.) ICWE 2011. LNCS, vol. 6757, pp. 152–166. Springer, Heidelberg (2011)
11. Nestler, T., Feldmann, M., Hübsch, G., Preußner, A., Jugel, U.: The ServFace Builder - A WYSIWYG Approach for Building Service-Based Applications. In: Benatallah, B., Casati, F., Kappel, G., Rossi, G. (eds.) ICWE 2010. LNCS, vol. 6189, pp. 498–501. Springer, Heidelberg (2010)
12. Belaunde, M., Hassen, S.B.: Service mashups using natural language and context awareness: A pragmatic architectural design. In: Proc. of EDOCW 2011 (2011)
13. Yu, J., Benatallah, B., Saint-Paul, R., Casati, F., Daniel, F., Matera, M.: A framework for rapid integration of presentation components. In: Proc. of WWW 2007 (2007)
14. Abiteboul, S., Greenshpan, O., Milo, T., Polyzotis, N.: Matchup: Autocompletion for mashups. In: Proc. of ICDE 2009 (2009)

visualRSS: A Platform to Mine and Visualise Social Data from RSS Feeds

Martin O'Shea and Mark Levene

Department of Computer Science and Information Systems,
Birkbeck, University of London, United Kingdom
{martin,mark}@dcs.bbk.ac.uk

Abstract. RSS, a popular method of syndicating frequently updated on-line content, allows data to be stored in a semi-structured, XML-based format. Much work has been carried out applying data mining techniques to RSS, but in this paper we propose the visualRSS (vRSS) application as a platform to mine and visualise data trends in RSS feeds, by tracking changes in keyword frequencies as a source of social data. Core components of vRSS's architecture to manipulate RSS feeds are described. We also present the results of vRSS's initial experimental usage involving 36 students in late 2011, concerning our research into preferences of mining types and visualisations.

Keywords: RSS feeds, keyword frequencies, visualisations, social data, data mining.

1 Introduction

XML has become the *de facto* means of exchange [1] for transmission of data on-line, either in the form of documents or information exchanged between databases. RSS ('Really Simple Syndication'), a dialect of XML, provides a popular method of syndicating and aggregating on-line content, and most commonly consists of frequently updated works such as blog entries, news headlines, audio and video media, and HTML. Typically, a feed is composed of a <channel> containing the feed's title and description, and within the <channel> are numerous <item> elements, each of which forms a posting to the feed. In turn, each <item> is made up of <title>, <description> and publication date <pubDate> elements.

As described in this paper, much work has focused on applying data mining techniques to RSS feeds to classify and cluster them. But this work may be constrained by the semi-structured nature of RSS, volume of available data and the frequent inclusion of other, often unstructured, content. Despite this, it is the authors' hypothesis that RSS contains undiscovered information which may be beneficial to end-users.

In a previous case study [2], we presented the results of an experiment concerning the feasibility of mining and visualising textual and numeric information from the *raw* data of small numbers of RSS feeds. Our current work is underpinned by the successful mining of textual data from RSS in this case study.

M. Grossniklaus and M. Wimmer (Eds.): ICWE 2012 Workshops, LNCS 7703, pp. 121–133, 2012.
© Springer-Verlag Berlin Heidelberg 2012

Moreover, we have extended this work to provide a variety of mining types to explore and visualise data trends in RSS by tracking changes in keyword frequencies. This is the basis of the visualRSS (vRSS) platform proposed in this paper, i.e. a research prototype to provide these services by integrating third-party products into a coherent and innovative toolset.

To allow it to be used by any class of user, vRSS employs several simple mining types for the specification of feeds and keywords. The application's outputs are a series of familiar visualisations including column and bar charts, treemap, pie chart and a wordcloud (sometimes known as a tag cloud), to display keyword frequencies as social data. By *social data*, we are not referring to data which represents user interaction within a social network such as Facebook or Twitter. Rather we define social data as actionable and potentially useful [3] information derived from datasets generated by social media [4], which may be relevant to anyone who cares to use it, e.g. to apply vRSS to feeds produced by news or financial sources, where the outputs are available for data warehousing, on-line trending in advertising and marketing, or in other big data analytics [5].

Therefore, this paper is written to describe vRSS and its use in the authors' research work. We begin by briefly discussing related work and we then describe vRSS and core components of it. We then summarise initial experimental use of vRSS together with the research aims and results of this work. We conclude by discussing our on-going work to classify RSS feeds by their keyword frequencies and analysing them for sentiment.

2   Related Work

Mining RSS falls within the scope of both textual and data mining. However, despite a massive corpus of available work in these areas, we focus explicitly upon RSS in the following brief literature review.

Thelwall et al. [6] distinguished between a *purist* mining of RSS as it is found, and a *pragmatic* use of extensive data cleansing. After using a purist approach to track stories in RSS feeds focusing on public fears about science, they concluded that, despite useful information in RSS, extensive and repetitive content requires data cleansing. This pragmatic approach has been more widely adopted in recent work clustering and classifying text from RSS feeds, of which [7], [8], [9] and [10] are examples. Roesler [11] has also identified caveats here concerning the number of documents or RSS feeds/items to be clustered, semantic and linguistic issues, and the time taken to cluster content especially in a real-time application.

Association rules have also been used to analyse news disseminated on the web: Hsu [12] has proposed the Web News Search System to discover 'useful' news, and Kittiphattanabawon and Theeramunkong [13] mined relations between Thai news articles concerning politics, economics and crime. A corollary of this concerns mining text snippets, e.g. the short RSS <title> element, which may not be sufficient for mining. Banerjee et al. [14] sought to improve the clustering of small pieces of text by supplementing their descriptions with text from Wikipedia. Phan et al. [15] again used Wikipedia and other sources to classify sparse text.

A detailed survey of methods available for the visualisation of text streams is given by Šilić and Bašić [16]. Wanner et al. [17] have visualised RSS data to reveal the sentiment of RSS news feed stories about the candidates during 2008's US presidential election campaign. This work is an example of the role of visualisation in social data analysis [18], i.e. to address the issues of whether visualisations enhance social networking and how users respond to them, how visualisations are used and the purposes they are used for. 10x10 [19] is an interactive exploration of the words and pictures in RSS feeds provided by several leading international news sources.

This role of visualisations though should not be confused with more typical social networking services like Facebook and MySpace. Instead, it is more related to data-centric social networking allowed by websites specialising in visualisa-tions, e.g. Many-Eyes, allowing users to upload data, visualise it on-line and append comments.

3   visualRSS: Exploring and Visualising Trends in RSS

vRSS is a research prototype written to explore and visualise data trends in RSS feeds by tracking changes in keyword frequencies, where resulting social data is available to users via on-screen displays and interactive visualisations (Fig. 1). Users are able to specify feeds and keywords for mining via three simple mining types:

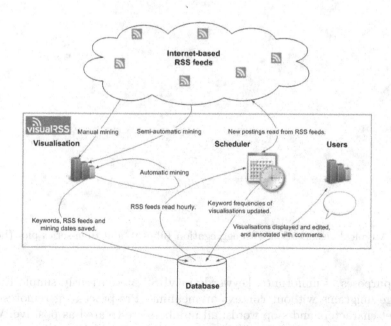

Fig. 1. A conceptual view of visualRSS

1. *Automatic mining* displays a current *buzz* of keywords in the *rssosphere*. It does this by using a subset of keywords mined hourly from the `<title>` elements of new postings to vRSS's pre-defined feeds: each keyword then has its frequency calculated from the `<description>` elements. Finally these frequencies are sorted in descending order, and the most popular keywords are determined as the subset.
2. *Semi-automatic mining* allows users to enter their own keywords, which search vRSS's pre-defined feeds to track topical issues.
3. *Manual mining* allows users to enter feeds and keywords of their own choice, to focus upon a particular subject(s).

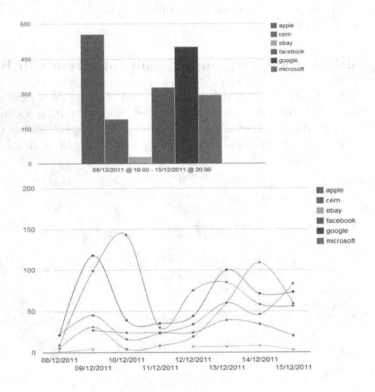

Fig. 2. A typical visualisation with aggregation (above), and time-series plot (below)

For purposes of uniformity, keywords in vRSS are currently simple English language unigrams without context or meaning. Pre-processing removes non-alphabet characters and stop words: all numbers are treated as positive. When they are defined using one of the mining types above, a wordcloud (or tag cloud) constantly displays current keyword frequencies from the appropriate feeds over the last 1 - 24 hours: see Fig. 3 for manual mining. Once a user is satisfied with their selection, a sample visualisation is created via Google Chart Tools [1], i.e. a bar or column chart, pie chart, wordcloud or treemap, which is used as the basis of a new *permanent* visualisation. If saved, the sample visualisation's type, RSS feeds, keywords and dates between which mining will occur, are persisted in vRSS's database. If a new RSS feed is defined by a user during manual mining, a new database table is dynamically created.

A saved visualisation includes two charts, e.g. Fig. 2 displays several IT-related keywords for a week in December 2011: aggregated frequencies are displayed in the user-selected type, i.e. in this example a column chart, and the time-series chart depicts frequency changes during the aggregation's period. Each saved visualisation also displays its component feeds and keywords. A keyword-based search facility also allows users to browse vRSS's feeds and visualisations.

4   Architecture

4.1   Implementation

vRSS's basic architecture forms a typical *n*-tiered web application rendered in Java servlets and JSPs within an Apache Tomcat container based over a MySQL database. To implement the application, numerous third-party products and web services are used on a *black box* basis as a *mash-up*. Moreover, no frameworks tools such as Spring are used in vRSS: instead each principal object type, e.g. visualisations, has a dedicated class implementing methods for the necessary object relational modelling for database interaction. As each method handles one operation per table(s), e.g. add row, get one or many rows, such methods are quickly written and customised: each of these methods also makes use of a simple connection pooling.

4.2   Anatomy of a Mining Type

The three mining types in vRSS all employ the same basic interface to allow keywords and feeds to be specified. A wordcloud showing keyword frequencies from the appropriate feeds over the last 1 - 24 hours is displayed at the top of the page, and dedicated controls per mining type are placed adjacent to this, e.g. as Fig. 3 for manual mining.

Behind each mining type, a simple hierarchy of classes maintains the feeds and current frequencies of keywords specified: these are illustrated in Fig. 4. The super class of this hierarchy is an RSS_Feed_Miner which includes dedicated naming elements and an RSS_Feed_Polling object. RSS feeds are stored in a series of parallel lists along with the RSS elements, categories and the mining type to be used. The RSS_Feed_Occurrence_Miner specialisation class for keyword frequencies maintains a *key-value*, i.e. word-frequency, hashmap, and is populated from the wordcloud displayed in Fig. 3. Thus, the frequency of a particular keyword is derived from all of the feeds stored in the super class when a mining

---

[1] https://developers.google.com/chart/

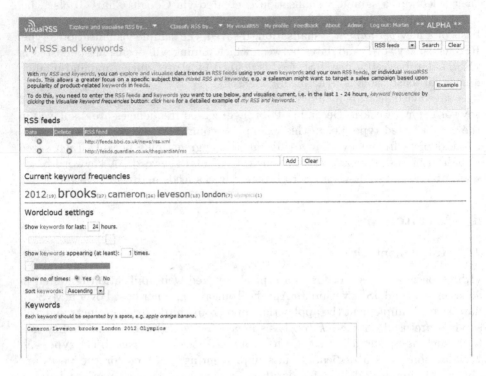

Fig. 3. A partial screenshot of manual mining in vRSS

type is used. The other specialisations illustrated are for future data mining of RSS feeds by vRSS which we describe later, and also for mining numeric data.

4.3 Polling and Indexing RSS Feeds

To maintain frequencies of keywords for visualising, vRSS relies on an index which is updated hourly with new postings mined from its pre-defined collection of RSS feeds. Thus, the index is structured as a series of M:N database relationships to record keyword frequencies from various `<item>` elements of RSS feeds on an hourly basis, i.e. Table 1 displays a simplified representation of the index.

The following pseudocode represents the basic hourly algorithm. The current polling date/time is determined (line 1) and two consecutive stages are executed: the first polls RSS feeds for new `<item>` elements whilst the second mines and disseminates this data to visualisations. Each stage is represented by the two `for` loops (lines 2 and 12):

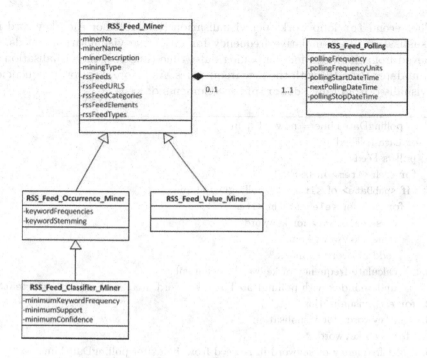

Fig. 4. vRSS's object hierarchy for storing RSS feeds and keywords

Table 1. A representation of the keyword index in vRSS

Polling date/time	Keyword	RSS feed	RSS Element	Frequency
29/04/2012 @ 11:00	$keyword_1$	$rssFeed_1$	`<title>`	4
29/04/2012 @ 11:00	$keyword_2$	$rssFeed_1$	`<description>`	2
29/04/2012 @ 12:00	$keyword_1$	$rssFeed_1$	`<title>`	6
29/04/2012 @ 12:00	$keyword_2$	$rssFeed_3$	`<description>`	1
29/04/2012 @ 12:00	$keyword_n$	$rssFeed_n$	`<description>`	3

The first of these loops (line 2) mines data from each RSS feed in vRSS: the address of each feed is polled (line 3) and the published date/time of each `<item>` in the feed is checked to determine if any new postings have been made during the polling date/time (line 5). For any new `<item>`, each `<element>` is parsed (lines 6 and 7), and new keywords are added to the index (lines 8 and 9): the frequency of each keyword per `<element>` is calculated in Lucene[2] and written to the index together with the feed, `<element>` and the polling date/time (lines 10 and 11). At the moment, only the frequencies of keywords from the `<description>` elements of each `<item>` are parsed when feeds are polled hourly. Postings from each feed are stored in dedicated database tables.

---

[2] http://lucene.apache.org/

The second **for** loop works per visualisation (line 12). For each keyword in a visualisation, its cumulative frequency for all of the visualisation's feeds, is retrieved from the index for the polling date/time (line 15): the visualisation is then updated (line 16) with the new frequencies. As before, keyword frequencies are visualised from only `<description>` elements of feeds.

```
1.  set pollingDateTime = now - 1 hour
2.  for each rssFeed
3.    poll rssFeed
4.    for each <item> in rssFeed
5.      if <pubDate> of <item> >= pollingDateTime
6.        for each for <element> in <item>
7.          parse <element> for keywords
8.          if new keyword found
9.            add keyword to index
10.         calculate frequency of keyword in element
11.         update index with pollingDateTime, keyword, freq., rssFeed and <element>
12. for each visualisation
13.   get keywords for visualisation
14.   for each keyword
15.     get frequency of keyword in rssFeed from index for pollingDateTime
16.   update visualisation with pollingDateTime, keywords and frequencies
```

4.4   Parsing an RSS Feed

During the polling process described above, vRSS uses the Rome API[3] to parse RSS feeds. Rome is based upon the JDOM XML parser and allows RSS and Atom to be parsed via a common `<SyndFeed>`, i.e. syndicated feed, model. The following Java extract from vRSS parses a feed's address:

```java
URL url = new URL(rssFeedURL);
URLConnection urlConn = url.openConnection();
XmlReader reader = new XmlReader(urlConn);
SyndFeedInput input = new SyndFeedInput();
SyndFeed rssFeed = input.build(reader);
```

Each `<item>` in a feed is a `<SyndEntry>` and API calls access each `<element>`:

```java
List<SyndEntry> rssFeedItems = rssFeed.getEntries();
for (SyndEntry rssFeedItem : rssFeedItems) {
    String title = rssFeedItem.getTitle();
    ...
}
```

---

[3] http://java.net/projects/rome

5 Initial Experimental Usage

5.1 Rationale and Objectives

Our previous case study [2] to mine and visualise data from RSS allowed both textual and numeric data. With vRSS though, we have suspended the mining of numeric data, e.g. exchange rate fluctuations from RSS, because of difficulties encountered by the experiment's participants. Instead, we have concentrated upon simplifying and extending our text mining by focusing on a variety of mining types to specify keywords and feeds to provide social data.

Therefore, to assess these techniques to the maximum possible real-world extent available to us at the time, an *alpha* version of vRSS was tested by 36 part-time MSc students of various employment and experience backgrounds, in a new experiment during late 2011. This has allowed us to research preferences and efficiencies of mining types and visualisations, distribution of categories of feeds visualised, and common usage of these amongst the mining types.

5.2 Discussion: An Analysis of Our Results

RSS Feeds and Categories. We provided our students with 57 RSS feeds arranged into seven generic categories, e.g. Business, Finance and Economics (BFE), Fashion, Celebrity and Lifestyle (FCL), Film, Music, News and Current Affairs (NCA), Science, Nature and Technology (SNT), and Sport. This corpus of feeds and categories were selected to be English language in content, global or regional rather than applicable to a specific country, and also to be wide-ranging and relevant in nature: the majority of feeds were present in the NCA (16) category and SNT (10) categories.

Keyword frequencies from each feed were recorded for 10 days prior to the experiment itself which lasted for a fortnight. We did not wish to bias our students in any way because we wanted to collect a wide variety of data for our research questions: therefore, the experiment was very *free* in format. Our students were able to choose keywords, add new feeds and to use the mining types without restriction: at the end of the experiment 202 feeds, including new categories such as Travel and Astronomy, were being mined hourly for new postings. The most popular feed categories were NCA with 52 feeds (25.74%), SNT with 39 feeds (19.30%), and Sport (31 feeds or 15.35%): least popular were Entertainment and Arts (EA) with 6 feeds (2.97%), and Travel with 5 feeds (2.48%). Figure 5 displays the distribution of mining types per feed categories with semi-automatic as favourite. Some 99 (73.33%) of visualisations covered two feed categories, whereas only five (3.70%) included all twelve categories.

Distribution of Visualisations. The 135 visualisations created by our students are displayed per RSS feed category in Fig. 6. The column chart was the most popular type with 107 instances (79.26%), despite alternatives such as word cloud and treemap, neither of which is reliant upon the association of words to specific colours to relate information.

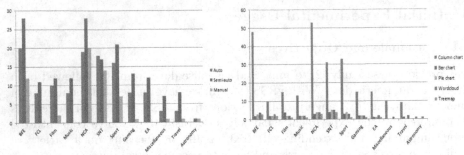

Fig. 5. Mining types per feed category   **Fig. 6.** Visualisations per feed category

Use of Mining Types to define RSS Feeds and Keywords. The majority of the 135 visualisations used different combinations of RSS feeds and keywords. But, in a small number of cases, students used the same feeds and keywords for semi-automatic and automatic mining: e.g. one student used keywords *economy, recession, depression, war* and *apocalypse* '*because of major events in current affairs*', where semi-automatic mining proved most successful because '*it tracked 4 keywords for 7 days*'. In this, and similar cases documented, automatic proved the least popular mining type because generic keywords convey '*less meaning and are less indicative of specifics*'. However, with automatic mining intended to provide a current *buzz*, this is not surprising.

6   Applications of visualRSS

In the experiment above, we also asked our students to propose applications for vRSS as a source of social data. Many of the suggestions made confirmed the authors' own opinions in areas such as:

– Business Intelligence: As a data source for big data analytics, or in turning unstructured data into tabular form for use in data mining fact and decision tables.

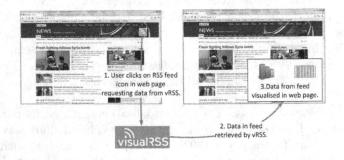

Fig. 7. vRSS as a web service

- Linguistics: To reveal geographical, cultural or political bias in news reporting, or calculating n-gram relationships between keywords to assist search engine results.
- Tracking and Trending: Where an organisation might place mouse-over adverts in web pages based upon popular keywords, or to track frequencies of keywords to determine market share.

More germane however, is the use of vRSS as a web service, i.e. as a browser plug-in or API to allow websites to display vRSSs outputs *on the fly* (Fig. 7).

7 Conclusion

In this paper, we have proposed the vRSS platform for exploring and visualising data trends in semi-structured RSS feeds by tracking changes in keyword frequencies. Major components of vRSS have been described and we have also presented a summary of our initial findings using vRSS. Though successful, this work was restricted to an experiment made up of a small user body in an ostensibly *class room* environment.

Our initial work also falls into the *purist* approach put forward by Thelwall et al. [6], where keywords are not extensively pre-processed in vRSS. This also contrasts with the approach taken by others, i.e. [14] and [15], in using external data sources to assist categorisation. vRSS differs from the related work we cite because it provides a coherent and innovative platform for aggregating information across RSS feeds. Furthermore, although vRSS's outputs are similar to others available, it must be remembered that RSS is a dialect of XML conforming to W3C standards, rather than a *proprietary* format belonging to a social network provider subject to the whims of a changing market.

Currently we are using decision trees to classify feeds into categories according to the presence of keywords at particular frequencies for varying 10, 20 and 30 day periods. This work re-uses the corpus of 57 feeds and seven categories described in our initial experimentation, and involves approximately 300,000 RSS feed <item> elements mined between August and October 2011. Further tests using Naive Bayes and SVM will also be carried out upon this corpus to compare the validity of the resulting classifications. We also plan to analyse our data for sentiment, and by relating the results to popular keywords revealed by our classification work, provide a finely-grained time-series analysis of RSS-based sentiment.

These extensions to vRSS extend our initial experimental work in providing social data from semi-structured RSS, which may be beneficial to end-users in the roles we have referred to.

Other future work also includes extending our current unigram keywords to include phrases and stemming.

References

1. Bray, T., Paoli, J., Sperberg-McQueen, C., Maler, E., Yeargeau, F.: Extensible markup language (xml) 1.0, 3rd edn. W3C Recommendation (2004), http://www.w3.org/TR/2004/REC-xml-20040204/
2. O'Shea, M., Levene, M.: Mining and visualising information from RSS feeds: a case study. IJWIS 7(2), 105–129 (2011)
3. Witten, I.H., Frank, E.: Data Mining: Practical Machine Learning Tools and Techniques, 2nd edn. Morgan Kaufmann Series in Data Management Systems. Morgan Kaufmann (2005)
4. Ohlhorst, F.: Tools to help analyze mountains of social data (2011), http://www.informationweek.com/thebrainyard/news/marketing/231002135/
5. Dumbill, E.: What is big data? An introduction to the big data landscape (2012), http://radar.oreilly.com/2012/01/what-is-big-data.html
6. Thelwall, M., Prabowo, R., Fairclough, R.: Are raw RSS feeds suitable for broad issue scanning? a science concern case study. J. Am. Soc. Inf. Sci. Technol. 57(12), 1644–1654 (2006)
7. Teng, Z., Liu, Y., Ren, F.: Create special domain news collections through summarization and classification. IEEJ Transactions on Electrical and Electronic Engineering 5, 56–61 (2010)
8. Getahun, F., Tekli, J., Chbeir, R., Viviani, M., Yetongnon, K.: Relating RSS News/Items. In: Gaedke, M., Grossniklaus, M., Díaz, O. (eds.) ICWE 2009. LNCS, vol. 5648, pp. 442–452. Springer, Heidelberg (2009)
9. Hu, C.L., Chou, C.K.: RSS watchdog: an instant event monitor on real online news streams. In: CIKM 2009: Proceeding of the 18th ACM Conference on Information and Knowledge Management, pp. 2097–2098. ACM, New York (2009)
10. Bossa, S., Fiumara, G., Provetti, A.: A lightweight architecture for RSS polling of arbitrary web sources. In: WOA (2006)
11. Roesler, R.: Relational RSS clustering techniques (2010), http://www.stanford.edu/class/cs229/proj2009/Roesler.pdf
12. Hsu, L.-F.: Mining on Terms Extraction from Web News. In: Pan, J.-S., Chen, S.-M., Nguyen, N.T. (eds.) ICCCI 2010, Part I. LNCS, vol. 6421, pp. 188–194. Springer, Heidelberg (2010)
13. Kittiphattanabawon, N., Theeramunkong, T.: Relation Discovery from Thai News Articles Using Association Rule Mining. In: Chen, H., Yang, C.C., Chau, M., Li, S.-H. (eds.) PAISI 2009. LNCS, vol. 5477, pp. 118–129. Springer, Heidelberg (2009)
14. Banerjee, S., Ramanathan, K., Gupta, A.: Clustering short texts using wikipedia. In: Proceedings of the 30th Annual International ACM SIGIR Conference on Research and Development in Information Retrieval, SIGIR 2007, pp. 787–788. ACM, New York (2007)
15. Phan, X.H., Nguyen, L.M., Horiguchi, S.: Learning to classify short and sparse text & web with hidden topics from large-scale data collections. In: Proceeding of the 17th International Conference on World Wide Web, pp. 91–100. ACM, New York (2008)
16. Šilić, A., Bašić, B.D.: Visualization of Text Streams: A Survey. In: Setchi, R., Jordanov, I., Howlett, R.J., Jain, L.C. (eds.) KES 2010, Part II. LNCS, vol. 6277, pp. 31–43. Springer, Heidelberg (2010)

17. Wanner, F., Rohrdantz, C., Mansmann, F., Oelke, D., Keim, D.A.: Visual sentiment analysis of RSS news feeds featuring the US presidential election in 2008.
In: IUI 2009 Workshop on Visual Interfaces to the Social and the Semantic Web,
VISSW (2009), Online Proceedings, http://ceur-ws.org/Vol-443/paper7.pdf
18. Viégas, F.B., Wattenberg, M., Heer, J., Agrawala, M.: Social data analysis workshop. In: CHI 2008: CHI 2008: Extended Abstracts on Human Factors in Computing Systems, pp. 3977–3980. ACM, New York (2008)
19. 10x10 (2012), http://www.tenbyten.org/

Extracting Models
from Web API Documentation

Rolando Rodríguez[1], Roberto Espinosa[1], Devis Bianchini[2], Irene Garrigós[3],
Jose-Norberto Mazón[3], and Jose Jacobo Zubcoff[4]

[1] WaKe Research, Dept. of Computer Science
University of Matanzas "Camilo Cienfuegos", Cuba
{rolando.rodriguez,roberto.espinosa}@umcc.cu
[2] Dept. of Information Engineering, University of Brescia, Italy
bianchin@ing.unibs.it
[3] WaKe Research, Dept. of Software and Computing Systems
University of Alicante, Spain
{igarrigos,jnmazon}@dlsi.ua.es
[4] WaKe Research, Dept. of Marine Sciences and Applied Biology
University of Alicante, Spain
jose.zubcoff@ua.es

Abstract. In order to develop web mashups, designers need an in-depth
understanding of each Web API they are using. However, Web API documentation is rather heterogeneous, represented by big HTML files or
collection of files in which it is difficult to identify elements such as API
methods and how they can be invoked. Models have been widely recognized as first-citizen artifacts for documenting software applications,
abstracting from implementation details, thus becoming good candidates
to raise the level of automation of web mashup development. In this paper we present an approach for extracting models from Web API documentation. Our contributions are (i) a metamodel for standardizing the
information extracted from Web APIs documentation; and (ii) a method
for the extraction of models by parsing HTML files containing the Web
API documentation, discovering useful data, and automatically generating the corresponding models (that conform to the defined metamodel).

1 Introduction

Web mashups are low-cost, personalized web applications, designed and implemented to be used for short periods of time and built starting from a set of
predefined Web APIs. The great success of Web APIs basically relies on a very
simple technological stack, based on HTTP, XML and JSON, and the extensive use of URIs. Nowadays, Web APIs are used to access and aggregate large
quantity of data, like Flickr and Facebook, or to expose on the web contents
from legacy systems. To promote the adoption of Web APIs for web mashup development, the ProgrammableWeb public repository[1] has been made available,

---

[1] http://www.programmableweb.com

M. Grossniklaus and M. Wimmer (Eds.): ICWE 2012 Workshops, LNCS 7703, pp. 134–145, 2012.
© Springer-Verlag Berlin Heidelberg 2012

where Web API providers share their own components and web designers can look for Web APIs they need to compose new web mashups without implementing them from scratch. Currently, the repository registers more than 6,000 Web APIs (a number that is continuously growing) and more than 6,600 user-defined mashups.

In this context, providing web designers with the required information to effectively find Web APIs they need and compose them in web mashups is becoming a more and more critical issue. Unfortunately, this task is hampered by the absence of a standard structure in Web API documentations (like the WSDL specification for SOAP-based Web services). On the one hand, Web API consumers are not constrained to adhere to any description language, on the other hand, information extracted from Web API documentation must be performed automatically, in a transparent way for consumers, starting from plain HTML documentation used to describe Web API usage.

For decades, models have provided developers with a standard and visual documentation for understanding software (e.g, UML in software engineering or ER model in databases). The same idea can be applied to Web APIs, where different kind of documentation formats may mislead designers. Having a common model can improve understanding and supporting them in using Web APIs. Also, if models are used, the level of automation of all the phases of Web mashup development is raised: semantic enrichment of Web API descriptions would be pursued to improve their selection [5] or to improve their automatic comparison for substitutability purposes (often referred to as *Web API migration* [2]); CASE tools may be implemented to ease web mashup composition and to enable automatic code generation [7].

Bearing these issues in mind, in this paper we introduce an approach for extracting models from Web API documentation. In particular, our contribution is twofold: (i) a metamodel for standardizing the data related to Web APIs documentation; and (ii) a method for extracting models (conformed to the Web API metamodel) by discovering useful data in the HTML files that contain the Web API documentation. Our aim is to perform a first step toward a computer-assisted extraction and semantic annotation of Web API models for web mashup composition purposes.

The paper is organized as follows: Section 2 provides an overview of the proposal and a motivating example. Our approach is detailed in Section 3, where the metamodel is described, and in Section 4, where the model extraction procedure from the Web API documentation is presented step by step with the help of the motivating example. A comparison with the state of the art to underline the cutting-edge elements of our proposal is discussed in Section 5. Finally, Section 6 closes the paper providing some hints about future work.

2   A Web API Model Extractor

Our approach aims at obtaining Web API models from a set of HTML files describing the Web API documentation. To do so, the first step concerns the analysis of a significant number of Web APIs with the aim of building a meta-model for them. Once we have the metamodel, a Web API model extractor is designed. This extractor is composed of two steps: (i) parsing the HTML files that contain the documentation in order to discover useful data, and (ii) creating a model (that conforms to the Web API metamodel) by using those data.

The problem addressed here is related to the one of designing proper wrappers to load contents of Web pages, such as Lixto[2], that has been developed for extracting product pricing from already known Web sources [3]. Nevertheless, Web API documentation is contained in rather heterogeneous (in format and content) and unfamiliar HTML files, thus hampering the task of discovering useful data, i.e. identify elements such as Web API methods (or operations), corresponding parameters to invoke them and which is the output provided by method invocations. Therefore, it is crucial to use some kind of "a priori" knowledge to identify the right portions of the HTML documentation which correspond to Web API elements. The documentation of a Web API is divided in two parts: a list of Web API operations, and a list of parameters of each Web API. After analyzing the structure of several Web API documentations (based on a representative population) on the ProgrammableWeb repository, we found that these two parts are represented in one or several web pages. We chose this repository since it is, to the best of our knowledge, the most complete collection of Web APIs shared among web mashup designers.

Our findings show that HTML documentation of any Web API presents recurrent patterns of tags (such as <ul>, <table> and so on) that can be used to discover useful data for our purpose. There are different tags used to highlight the name of the operations or parameters, e.g. <h1> or <b>, that can be considered as well. In order to know the most used tags for representing operations and their parameters, we conducted an analysis of a random sample of 30 Web APIs selected from the ProgrammableWeb site. This representative sample gives us enough information about tags used for enclosing operations and parameters. We use the ANalysis Of Variance [15] (ANOVA) technique, which is the most appropriate test with which to discover the most frequent tags. In our experiment, ANOVA is used to compare the means of usage of all tags by computing $p-values$, thus determining which are the most frequent tags from the analysis of the random sample. As a result, we can conclude that the <ul> and <ol> tags were the most used (ANOVA $p-value = 0.0196$) for enclosing lists of operations, while <table> was the main significantly different tag for enclosing parameters (ANOVA $p-value = 0.0136$). As a matter of fact, in this paper, we focus on these more used tags according to the results of our empirical analysis. Moreover, some recurrent terms contained in Web API documentations, such as *service, api, operation, inputs, outputs, method, parameter* and so on, could be exploited as additional knowledge to guide the discovery of useful data.

For the sake of understandability, a running example based on a Web API from ProgrammableWeb is presented throughout the paper. The running example is

---

[2] http://www.lixto.com/

based on the Zillow API[3], which provides real estate and mortgage data. Among the data about the Web API that can be extracted from ProgrammableWeb, there is the Zillow Web API documentation URL from which to obtain the list of operations of the API (as shown in Fig. 1(a)). In this figure, it is marked that each of the items representing an operation refers to a URL in which information of the parameters is defined. These parameters are described in a table as shown in Fig. 1(b). Throughout the paper, our approach is applied to Zillow Web API to show how a model is obtained from this documentation.

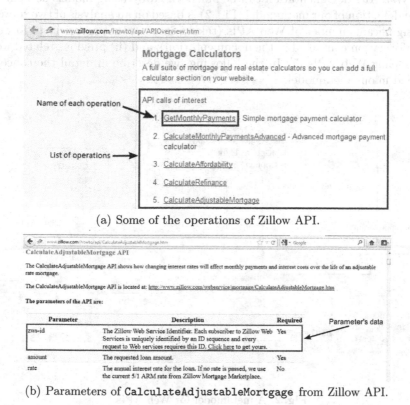

(a) Some of the operations of Zillow API.

(b) Parameters of `CalculateAdjustableMortgage` from Zillow API.

Fig. 1. Sample screenshots of the Zillow Web API documentation

3   A Metamodel for Web APIs

Under the model-driven umbrella, and according to [11], "a model is a description of (part of) a system written in a well-defined language", while "a well-defined language is a language with well-defined form (syntax), and meaning (semantics), which is suitable for automated interpretation by a computer". Therefore, on the one hand, a model must focus on those important parts of a system, thus avoiding

---

[3] http://www.programmableweb.com/api/zillow

superfluous details. On the other hand, well defined languages can be designed by means of metamodeling [4], which provides the foundation for creating models in a meaningful, precise and consistent manner.

Our Web API metamodel contains those useful concepts for representing models of a Web API in a standardized manner, thus dealing with the heterogeneity of Web API documentation. As aforementioned, models of Web APIs (based on our metamodel) can support web mashup designers during Web API retrieval and composition from huge repositories. Interestingly, the rough process of creating Web API documentation can be ameliorated by using models as well.

The definition of our metamodel (Fig. 2) is based on an analysis of two sources: (i) a significant number of Web APIs (taking into account a variety of formats and information contained in the documentation), and (ii) previous related work on modeling Web APIs [5]. In the following, we describe in detail the concepts included in our metamodel.

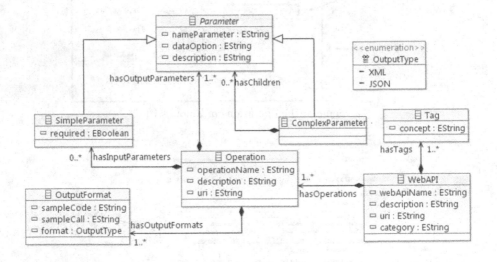

Fig. 2. A metamodel for Web APIs

WebAPI. This is the main container class for the other elements in the Web API model. It defines a name and a general description of the Web API. The `WebAPI` class contains a category which the Web API belongs to, a set of operations that can be called with the Web API and a URI from which the Web API documentation can be accessed. It contains a set of tags with which is semantically annotated.

Tag. This class defines a set of concepts with which the Web API can be semantically annotated.

Operation. It describes the methods implemented within the Web API. Each operation has a name and a description to explain the functionality of the operation. The class `Operation` can have zero or more input parameters, but it must always contain, at least, one output parameter. Since Web APIs may output results from method invocations according to several formats (e.g. XML or JSON), the metamodel contains the `OutputFormat` class associated to each operation. An output parameter of an operation may be simple or may contain a collection of parameters nested with their respective values. i.e., a complex parameter.

Parameter. It is an abstract class that represents either an input or an output parameter. This class contains the name of the parameter, a value type for that parameter, and a description. The `Parameter` class is the base class for defining simple and complex parameters.

SimpleParameter. This class inherits from the `Parameter` class and defines a simple input or output parameter for an operation. In the context of Web APIs, *simple* means that the parameter is in the form `attribute=value`, where value is a simple type. This class contains a boolean attribute to indicate if the parameter is required or not. The `SimpleParameter` class can be used as an input parameter or as part of an output parameter.

ComplexParameter. It inherits from the `Parameter` class and represents a complex parameter type. This class can contain other parameters (by means of the `hasChildren` association) that give it the *complex* nature, as being related to other parameters. As shown in Fig. 2, the `ComplexParameter` class can be only used as an output parameter.

OutputFormat. This class represents the information related to the different formats that can be returned in an output of each Web API. It stores the name of the format (by means of an enumeration called `OutputType`) and sample excerpts of source code.

While required data for creating `WebAPI` and `Tag` classes can be acquired from the ProgrammableWeb site, data for creating the remainder of the classes are found in the specific Web API documentation (see Fig. 1).

Our Web API metamodel has been implemented by using the Eclipse Modeling framework (EMF)[4]. The EMF project is a modeling framework and code generation facility for building applications based on a structured model and metamodels.

4   Model Extraction from Web API Documentation

Our approach for extracting models from Web API documentation has two main stages: (i) parsing HTML pages containing the documentation of the Web API to discover required data (i.e., generic Web API data, operation data and parameters data), and (ii) using these data for generating a model of the Web API (conformed to the metamodel). An overview of our approach is shown in Fig. 3.

---

[4] http://www.eclipse.org/emf

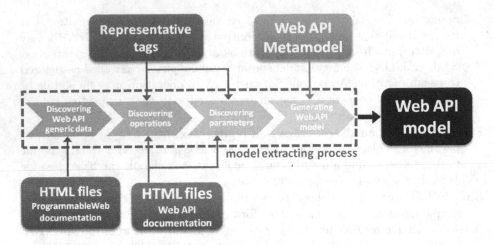

Fig. 3. Overview of our Web API model extractor

4.1 Discovering Data from Web API Documentation

The first step when collecting data is invoking methods from the ProgrammableWeb site to extract useful information about Web APIs[5]. In particular, they enable:

- to retrieve Web APIs by category or tags; given a category c, the `api.programmableweb.com/apis/-/c` method is invoked and the list of Web APIs that have been categorized in c is returned; within the ProgrammableWeb repository Web APIs are classified in 67 categories such as `mapping`, `payment`, `search`; tag-based Web API retrieval is performed in the same way;
- to retrieve the details of a given Web API; given a Web API W, the `api.programmableweb.com/apis/W` method is invoked to retrieve all the detailed information about the Web API W.

Once data from ProgrammableWeb site has been acquired, the URI of the Web API documentation is used for obtaining the remainder of data. A set of steps and heuristics for parsing Web API documentation have been defined and implemented in a well-known tool for defining ETL (Extract/Transform/Load) processes, named Pentaho Data Integration (aka Kettle)[6].

According to our preliminary statistical study, operations are mainly represented as `<ol>` or `<ul>` tags. Enclosed by these tags each operation is contained in a `<li>` tag with some decoration to visually highlight the name of the operations, e.g., underlined (`<u>`), bold faces (`<b>`), header type (`<h1>`) and so on[7]. In order to discover these data, the steps performed are as follows:

---

[5] http://api.programmableweb.com/
[6] http://kettle.pentaho.com/
[7] There are alternatives, e.g. combinations of `<span>` and `<div>` tags intentionally marked with `id` or `class` that are then defined in style sheets. Considering these tags is part of our future work.

1. cleaning the HTML page in order to get a well-formed XML document suitable for further processing; specifically, HtmlCleaner[8], an open-source HTML parser written in Java, is used;
2. extracting every piece of HTML code between tags that structure the required data; in this case, the focus is on the <ul>, <ol> and <li> tags;
3. applying several heuristics in order to ameliorate the detection of operation names, namely:
   - discard those pieces of HTML code in which the word *operation* or a synonym such as *method* or *call* are not presented in the previous piece of code; a thesaurus has been properly created to consider these terms;
   - text enclosed by style tags such as <h1> or <b> is likely to represent operations, since they are normally highlighted due to its importance for documentation purposes;
   - text enclosed by <a> tags is likely to represent operations, since it refers to the URL of the documentation of the operation; for example, <li><h4><a href=''operations/getusers.html''>GetUsers</a>..., where GetUsers is the name of the operation, and the URL to get the documentation of that operation is operations/getusers.html.

In our running example, the Web page of the Zillow API documentation is http://www.zillow.com/howto/api/APIOverview.htm. A sample excerpt is acquired and shown as follows:

```
<div class="api-overview">
 <h4>Home Valuation</h4>
 <p>Search results list, Zestimate<sup>&reg;</sup>, Rent Zestimate<sup>&reg;</sup>,
    home valuations, home valuation charts, comparable houses, and market trend charts.</p>
 <p class="no-margin">API calls of interest:</p>
 <ul>
  <li><a href="/howto/api/GetZestimate.htm">GetZestimate</a></li>
  <li><a href="/howto/api/GetSearchResults.htm">GetSearchResults</a></li>
  ...
 </ul> </div>
```

Our ETL process provides the functionality required for detecting that this piece of HTML code contains the required data, parsing these data and extracting the name of each operation (enclosed in each <li> tag) together with the corresponding URL (combination of the current URL and the *href* attribute of the <a> tag). For example, GetZestimate is an operation and the URL that provides information about it is http://www.zillow.com/howto/api/GetZestimate.htm..

Next step is using each of the retrieved URL to navigate through documentation in order to acquire the information related to each operation. Note that the URL can be the same in which the operations are listed (i.e., operations and parameters can be in the same website). The steps to perform are as follows:

1. recovering each operation website;
2. cleaning the HTML page in order to get a well-formed XML document as aforementioned;

---

[8] http://htmlcleaner.sourceforge.net/

3. focusing on pieces of code enclosed by <table> tags;
4. discarding those pieces of HTML code in which the words *parameter* or *response* or some synonyms are not presented in the previous piece of code (also for this purpose, we rely on the thesaurus of potentially related terms);
5. extracting data from tables; the header of the table indicates the name of the concept (parameter, description, etc.) and other rows indicate values; data from these tables can be extracted from <tr> and <td> or <th> tags.

Recalling our running example, a sample excerpt of code for GetZestimate operation is as follows:

```
<h4>The parameters of the API are:</h4>
<table class="improvements" summary="parameters_of_the_GetZestimate_API">
 <thead>
  <tr>
   <th>Parameter</th><th>Description</th><th>Required</th>
  </tr>
 </thead>
 <tbody>
  <tr>
   <td>zws-id</td>
   <td>The Zillow Web Service Identifier. Each
   subscriber to Zillow Web Services is uniquely
   identified by an ID sequence and every request
   to Web services requires this ID.</td>
   <td>Yes</td>
  </tr>
   ...
 </tbody>
</table>
```

Parameters are structured in tables in which the first row indicates that the first cell is the Parameter, the second one is the Description and, finally, the third one indicates if the parameter is Required or not. In the code excerpt of our running example above, zws-id is considered as a required parameter, being The Zillow Web Service Identifier... its description.

4.2   Creating a Web API Model

Once we have acquired data required from the Web API documentation, the corresponding model is created. Our metamodel has been included in an EMF plugin that contains all the new functionality required to generate Web API models, since EMF provides facilities for dynamically creating models that conform to a metamodel. To this aim, from the metamodel, several libraries can be derived:

com.wake.model.webapi.WebAPI. It contains general code for interfaces and factories to create the Java class to allow web designers to create elements of a model dynamically.

com.wake.model.webapi.WebAPI.impl. It contains specific code for generating Java classes tailored to our metamodel.

com.wake.model.webapi.WebAPI.util. It contains the AdapterFactory that provides facilities for creating classes via create() methods and giving them values via *getter* and *setter* methods.

Fig. 4 shows the Web API model extracted from our running example. The WebAPI class *Zillow API* and all the data related to it, including operations and parameters, are generated.

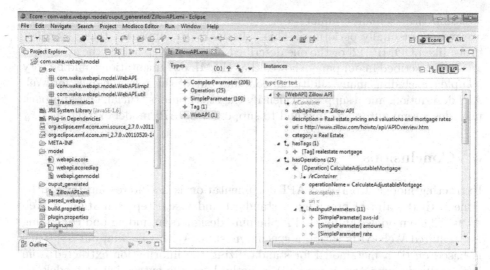

Fig. 4. Sample model of Zillow Web API

5   Related Work

We compared our approach with other related efforts, distinguishing among approaches which impose their own model to which API developers must adhere [1,8], approaches which automate the extraction of models from API documentation [6,9,14], approaches which provide a slight support for structuring the API documentation [12,13].

Some solutions such as WADL (Web Application Description Language) [8] have been developed for Web APIs to be the counterpart of the WSDL standard. In [1] a formal model based on Datalog rules is proposed to capture all the aspects of a mashup component or Web API (called there *mashlet*). Unfortunately, these proposals are too complex to be adopted in a Web 2.0 context, where Web APIs providers do not want to be hampered by the adoption of new, high-level, abstract languages or formalisms and prefer to use plain HTML documentation (on which they are more skilled).

The application of Model Driven Engineering techniques to extract models from Web APIs code has been described in [9], that is focused on object-oriented API specification. The tool described in [9] is designed to obtain model from API source code, while our goal is to start from plain, unstructured HTML documentation. Also approaches like MoDisco [6] and SM@RT [14] only work when the source code is available. Wazaabi[9] extracts GUI models from SWT, JFS and Swing, working only with these kinds of APIs.

The problem of supporting the structuring of Web APIs starting from HTML documentation has been addressed in tools like SWEET [13], which enables the use of the hRESTS formalism to identify the Web API elements (methods, inputs, outputs and so on) within the HTML documentation, with the goal of

---

[9] http://wazaabi.org

assisting their semantic annotation. Within the SWEET tool, all these tasks are mainly manually performed. This is basically the approach taken by other tools, like LOOMP [12] or the one described in [10]. Nevertheless, the statistical analysis described in our paper showed that HTML documentation could be very complex, including many additional contents out of the relevant ones for Web API description, and a support to identify the latter ones is crucial. Our approach provides a semi-automated method to support Web API model extraction.

6   Conclusions

Extracting models from Web API documentation is an interesting task to be done with the aim of providing a standard and visual representation of Web APIs. These models can be used for helping designers in finding and combining the required Web APIs within a specific mashup. With this aim, our approach is based on (i) a metamodel for standardizing the information extracted from Web APIs documentation; and (ii) a method for the extraction of models by parsing HTML files containing the Web API documentation, discovering useful data, and automatically generating the corresponding models (that conform to the defined metamodel).

As a short-term future work, several experiments will be conducted in order to validate our approach. Our experiments will consist of using our approach for obtaining models for each Web API documentation in the ProgrammableWeb site and manually comparing several measures (e.g., quantity of operations and parameters correctly retrieved) to study precision and recall. As a long-term future work, our plan is using our model-driven approach for guiding users in the process of discovery, semantic annotation and composition of Web APIs. As a matter of fact, our next step in this sense will be the definition of measures and techniques for increasing the level of automation in the semantic annotation of the Web APIs.

Acknowledgements. This work has been partially funded by IN.MIND project from University of Alicante (Spain), and MANTRA project (GV/2011/035) from Valencia Government (Spain).

References

1. Abiteboul, S., Greenshpan, O., Milo, T.: Modeling the Mashup Space. In: Proc. of the Workshop on Web Information and Data Management, pp. 87–94 (2008)
2. Bartolomei, T.T., Czarnecki, K., Lämmel, R., van der Storm, T.: Study of an API Migration for Two XML APIs. In: van den Brand, M., Gašević, D., Gray, J. (eds.) SLE 2009. LNCS, vol. 5969, pp. 42–61. Springer, Heidelberg (2010)
3. Baumgartner, R., Gottlob, G., Herzog, M.: Scalable web data extraction for online market intelligence. PVLDB 2(2), 1512–1523 (2009)
4. Bézivin, J.: On the unification power of models. Software and System Modeling 4(2), 171–188 (2005)

5. Bianchini, D., Antonellis, V.D., Melchiori, M.: Semantics-Enabled Web API Organization and Recommendation. In: Proc. of International Workshop on Web Information Systems Modeling, WISM 2011, Brussels, Belgium, pp. 34–43 (2011)
6. Bruneliere, H., Cabot, J., Jouault, F., Madiot, F.: MoDisco: a generic and extensible framework for model driven reverse engineering. In: Proceedings of the 25th International Conference on Automated Software Engineering (ASE 2010), pp. 173–174 (2010)
7. Cappiello, C., Matera, M., Picozzi, M., Sprega, G., Barbagallo, D., Francalanci, C.: DashMash: A Mashup Environment for End User Development. In: Auer, S., Díaz, O., Papadopoulos, G.A. (eds.) ICWE 2011. LNCS, vol. 6757, pp. 152–166. Springer, Heidelberg (2011)
8. Hadley, M.: Web application description language. Tech. rep., W3C (2009)
9. Izquierdo, J.C., Jouault, F., Cabot, J., Molina, J.G.: API2MoL: Automating the building of bridges between APIs and Model-Driven Engineering. Information and Software Technology 54, 257–273 (2012)
10. Kiryakov, A., Popov, B., Terziev, I., Manov, D., Ognyanoff, D.: Semantic annotation, indexing, and retrieval. Journal on Web Semantics 2, 49–79 (2004)
11. Kleppe, A., Warmer, J., Bast, W.: MDA Explained. The Practice and Promise of The Model Driven Architecture. Addison Wesley (2003)
12. Luczak, M., Heese, R.: Linked Data Authoring for non-Experts. In: Proceedings of the Workshop on Linked Data on the Web (2009)
13. Maleshkova, M., Pedrinaci, C., Domingue, J.: Semantic annotation of Web APIs with SWEET. In: Proc. of the 6th Workshop on Scripting and Development for the Semantic Web (2010)
14. Song, H., Xiong, Y., Chauvel, F., Huang, G., Hu, Z., Mei, H.: Generating Synchronization Engines between Running Systems and Their Model-Based Views. In: Ghosh, S. (ed.) MODELS 2009. LNCS, vol. 6002, pp. 140–154. Springer, Heidelberg (2010)
15. Winer, B., Brown, D., Michels, K.: Statistical Principles in Experimental Design. McGraw-Hill (1991)

Identifying and Modelling Complex Workflow Requirements in Web Applications

Mario Matias Urbieta[1,2], Gustavo Rossi[1,2], Silvia Gordillo[1,3], Wieland Schwinger[4], Werner Retschitzegger[4], and María José Escalona[5]

[1] LIFIA, Facultad de Informática, UNLP, La Plata, Argentina
{murbieta,gustavo,gordillo}@lifia.info.unlp.edu.ar
[2] Conicet
[3] CiCPBA
[4] Department of Cooperative Information Systems,
Johannes Kepler University Linz
{wieland.schwinger,werner.retschitzegger}@jku.at
[5] IWT2 Group. University of Seville, Spain
mjescalona@us.es

Abstract. Workflow plays a major role in nowadays business and therefore its requirement elicitation must be accurate and clear for achieving the solution closest to business's needs. Due to Web applications popularity, the Web is becoming the standard platform for implementing business workflows. In this context, Web applications and their workflows must be adapted to market demands in such a way that time and effort are minimize. As they get more popular, they must give support to different functional requirements but also they contain tangled and scattered behaviour. In this work we present a model-driven approach for modelling workflows using a Domain Specific Language for Web application requirement called WebSpec. We present an extension to WebSpec based on Pattern Specifications for modelling crosscutting workflow requirements identifying tangled and scattered behaviour and reducing inconsistencies early in the cycle.

Keywords: Requirements, Workflow, Crosscutting, Model-driven paradigm, Web application.

1 Introduction

Nowadays business must adapt to global trends in order to keep users engaged; unplanned marketing campaigns, season promotions (final season sales), crisis management, among others business requirements are examples of unexpected requirements that stress the whole applications' infrastructure.

We will focus on the problem produced by those requirements that demand business processes change according to the users' context. Depending on context variables like current day, payment method, active market campaign, accessing device, etc. the system may modify the underlying workflow model; this may imply execut-

M. Grossniklaus and M. Wimmer (Eds.): ICWE 2012 Workshops, LNCS 7703, pp. 146–157, 2012.
© Springer-Verlag Berlin Heidelberg 2012

ing a slightly different workflow providing adaptations which support new requirements like discounts and free-shipping, or introduces new workflow steps like new forms to be filled, etc. Unfortunately, these changes may affect different application´s features. In Web Applications these changes compromise several applications' tiers (model, navigation, and interface). When the underlying workflow changes, user interfaces may, for example, introduce a new form that will demand new view controllers that orchestrates validation and navigation, and finally the business model must be modified for supporting new entities' forms and fields.

To make matter worst, when new concerns are unforeseen and unpredictable like Crisis Management[7] or Volatile requirements[8], these requirements are usually introduced in an ad-hoc way. The inadequate implementation of these changes may lead to a decay of software quality compromising application maintenance, stability, and complexity, and finally the application's budget.

In this paper we present a model-driven approach for analysing and modelling workflow changes in Web adaptations in the early stage of requirement gathering. The main contribution is a model-driven approach for dealing with base and adaptation requirements. It is based on a clear separation of concerns applied in the early phase of the software development process. The approach allows defining symmetrically both base and adaptation requirements; later these models are used for implementing test suites that assess the final application behaviour.

The rest of the paper is structured as follows: in Section 2 the problem will be motivated with simple but illustrative examples; in Section 3, we discuss some related work; in Section 4, we present some background themes; in Section 5, we introduce an extension for WebSpec that uses Pattern Specification; and in Section 6 we present our model-driven approach for modelling workflow changes in Web Application and in Section 7, a running example is presented; finally in section 8 we conclude and discuss some further work we are pursuing.

2   Motivating Example

We motivate our research with an example in the e-commerce domain. In the checkout process for buying selected items, the user must follow a simple workflow presenting several steps such as choosing the wrapping configuration (regular or special for birthday), selecting the shipping address, and the payment method, etc. Suppose an unforeseen event such as a catastrophe that leads to a donation campaign. We may require the introduction of a new donation step in the workflow, where users can choose between different pre-set amounts of money to donate. This change will require at least a set of modifications:

- Implement a page that holds a donation form with its corresponding fields;
- The corresponding step must be placed in the workflow and the workflow must be modified to be coherent;
- New data needs to be stored and therefore we need to add persistence machinery for these data;
- Navigation models demands modification to let users navigate to their donations for example.

In this case the set of changes must be present only when the catastrophe campaign is active otherwise they make no sense. In the mid-term we have an adaptation requirement (the existing of a catastrophe and the donation campaign) which lead to a "context-aware" workflow behaviour.

Additionally, the impact in the application of the adaptation may not be simple; that is, the introduction of this adaptation may cross other workflows such as ticket booking for a recital, product pre-order, etc. Therefore, the way in which the adaptation requirements are modelled is critical to assure that they correctly implemented.

To make matter worst, the incoming of new context-aware requirements that cross-cut several workflows make the situation more complex since different business domains are compromised by the same set of events.

3   Related Work

Adams [1] et al. presents the soviet "Activity Theory" as a driver for a more flexible and better directed workflow support. A subset of the main theory's principles highlights the need of context awareness in each possible workflow action execution. The authors propose a set of criteria as requirements of Workflow Management Systems (WfMSs). One criteria "adaptation by reflection" promotes flexible, dynamic and evolving workflows. In this case, systems must record derivations (exceptional flows in the workflow definition) capturing its reasons and its resolution that later can become part of the next workflow instantiation. Although this attempt will help to implement awareness workflows, it works reactively from exception instead of being a proactive solution. As exceptions are captured in real-time, the solution recorded is ad-hoc and isn´t neither modelled nor optimized by domain experts. This work was assessed with the implementation of a WfMS so called YAWL [2] that allows implementing dynamic workflows. The platform defines Worklet as a reusable unit of work. Each time a workflow derivation event is detected it is either possible to choose an already defined worklet or define a new one.

AO4BPEL [3] is an aspect-oriented extension to BPEL that allows describing workflow´s crosscutting behaviour. The extension comprises a language that is used to declare aspects and an execution engine that is responsible of weaving core workflows with workflow aspects. The language introduces constructors for pointcut, jointpoint and advice concepts. It is noteworthy that the extension supports process-level aspects being activated in all workflow instances and instance-level being activated on certain instance of the workflow. AO4BPEL is a powerful tool for describing aspects in Business Process models but aspects are taken into account later (in the design phase) where crosscutting can not be identified and checked with stakeholders.

We are not aware about any approach that allows identifying workflows and specifying its aspects in the requirement gathering phase in such a way that the whole application behaviour is described allowing assessing its behaviour first with the user and later by automatic testing.

4   Background

In this section we introduce some base work which we have used in our approach, namely WebSpec for modelling workflow requirements and Pattern Specifications for specifying the binding of requirements belonging to different concerns.

4.1   WebSpec

WebSpec [9] is a visual language; its main artefact for specifying requirements is the WebSpec diagram which can contain *interactions, navigations* and *rich behaviors.*

A WebSpec diagram defines a set of scenarios that the web application must satisfy. An *interaction* (denoted with a rounded rectangle) represents a point where the user can interact with the application by using its interface objects (widgets). *Interactions* have a name (unique per diagram) and may have widgets such as labels, list boxes, etc. In WebSpec, a *transition* (either *navigation* or *rich behavior*) is graphically represented with arrows between *interactions* while its name, precondition and triggering actions are displayed as labels over them. In particular, its name appears with a prefix of the character '#', the precondition between {} and the actions in the following lines.

The scenarios specified by a WebSpec diagram are obtained by traversing the diagram using the depth-first search algorithm. The algorithm starts from a set of special nodes called "starting" nodes (*interactions* bordered with dashed lines) and following the edges (*transitions*) of the graph (diagram).

As an example of WebSpec's concepts we present in Fig. 1 the specification for the user story: "As a customer, I would like to search products by name and see their details" in an e-commerce application. *Home* represents the starting point of the specification and it contains 2 widgets: *searchField* text field and *search* button (see [9] for further details).

Fig. 1. WebSpec diagram of the *Search by name* scenario

WebSpec has a supporting tool [16] with features that allows, in the early phases of requirement gathering, realizing simulation of application interaction against mock interfaces and generating independent Web tests for testing the final development result.

4.2   Pattern Specification

Pattern Specifications (PSs) [6] is a tool for formalizing the reuse of models. Originally the notation for PSs was presented using the Unified Modelling Language (UML) as a base but in this work we will instead use the concept in the WebSpec realm. A Pattern Specification describes a pattern of structure defined over the roles which participants of the pattern play. Role names are preceded by a vertical bar ("|"). A PS can be instantiated by assigning concrete elements to play these roles.

5   Crosscutting Behaviour Modelling Using Pattern Specification

WebSpec provides a powerful language for describing user's interaction of Web application as it was introduced in previous section. Nonetheless it lacks a means for portraying generalization of interaction patterns; for example, common patterns required in determined workflows' points (tasks or transitions) that stop the workflow execution up to the manager authorizes to continue, or landmarks-like behaviour where a given subworkflow can be accessed from steps belonging to a main workflow. This restriction increase size and complexity of diagrams, and effort to document the requirement. So, we propose the use of Pattern Specifications (PS) where, in our case, a role is a specialization of a WebSpec *Interaction* restricted by additional properties that any *Interaction* fulfilling the role must possess. A model conforms to a PS if its model elements that play the roles of the PS, satisfy the properties defined by the roles.

In Figure 2, a requirement that generalizes an interaction pattern defines two roles: |*sourceInteraction* and |*targetInteraction*. The |*sourceInteraction* role (notice that role's name starts with "|") demands a widget of type Label called *mandatoryWidget* that must be present in the *Interaction* that conforms the role, and defines a new widget of type TextField called *introducedWidget* that will be part of conforming *Interaction*. The |*targetInteraction* role is analogous to the previous role; it demands a widget of type Combobox called *mandatoryWidget* to be part of the interaction that matches the role. Finally, when both roles are bound in a given diagram, a new interaction is introduced with the corresponding transitions called *IntroducedInteraction* as it is defined in Figure 2.

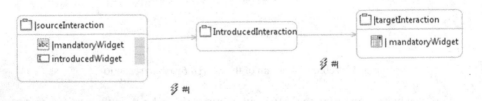

Fig. 2. Introducing interactions and elements in a Workflow requirement

In Figure 2, PS was used for introducing a new *Interaction*. Alternatively, it can be used for defining constraints over a diagram that may lead to an overriding of existing definitions. E.g. Navigations preconditions and actions may be introduced by PS in order to enrich the scenario for making consistent a set of changes. This kind of situations is usually present in adaptive requirements where some behaviour is intended to be replaced by other.

In Figure 3, we show a generalization of a Web application requirements that provides the option for donate. This introduces a banner between two roles describing the donation goal and allows traversing towards a donation form. This requirement can be instantiated in Figure 1 example where |stepOne role is bound with the *Home* interaction and |stepTwo with the *SearchResult* interaction.

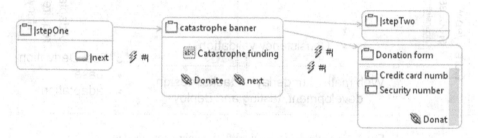

Fig. 3. Donation requirement model using PS

5.1   Yet Another AOSD Visual Language?

Although there are several AOSD (Aspect-Oriented Software Development) formal and visual languages already defined for almost any model of a Web application (conceptual, navigational, and interface models), none of them covers requirement gathering phase and indeed these are focused on describing just functional features closer to the conceptual model [17].

Tackling crosscutting workflow behaviour in the early requirement analysis phase allows identifying crosscutting behaviours in the system, and context variables that rules adaptation behaviour. The use of WebSpec with PS, will help to separate matter of interest in (WebSpec) requirement diagrams and thus in the whole System Requirement Specification (SRS) documents.

In this case, the extension provided for WebSpec using PS not only allows defining high level reusable requirements for Web Applications; it also helps to derive the set of tests that will be used for validating the final result of the application design and implementation.

6   Our Approach in a Nutshell

Next, we will present our approach to identify, design and implement adaptive requirements in Web Workflows. The approach is based on the idea that any adaptive requirement must be treated as first–class; as a consequence we consider these requirements as belonging to separate concern[1] [11] allowing us to isolate, model and later compose both core application workflows with adaptive requirements. In this aspect we focus on Web workflow requirements, specifically in analysis and modelling aspects. Their impact in different application tiers has been already presented in[14,12].

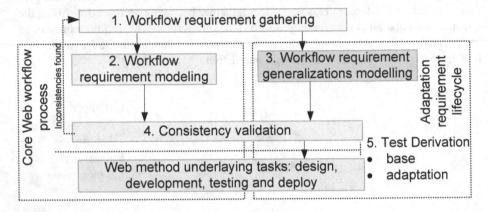

Fig. 4. Overall schema for workflow requirement modelling

The approach comprises a set of steps that are depicted in Figure 4 and described below:

Step 1: **Workflow requirement gathering**. Using well-known requirement elicitation techniques such as meetings, surveys, Joint Application Development (JAD), etc. a Software Requirement Specification (usually in natural language) is produced. In the case of an agile underlying development process, a briefer description is usually produced with user stories [4].

Step 2: **Workflow requirement modelling**. Web application requirements are formalized using a requirement Domain Specific Language (DSL). This formalization is essential during the requirement gathering process with stakeholders. By means of using a requirement DSL, the tasks such as tests derivation and scenarios simulations can be automated easily. In this work, we selected WebSpec as requirement DSL.

Step 3: **Workflow requirement generalizations modelling**. Base Workflow changes are modelled using the Pattern Specification extension for the requirement DSL; in this paper we exemplify with the WebSpec extension.

Step 4: **Consistency validation**. Syntactic and semantic analysis is performed over requirements. By means of an algebraic comparison of models, candidate

---

[1] In software engineering a concern represents a matter of interest that groups a coherent set of requirements.

structural and navigational conflicts are detected. On the other hand, candidate conflicts are analyzed and semantic equivalences are detected. For each candidate conflict, both the new requirement and the compromised requirement are translated from a high abstraction level (the requirements DSL) to a minimal form, using an atomic constructor in order to detect semantic differences. Semantic equivalences between requirements are detected for warning requirement analysts. For more information see [13].

In the case of adaptation requirements, a previous weaving is performed among both kind of requirements obtaining instantiated PS.

Step 5: **Test derivation**. In this step, both traditional WebSpec diagram and WebSpec PS extension are processed for producing tests that allow validating the final Web Application. This also allows assessing the set of requirement with users by using simulations in the early stages of UI mocking. Later the same tests are used in the testing phase of the software development process.

In the following section we present a simple but illustrative example for modeling workflow requirements. First, a simple workflow for checking out products in an e-commerce Web application is modelled using WebSpec. On the other hand, a simple requirement that introduces context awareness in the workflow is designed using PS.

6.1   Requirement Gathering (Step 1)

We use as a running example the development of an e-commerce site. In Figure 5, user stories [4] derived from gathered requirements are shown. There are three user stories: "Checkout process" (US1), "Reduced checkout process from smartphone" (US2), and "Ordering a product" (US3). The first, on the left-hand side, defines a basic workflow for checking out selected products in a straightforward way where issues such as product wrapping, delivery and payment method must be covered. In the middle, it is required that the delivery configuration step in the workflow must be removed and in its place the current location is used for setting up the shipping address. Finally, on the right-hand side, a user story defines another view point of the checkout process defined by a different stakeholder.

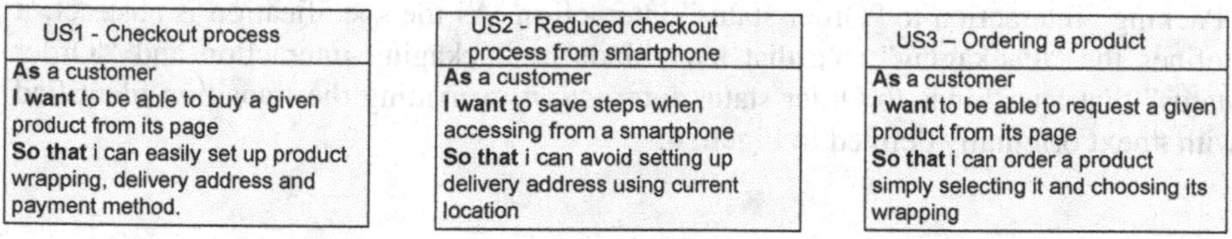

US1 - Checkout process	US2 - Reduced checkout process from smartphone	US3 – Ordering a product
As a customer I want to be able to buy a given product from its page So that i can easily set up product wrapping, delivery address and payment method.	As a customer I want to save steps when accessing from a smartphone So that i can avoid setting up delivery address using current location	As a customer I want to be able to request a given product from its page So that i can order a product simply selecting it and choosing its wrapping

Fig. 5. Application's user stories

6.2   Workflow Requirement Modelling (Step 2)

For this step we will adopt a workflow's definition presented in [15] where a workflow has as a main objective to deal with a case. A workflow has a set of elements that allows achieving the objective: a state and a set of interconnected task where each one can have conditions that enable its execution. From this definition, we claim that WebSpec can help modelling Workflows requirement from a user interaction perspective. User stories define the case that motivates workflow design with WebSpec. WebSpec *interaction* are used for presenting available tasks and state information, meanwhile *transition* are used for describing workflow conditions and state changes. Therefore workflows are described in a WebSpec scenario that comprises a set of (WebSpec) *interactions* and *transition*. Each *Interaction* describes the expected workflow's input and output using widgets (Labels, Radio Button, etcs.) meanwhile *transitions* represents actions that application must perform with its corresponding guard.

In Figure 6, the checkout process in a Web application is depicted as a set of interactions where the user is able to select a product for start setting out its purchase (interaction *Products*); next she is able to choose whether a simple or gift wrap should be used; next, delivery information must be introduced such as address and city; and finally the list of current orders is shown.

Fig. 6. WebSpec scenario for Checkout process based on US1

6.3 Workflow Requirement Generalizations Modelling (Step 3)

So far, we have modelled workflows in Web application using WebSpec. Sometimes there are requirements, such as US2 – "Reduced checkout process from smartphone", that introduce enhancements over main workflows like adaptations or temporal changes. In order to model this kind of requirements, we will use the proposed extension of WebSpec that introduces PS concepts for generalizing behaviours.

In Figure 7, User Story 2 (US2) is modelled overriding the default navigation presented in Figure 6 where delivery information specification (Delivery *interaction*) is by-passed, and, instead, Order Status *interaction* is exhibited after selecting Packaging configuration. This "by passing" is achieved defining a transition that goes from "Packing" interaction to "Order status" interaction. As the specification is abstract, it defines the "|Packaging" role that later binds to Packaging interaction and "|Order status" that later binds to Order status *interaction* overriding the transition identified with #next originally defined in Figure 6.

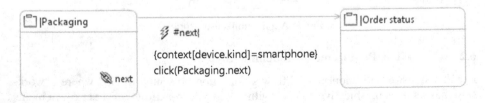

Fig. 7. WebSpec diagram for "Reduced checkout process for smartphones" user story

The semantic result of this adaptation can be seen in Figure 8 where Delivery interaction is not part of the workflow any more.

For example, the requirement modeled in Figure 3, donation requirement can also be introduced in the checkout by binding "|stepOne" role with "Packaging" and "|stepTwo| with Order status. After weaving diagrams, it is possible to donate to catastrophe help´s funding after performing the checkout process. For the sake of space, we are not showing the weaving result.

Fig. 8. Resulting WebSpec diagram after composing requirements

Although roles in this example only bind to one *interaction,* it is possible to have situations were a role may be bound to several interactions when having scattered behaviour.

6.4 Consistency Validation (Step 4)

Conflicts between requirements may arise when two (or more) stakeholders have a different point of view for a given workflow requirement. These situations present themselves as structural or navigational inconsistencies. The former type corresponds to a difference in the data belonging to a business concept meanwhile the latter defines a difference in the way interaction occurs. For more information see [13].

User story US3 proposes a slightly different workflow with respect to the one presented in Figure 6 corresponding to US1. The proposed workflow differs from the one in US1 in the way it is navigated and the data handled.

In Figure 9 a navigational conflict and a structural conflict are highlighted with an ellipse. The navigational conflict is present since it is possible to browse from the Product *interaction* towards Packaging and Delivery *interactions* defined in S1 and S3 respectively. On the other hand, the structural conflict occurs in a contradiction in the way in which the City and Country widgets are defined in the Delivery interaction; in US1 they are expected as Labels but in US3 they are expected as Combobox widgets.

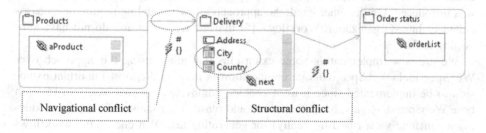

Fig. 9. WebSpec scenario for Checkout process based on US3

6.5   Test Derivation (Step 5)

Once all scenarios were described, design and further development tasks can start. The information gathered so far allows generating both core workflow and workflow's adaptation tests. That is, main workflow's tests are derived for checking navigation, and inputs/outputs from each user interaction step in the workflow. Complementary, specific tests are derived for those WebSpec diagrams that bind any adaptations (WebSpec diagrams that generalize behaviour using PS) where these validate the behaviour corresponding to the base workflow woven with adaptation requirement models.

In Code 1, we can see the result of the automatic test generation feature of WebSpec that checks the workflow of Figure 6. Besides, Code 2 shows a test case that checks the described mobile adaptation (see Figure 7 for adaptation design and Figure 8 for the resultant Workflow). Both tests uses the Selenium [10] engine for executing actions, assessments, and navigation automatically like a user would do.

```
public void
testCheckoutWflow(){
sel.click("id=aProduct");
sel.waitForPageToLoad("30000");
sel.select("id=Simple", "1");
sel.click("id=next");
sel.waitForPageToLoad("30000");
sel.type("id=Address", "..");
sel.click("id=next");
sel.waitForPageToLoad("30000");
}
```

Code 1. Checkout workflow test case

```
public void testMobCheckoutWflow(){
//context configuration
configureContextForMobileDevice()
sel.click("id=aProduct");
sel.waitForPageToLoad("30000");
sel.select("id=Simple", "1");
sel.click("id=next");
sel.waitForPageToLoad("30000");
//removed by "Reduced checkout
// process for smartphones" req.
}
```

Code 2. Reduced Checkout workflow for mobile access test case

7   Conclusions and Future Works

In this work we have presented a novel approach for modeling Workflows in Web applications for both traditional requirements as well as crosscutting one. By using WebSpec diagrams, workflows were modeled as a set of *interactions* representing their steps and *transitions* for defining interactions' connections. In this work, a PS extension for WebSpec, allowing easily specify crosscutting workflow's behavior, was introduced. On the other hand, the approach allows modeling requirements associated to Inter-Organization Workflows [5] that, as we are aware, do not have supporting tools.

We are now implementing some extensions that allow using this approach over WebSpec tool. WebSpec diagram composition is may be the most important extension to be implemented since it must enable composing diagrams based on PS with base WebSpec diagrams. Next, the tool should reason over the set of diagram producing a semantic view (used internally) for generating tests that checks the workflows including the adaptation behaviour specified with PS.

Finally, UML class diagrams and business process models can be sketched from WebSpec diagrams by reasoning over them. Heuristics must be studied in order to produce accurate design models. Obtained UML and business process modes can be used also for producing prototype applications.

Acknowledgment. This work has been funded by the österreichische Agentur für internationale Mobilität und Kooperation in Bildung, Wissenschaft und Forschung (OeAD) under grant AR 21/2011.

References

1. Adams, M., Edmond, D., ter Hofstede, A.H.M.: The Application of Activity Theory to Dynamic Workflow Adaptation Issues. In: PACIS 2003 Proceedings. Paper 113 (2003)
2. Adams, M., ter Hofstede, A.H.M., Edmond, D., van der Aalst, W.M.P.: Worklets: A Service-Oriented Implementation of Dynamic Flexibility in Workflows. In: Meersman, R., Tari, Z. (eds.) OTM 2006. LNCS, vol. 4275, pp. 291–308. Springer, Heidelberg (2006)
3. Charfi, A.: Aspect-Oriented Workfow Languages: AO4BPEL and Applications. Phd thesis, Fachbereich Informatik, der Technischen Universit at Darmstadt (2007), http://d-nb.info/985111321
4. Cohn, M.: Succeeding with Agile: Software Development Using Scrum, 1st edn. Addison-Wesley Professional (2009)
5. Divitini, M., Hanachi, C., Sibertin-Blanc, C.: Inter-organizational workflows for enterprise coordination. In: Coordination of Internet Agents, pp. 369–398. Springer, London (2001)
6. France, R., Kim, D., Ghosh, S., Song, E.: A UML-Based Pattern Specification Technique. IEEE Transactions on Software Engineering 30(3) (2004)
7. Luecke, R.: Crisis Management: Master the Skills to Prevent Disasters. Harvard Business Press Books (2004) ISBN: 978-1591394372
8. Moreira, A., Araújo, J., Whittle, J.: Modeling Volatile Concerns as Aspects. In: Martinez, F.H., Pohl, K. (eds.) CAiSE 2006. LNCS, vol. 4001, pp. 544–558. Springer, Heidelberg (2006)
9. Luna, E.R., Garrigós, I., Grigera, J., Winckler, M.: Capture and Evolution of Web Requirements Using WebSpec. In: Benatallah, B., Casati, F., Kappel, G., Rossi, G. (eds.) ICWE 2010. LNCS, vol. 6189, pp. 173–188. Springer, Heidelberg (2010)
10. Selenium, http://seleniumhq.org/
11. Sutton, S., Rouvellou, I.: Modeling of Software Concerns in Cosmos. In: Proc. of ACM Conf. AOSD 2002, pp. 127–133. ACM Press (2002)
12. Rossi, G., Urbieta, M., Ginzburg, J.: Modular and Systematic Interface Design for Rich Internet Applications. In: Murugesan, S. (ed.) Handbook of Research on Web 2.0, 3.0, and X.0: Technologies, Business, and Social Applications, pp. 59–74 (2010)
13. Urbieta, M., Escalona, M.J., Luna, E.R., Rossi, G.: Detecting Conflicts and Inconsistencies in Web Application Requirements. In: Harth, A., Koch, N. (eds.) ICWE 2011 Workshops. LNCS, vol. 7059, pp. 278–288. Springer, Heidelberg (2012)
14. Urbieta, M., Rossi, G., Distante, M., Ginzburg, J.: Modeling, Deploying, and Controlling Volatile Functionalities in Web Applications. International Journal of Software Engineering and Knowledge Engineering (IJSEKE) 22(1), 129–155 (2012)
15. van der Aalst, W.M.P., van Hee, K.: Workflow Management Models, Methods, and Systems. The MIT Press (2004) ISBN: 978-0262720465
16. WebSpec Language, http://code.google.com/p/webspec-language/
17. Wimmer, M., Schauerhuber, A., Kappel, G., Retschitzegger, W., Schwinger, W., Kapsammer, E.: A survey on UML-based aspect-oriented design modeling. ACM Comput. Surv. (CSUR) 43(4), 28 (2011)

Requirements Models as First Class Entities in Model-Driven Web Engineering*

Nora Koch[1,2] and Sergej Kozuruba[1]

[1] Ludwig-Maximilians-Universität München, Germany
[2] NTT DATA

Abstract. The relevance of a detailed and precise specification of the requirements is well known; it helps to achieve an agreement with the customer on software functionality, user friendliness and priorities in the development process. However, in practice, modeling of requirements is avoided in many projects, in particular in the Web domain, mainly due to short time-to-market. The objective of this work is to make requirements modeling more attractive providing a win-win situation. On the one hand such models are used to improve the developer-customer communication and on the other hand to generate draft design models, which can be used in further steps of a model-driven development approach, and therefore reduce the developers' efforts. We concretize the approach presenting a domain specific modeling language defined as an extension of the UML-based Web Engineering (UWE) profile and a set of model transformations defined to generate the content, navigation and presentation models of web applications. A social network application is used to illustrate UWE requirements and design models.

1 Introduction

The first steps in a software development project comprise the elicitation, specification and validation of requirements of the new web system to be built. This is also valid in reengineering projects. Mainly elicitation but also the other two activities require intensive communication with the customer in order to reach an agreement on functionality, technologies and priorities. For the specification, different techniques, methods and tools have been developed, such as building models of the application. The more accurate the models produced in this early phase of the software development life cycle (SDLC), the less error-prone the code of the software. This relationship between the quality of the requirements specification and the implemented system has been analyzed and confirmed several times [9]. However, more often than not, only sketches of models are produced and the implementation phase is started too early. Even if requirements are specified, they are often partially ignored by developers. Generally, the time invested in the requirements specification is seen as partially wasted.

In this work we focus on web software and show how to move developers' efforts from the design to the requirements phase of the SDLC. This objective is achieved

* This work has been partially sponsored by the EU project ASCENS, FP7 257414, the EU-NoE project NESSoS, GA 256980, and the DFG project MAEWA II, WI 841/7-2.

M. Grossniklaus and M. Wimmer (Eds.): ICWE 2012 Workshops, LNCS 7703, pp. 158–169, 2012.
© Springer-Verlag Berlin Heidelberg 2012

through two changes in the development process: (1) Building annotated requirements models (more effort) and (2) Generating the design models from the requirements models in a semi-automatic way (less effort). Note that our goal is not the automatic generation of the complete application (proved to also have severe limitations), but instead to use model-driven engineering (MDE) to ease developers' work in several steps, to manage the complexity of web applications, and scalability aspects in the development. The benefits are better requirements models improving the communication between customers and developers, supporting the decision process and resulting in more stable web applications. In our previous work [5] we presented the results of a detailed assessment of the application of our approach showing that the effort reduction reached is calculated to be between 26% and 77%.

We present a domain specific modeling language (DSML), which provides the annotations needed to enrich standard requirements models with web features and to reduce model-complexity. The models specified with the DSML are used in the model transformations of the MDE process to generate the design models of the web applications. Although the approach is generic and the idea of a DSML in an early development phase of web applications could be applied for any model-driven approach, we selected the UML-based Web Engineering (UWE) [6] to illustrate the approach, and as an example we use a social media application, called *Linkbook*.

The remainder of this paper is structured as follows: Section 2 gives an overview of UWE modeling features focusing on requirements models. In Sect. 3 we present the model-to-model transformations showing how draft models are generated. Section 4 describes the tools that support the model-driven process. Finally, Sect. 5 discusses related work and in Sect. 6 we give an outlook on future steps in the use of our model-driven development approach.

2   Modeling Requirements of Web Applications

The specification of web applications focus on building a model of the functional requirements. For the modeling task, different languages can be used, such as BPMN [10], UML [11] or a DSML, such as the Navigation Development Technique (NDT) [3] or the UML-based Web Engineering (UWE) [6] approach. We selected the latter to exemplify our approach.

UWE comprises a notation, a method and tool support. The notation is defined as a UML profile [11], i.e. using the extension mechanism provided by the UML itself, which allows for the refinement of UML in a strictly additive manner by stereotypes, tag definitions and constraints, providing the required additional annotations. The cornerstones of the UWE method are the principle of separation of concerns and a model-driven approach. As UWE tool we use the MagicUWE plugin implemented for MagicDraw (see Sect. 4) and the UWE4JSF eclipse plugin for the code generation.

Case Study. To illustrate the modeling features of the DSML and the results of the model transformations, we selected the *Linkbook* rich internet application. This is a social network platform to share favorite web pages with friends, similarly to other social networks that enable the sharing of posts or pictures. The network distinguishes between two kinds of users, guests and registered users, and provides the usual functionality for logging in and out, as well as for registering. The homepage of the application shows a list of favorites website entries (referred to in the diagrams as link infos) grouped by categories, and offers search facilities over the available link info and the user comments. Registered users also have the option to comment link infos and switch to their personal view where they can add new entries as well as sort or remove entries from the list of favorites. The network functionality is provided by managing the list of friends providing access to the list of favorites of all friends.

Fig. 1 depicts a subset of the use cases of the *Linkbook* application. It illustrates the use of the UWE profile to annotate UML model elements supplying them with specific web semantics, e.g. distinguishing between «browsing» (□) and «processing» (Σ) use cases. The former represents pure navigation; the latter, workflow functionality. Examples for these two types of use cases – browsing and processing – are BrowsingLinkInfo and AddFriend, respectively. We introduce groupings of functionality using UML packages, for example, the packages Authentication and New. All of the model elements contained in the package adopt the stereotype of the package, which is then the only one that needs to be made explicit.

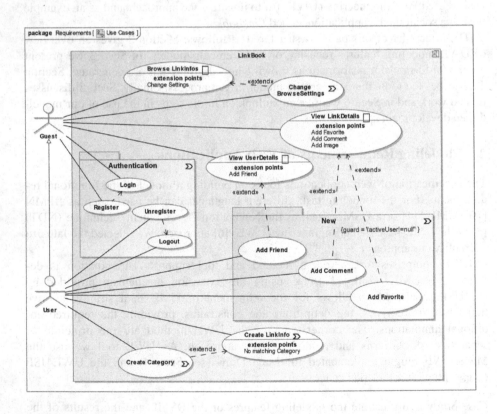

Fig. 1. *Linkbook*: Functional requirements modeled with use cases (excerpt)

Each use case can be refined by a detailed description or a graphical representation of the workflow associated to it. UML activity diagrams can be used for the visual representation as shown in Fig. 2 for the CreateLinkInfo workflow. Here we also use different stereotypes of the UWE profile to enrich the semantic of the activity diagram with web specific concepts. The objective is to specify:

- the actions which are part of the workflow, i.e. ShowForm, EnterData, sub-workflow CreateCategory and SaveLinInfo in our example;
- input and output information, given by pins (like name, address, description, category) or objects (linkinfo);
- decisions (not present in this example);
- features regarding the richness of the user interface, like the tag live validation for the input fields name and address;
- kind of visualization, e.g. the tag lightbox for the action ShowForm; and
- type of user-system interaction, indicating additional semantics such as validation and confirmation of the user input by the tag validated for EnterData and the tag confirmed for SaveLinkInfo.

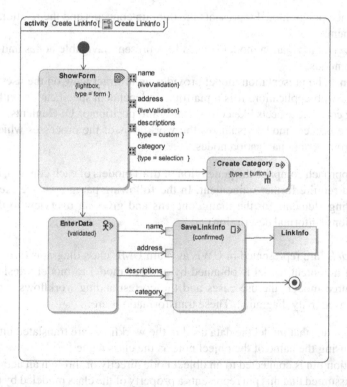

Fig. 2. *Linkbook*: Example of workflow represented as UML activity diagram

This CreateLinkInfo workflow depicts three different stereotyped actions: (1) «displayAction» (), used to visualize explicit presentation of elements; (2) «userAction» ()

that defines a point in the process flow when the user is asked to input data; and the (3) «systemAction» (▯») that indicates a step of the process flow where the application is processing some data.

3   Transformations and Model Generation

In the previous section we described the source models of the transformations, i.e. the requirements models. In this section we present the target, i.e. the design models and the model transformations that generate design models from requirements specification.

Our modeling approach for the design phase follows the principle of "separation of concerns" building separate models for views of the navigation, content, presentation, processes, etc. in the same way other web development methods do, such as OOHDM [14], OOHRIA [8], OOWS [15] and WebML [2], among others. The set of model types is a highly flexible and modular modeling framework providing the basis for the model-driven engineering (MDE) development process. Each model type has clear aims:

Content. The content model represents the domain concepts and the relationships between them.
Navigation. The navigation model is used to represent navigable nodes and the links between nodes.
Presentation. The presentation model provides an abstract view on the user interface (UI) of a web application. It is a platform-independent specification without considering concrete aspects like colors, fonts, and position of UI elements.
Process. The process model visualizes the workflows of the processes which are invoked from certain navigation nodes.

Our MDE approach comprise the generation of draft models of each concern, i.e. initial versions that require further refinement. In the following paragraphs we sketches the main modeling elements for the main concerns and gives an overview to the model transformations (informal description).

Content models are represented in UWE as plain UML class diagrams (see Fig. 3). A first draft of a content model is obtained by a set of model-to-model transformations using as source models the use cases and the corresponding workflows (graphically represented as activity diagrams). These transformations are:

- Objects nodes that model the data used in the workflows are translated into content classes using the name of the object note as the class name.
- If an action pin is connected to an object node directly or through an action, then it can be assumed that this pin represents a property of the class modeled by the object node. In that way, the name of the pin is used to determine whether an attribute or association is created by comparing the name with existing content classes.

Figure 3 shows the content model of the *Linkbook* web application that results from the above described transformations applied to the uses cases of Fig. 1.

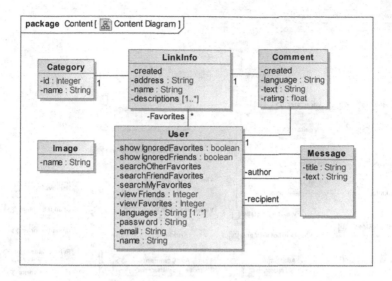

Fig. 3. *Linkbook*: Generated content model

Navigation models describe the navigation structure of a web application using a set of stereotyped classes defined for the web domain, such as navigation classes and links, menus, etc. Figure 4 depicts a first approach to the *Linkbook* navigation model which was generated based on the requirements models.

The following is a very brief overview of some modeling elements part of the UWE profile. A «navigationClass» (visualized as □) represents a navigable node of the hypertext structure; a «navigationLink» shows a direct link between navigation classes. Alternative navigation paths are handled by «menu» (▤) and the so-called access primitives are used to reach multiple instances of a navigation class («index», ≡), or to select items («query», ▨). Web applications frequently support business logic as well. An entry and/or exit points of the business processes is modeled by a «processClass» (Σ) in the navigation model, the linkage between each other and to the navigation classes is modeled by a «processLink».

The model transformations from requirements (use cases and workflows) to the navigation structure model encompass the following steps:

– Creation of «navigationClass»es for «browsing» use cases; «processing» use cases are transformed into «processClass»es.
– Tagged values of the use cases are transformed into equally named tags of the generated classes.
– Relationships between use cases are translated into associations between created navigation and process classes. The associations are stereotyped with «processLink» if at least one related class is a «processClass» and «navigationLink» otherwise.

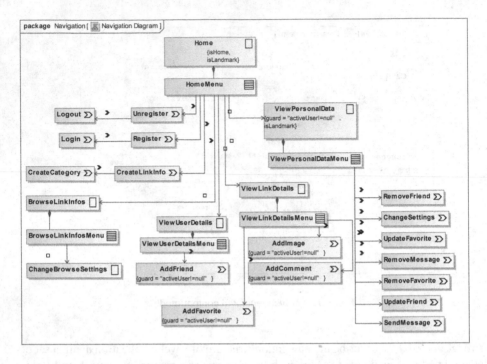

Fig. 4. *Linkbook*: Generated navigation model

- A «menu» is introduced whenever a navigation class has several outgoing links. The source of the links is changed to the «menu», which is connected to the navigation class by a composition.
- A navigation class can be created to serve as home of the application, if it has not been modeled explicitly.

In addition, each process class included in the navigation specification can be modeled as a detailed workflow in the form of a UML activity diagram (not included in this work). It is the result of a refinement process that starts from the workflow of the requirements model.

Presentation models are designed based on the information provided by the navigation models and the information available in workflows of the requirements models, e.g. rich UI features. A UML nested class diagram is selected as visualization technique. The presentation model describes the basic structure of the user interface, i.e., which UI elements (e.g. text, images, anchors, forms) are used to represent the navigation nodes.

The basic presentation modeling elements are the «presentationGroup» which are directly based on nodes from the navigation model, i.e. navigation classes, menus, access primitives, and process classes. A presentation group (▣) or a «form» (🗎) are used to include a set of other UI elements, like «text» (≈), «textInput» (▥), «button» (●), «selection» (✎), etc.

The top level elements of the presentation model are classes with the stereotype
«presentationGroup». The second level of presentation elements consists of input and
output elements. The presentation model similarly to the navigation model requires a
main class, which is not modeled explicitly during the requirements specification. This
presentation group is named «Home» and contains all presentation groups created from
use cases inside a class «presentationAlternatives» and an anchor for every presentation
group.

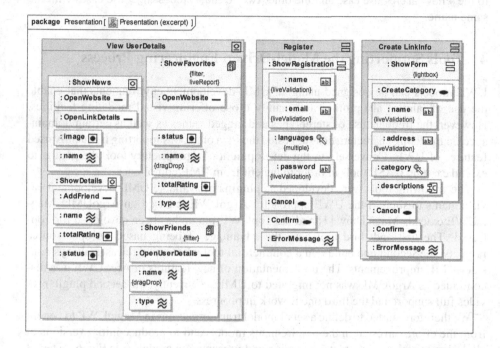

Fig. 5. *Linkbook*: Presentation model generated by transformations (excerpt)

The following model transformations are defined to transform requirements (use
cases and workflows) into a presentation model:

- Creation of «presentationGroup»es for «browsing» use cases; «processing» use
  cases are transformed into «inputForm»s.
- An «inputForm» is also created for each «displayAction».
- Elements of type «displayPin» and «interactionPin» are translated as presentation
  properties part of the «inputForm»s that were generated for the «displayAction»;
  the stereotype of the presentation class is computed from the type tag.
- Tags (with exception of type), mainly used for modeling RIA features, are added to
  the corresponding input elements.

   – An action of type «systemAction» with a tagged value confirmed set to true is translated into two classes of stereotype «button» named OK and Cancel; an action of
type «userAction» with a tagged value validated set to true is translated to a class
of stereotype «text» to show the errors of the validation.

Fig. 5 shows an excerpt of the presentation model including the presentation groups
ViewUserDetails, Register and CreateLinkInfo that were automatically generated by the
model-to-model transformations defined above. The first presentation group is related
to the «navigation» use case and the other two to the «processing» use cases with the
same name.

4 Tools Supporting the Model-Driven Engineering Process

UWE models can be designed using all UML development environments that enable
the use of (almost all) profiles and mainly those offering visual modeling facilities.
However, the frequent use of stereotypes and tagged values as well as certain domain-
specific modeling characteristics suggested the idea of a tool supporting frequently used
features of UWE. Conversely to the development of a proprietary tool, the goal is to
extend existing CASE tools in order to benefit from UML compliance.

The following tools were developed as plugins of available UML development environments to support the UWE approach : ArgoUWE is based on ArgoUML, MagicUWE extends MagicDraw [1] and the TopUWE-plugin has been developed for Top-
Cased. The first and third tool have the advantage of being based on open-source
projects; the second one builds on a commercial tool whose new releases always consider UML improvements. The implementation of new features in ArgoUWE was dis-
continued as ArgoUML was not migrated to UML2. Currently, the second plugin provides full support and the third one is work in progress.

We therefore started to define a set of model transformations in MagicUWE to benefit
from the efforts invested in the requirements models and to produce initial versions of
all design models, i.e. content, navigation and presentation models (see Fig. 6). The set
of transformations implemented are:

   – requirements to content,
   – requirements to navigation,
   – requirements to process, and
   – requirements to presentation.

The goal of these plugins are the computer aided design of web applications using the
UWE approach. They offer to the designer, in addition to the use of the UWE profile, aid
for the selection of the model elements, transformations for the automatic generation of
sketches of models (see transformations options in Fig. 6) or the refinement of certain
parts (aspects) of the models. Thus, the UML CASE tools are customized to the specific
modeling domain of web software by specific plugins. Code generation is supported by
the UWE4JSF tool [7].

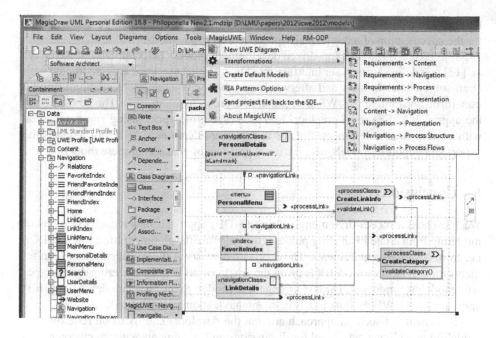

Fig. 6. MagicUWE: Tool support for modeling and transforming

5   Related Work

Several model-driven web engineering methods have been put forward during the last decade, only some of them include explicitly requirements specification in their software development process. The survey of Valderas and Pelechano [16] presents a detailed analysis of the model-driven characteristics of the most relevant methods.

OOHDM [14] defines a proprietary notation called user interaction diagrams used to refine use cases. Only UIDs are used to derive conceptual models, but there is no tool supporting the MDE process. Similarly, the previous version of UWE [4] that included a notation for requirements specification called WebRE, did not provide tool support for model transformations, but for the modeling as it is UML compliant. The Web Modeling Language (WebML) is supported by WebRatio, a commercial tool that is in use in many real projects. This implies a lot of experience in requirements specification, but the requirements models – use cases and textual specification – proposed by WebML [2] are not fully integrated in the automated generation of the web applications. The most complete approach is presented by Object-Oriented Web Solutions (OOWS) [16], which includes a task taxonomy, description of user tasks and system data. The notations used are task trees and activity diagrams, and the MDE process is fully supported by a graph-transformation-based tool. The drawback of this approach is the complexity of the requirements model and the need of proprietary tool support due to the use of a mix of techniques. The main focus of the Navigational Development Technique (NDT) is the requirements analysis phase [3]. The NDT Suite has been developed to support this very detailed template-based approach. Although NDT is useful for the requirements elicitation, the approach of textual templates are less appropriate for the specification of navigational aspects of web applications.

More recently, the Mockup-driven development process (MockupDD) of Rivero *et al.* [13] was defined using user interface mockups. Digital mockups are constructed with open-source mockup tools and afterwards enriched with annotations enabling smooth transformations into e.g. UWE navigation and presentation models. The advantage of the approach is the use of graphical user interface prototypes, easing communication with customers and designers. But the use of more than one CASE tool requires the export and import of models with the usual problem of visualizing these models.

6   Conclusions

We presented a model-driven engineering (MDE) approach that moves the focus of modeling from a late to an early phase in the software development life cycle (SDLC), i.e. from design to requirements. The approach consists of the specification of requirements models (source models)(1) using the UML-based Web Engineering domain specific modeling language(2), transforming these models to the target models (3), i.e. first approaches of UWE design models (content, navigation, presentation).

The benefits of such an approach are that the developer can focus on requirements modeling providing a better tool for discussions and agreements with the customer. On the other hand the generation of basic design models provides an effort reduction of the time consuming task of building these design models. Although the approach is generic and the idea of a DSML in an early development phase of web applications could be applied for any model-driven approach, we selected the UML-based Web Engineering (UWE) [6] to illustrate the approach. As an example we use a social media *Linkbook* application. Model transformations are tool supported in the CASE tool MagicUWE.

An evaluation of the approach comparing automatic generated and manually created design models was performed; the results are included in our previous work [5]. We plan to corroborate the evaluation results with empirical data obtained by groups of students that will manually create the design models. A future task would be the implementation of the model transformations as plugin of an open source tool, probably TopCased.

References

1. Busch, M., Koch, N.: MagicUWE – A CASE Tool Plugin for Modeling Web Applications. In: Gaedke, M., Grossniklaus, M., Díaz, O. (eds.) ICWE 2009. LNCS, vol. 5648, pp. 505–508. Springer, Heidelberg (2009)
2. Ceri, S., Brambilla, M., Fraternali, P.: The History of WebML: Lessons Learned from 10 Years of Model-Driven Development of Web Applications. In: Borgida, A.T., Chaudhri, V.K., Giorgini, P., Yu, E.S. (eds.) Conceptual Modeling: Foundations and Applications. LNCS, vol. 5600, pp. 273–292. Springer, Heidelberg (2009)
3. Escalona, M.J., Aragón, G.: NDT. A Model-Driven Approach for Web Requirements. IEEE Trans. Softw. Eng. 34(3), 377–390 (2008)
4. Escalona, M.J., Koch, N.: Metamodelling the Requirements of Web Systems. In: Rev. Sel. Papers Int. Conf. Web Information Systems and Technologies (WEBIST 2005–2006). LNBIP, vol. 1, pp. 267–280 (2007)

5. Koch, N., Knapp, A., Kozuruba, S.: Assessment of Effort Reduction due to Model-to-Model Transformations in the Web Domain. In: Brambilla, M., Tokuda, T., Tolksdorf, R. (eds.) ICWE 2012. LNCS, vol. 7387, pp. 215–222. Springer, Heidelberg (2012)
6. Koch, N., Knapp, A., Zhang, G., Baumeister, H.: UML-Based Web Engineering: An Approach Based on Standards. In: Olsina, et al. [12], ch. 7, pp. 157–191
7. Kroiss, C., Koch, N., Knapp, A.: UWE4JSF: A Model-Driven Generation Approach for Web Applications. In: Gaedke, M., Grossniklaus, M., Díaz, O. (eds.) ICWE 2009. LNCS, vol. 5648, pp. 493–496. Springer, Heidelberg (2009)
8. Meliá, S., Gómez, J., Pérez, S., Díaz, O.: A Model-Driven Development for GWT-Based Rich Internet Applications with OOH4RIA. In: ICWE 2008 Proceedings of the 2008 Eighth International Conference on Web Engineering, pp. 13–23. IEEE Computer Society, Washington, DC, USA (2008), ISBN: 978-0-7695-3261-5, doi:10.1109/ICWE.2008.36
9. Mendes, E., Mosley, N. (eds.): Web Engineering. Springer, Berlin (2006)
10. Object Management Group. Business Process Model and Notation, version 2.0. Specification, OMG (January 2011), http://www.omg.org/spec/BPMN/2.0/
11. Object Management Group. Unified Modeling Language: Superstructure, version 2.4. Specification, OMG (August 2011),
    http://www.omg.org/spec/UML/2.4.1/Superstructure/PDF/
12. Olsina, L., Pastor, O., Rossi, G., Schwabe, D. (eds.): Web Engineering: Modelling and Implementing Web Applications. Human-Computer Interaction Series, vol. 12. Springer (2008)
13. Rivero, J.M., Grigera, J., Rossi, G., Luna, E.R., Koch, N.: Towards Agile Model-Driven Web Engineering. In: Nurcan, S. (ed.) CAiSE Forum 2011. LNBIP, vol. 107, pp. 142–155. Springer, Heidelberg (2012)
14. Rossi, G., Schwabe, D.: Modeling and Implementing Web Applications with OOHDM. In: Olsina, et al. [12], ch. 6, pp. 109–155
15. Valderas, P., Fons, J., Pelechano, V.: From Web Requirements to Navigational Design – A Transformational Approach. In: Lowe, D.G., Gaedke, M. (eds.) ICWE 2005. LNCS, vol. 3579, pp. 506–511. Springer, Heidelberg (2005)
16. Valderas, P., Pelechano, V.: A Survey of Requirements Specification in Model-Driven Development of Web Applications. ACM Trans. Web 5(2), 10 (2011)

How the Web of Things Challenges Requirements Engineering*

Pete Sawyer, Animesh Pathak, Nelly Bencomo, and Valérie Issarny

Inria Paris-Rocquencourt, France
p.sawyer@lancaster.ac.uk,
{animesh.pathak,nelly.bencomo,valerie.issarny}@inria.fr

Abstract. As a subset of the Internet of Things (IoT), the Web of Things (WoT) shares many characteristics with wireless sensor and actuator networks (WSANs) and ubiquitous computing systems (Ubicomp). Yet to a far greater degree than the IoT, WSANs or Ubicomp, the WoT will integrate physical and information objects, necessitating a means to model and reason about a range of context types that have hitherto received little or no attention from the RE community. RE practice is only now developing the means to support WSANs and Ubicomp system development, including faltering first steps in the representation of context. We argue that these techniques will need to be developed further, with a particular focus on rich context types, if RE is to support WoT application development.

Keywords: Web of Things, Context, Requirements Engineering.

1 Introduction

Requirements engineering (RE) [7] has evolved to discover, model, specify and manage the required and desired properties of software systems. However, conventional RE makes an assumption that the knowledge from which the requirements will be formulated exists *a-priori*, even though the knowledge may be fragmentary, distributed and tacit. Thus, although their discovery may take significant effort, the requirements *are* discoverable using the appropriate RE practices.

However, the last decade or so has seen the emergence of new types of systems where this assumption does not hold. Two prime examples of such systems are ambient, ubiquitous and pervasive (Ubicomp) systems, and wireless sensor and actuator networks (WSANs). Conventional RE is ill-equipped to discover, model, specify and manage these systems' requirements because incomplete knowledge of the context under which they must operate is available at design time. While some progress has been made, by (e.g.) maintaining requirements models that support reasoning over context at runtime, the IoT and, even more recently, the WoT have now emerged to compound the challenge for RE.

---

* This work was supported in part by the European Commission FP7 CHOReOS and NESSOS projects, and the ANR Murphy project.

M. Grossniklaus and M. Wimmer (Eds.): ICWE 2012 Workshops, LNCS 7703, pp. 170–175, 2012.
© Springer-Verlag Berlin Heidelberg 2012

It could be argued that the RE-significant characteristics of the IoT and WoT [3] are simply the union of those of Ubicomp (primarily heterogeneity among devices) and WSANs (primarily large scale). Certainly, context and design-time uncertainty need to be handled, implying that many IoT and WoT applications need to be requirements-aware [12]. However, the WoT adds something that is significantly new; the ambition to seamlessly fuse physical and information objects. The contribution of this position paper is to argue that this fusion of the physical and virtual requires reasoning about kinds of context that have hitherto been neglected by RE: *personal*, *social* and *information* context.

2   The Web of Things

The IoT [8] has been defined as [2] *"A global network infrastructure, linking physical and virtual objects through the exploitation of data capture and communication capabilities."*

The IoT builds upon ideas already developed in WSANs and Ubicomp and the WoT can be considered to be that subset of the IoT that uses web standards to connect physical objects and information resources seamlessly. The rationale for the WoT is that the use of web standards should ease the integration of new smart objects as well as making the developer's job easier. The ever-increasing abundance of existing web-enabled devices such as smart phones, and the expected web-enablement of everyday objects that is envisioned by Ubicomp (fridges, cars, etc.) is bringing the WoT closer to realization. We expect to see increased adoption of WoT concepts in the fields as diverse as personal health, inventory management, and domestic energy usage monitoring, which bring to the fore the dual challenges of scale and heterogeneity.

WoT application development is envisaged to span a range of project types from ad-hoc user-developed Mashups, through domain-expert application programming to conventional commercial development by software professionals. Our interest in this paper is towards the latter end of the range and we are particularly interested in how and whether RE may be usefully applied to WoT application development. If RE can be adapted to support the understanding of and reasoning about the WoT problem and solution domains in a way that helps domain experts and developers communicate the application requirements, then the same techniques may also prove useful to domain experts developing their own applications. In any case, evidence from experience with service-based systems suggests that integration standards don't make the need for rigorous development processes and practices (whether these are conventional or agile) go away. This is particularly true where the problem includes multiple stakeholders, legacy systems and all the other scale-and complexity-related factors that are a routine feature of software development projects.

3   Illustrative Application

To illustrate the WoT, consider a *Liveliness Indicator* application. This is conceived as a cost-effective method of determining the relative *liveliness* of different city locations, such as city squares, parks, areas of a university campus, etc. Such an application might be useful for tourists during city festivals, for example to help tourists find street theatre during the Edinburgh Fringe.

The application is based on an assumption that ambient noise is an indication of human activity, in which the more noise (filtered to remove, e.g., traffic noise) there is, the livelier is the location. The application would display liveliness indicators for the city, and depending on the user's preferences, the application would recommend a location to visit. Thus if the user was a student wishing to study for an exam, a quiet park might be a suitable option. If they were looking for somewhere to celebrate after finishing their exam, a lively square might be chosen.

Figure 1 shows a very simple i* [17] Strategic Dependency Model indicating as circles the primary agents; a *Noise data provider*, the user of the application *Liveliness user*, and the application itself *Liveliness Indicator*. The Liveliness user has a goal depicted by ellipses, to *Find suitably lively location* and satisfaction of this goal is dependent on the Liveliness Indicator application. This dependency is indicated by the direction of the 'D' characters on the arcs that connect the goal to the *dependee* and *dependum* agents. The Liveliness Indicator itself, is dependent on the Noise data provider to provide resources in the form of *Noise data* and *Location data* depicted as rectangles. Finally, the Noise data provider has a reciprocal dependency on the Liveliness Indicator to satisfy a QoS requirement, represented here as the *softgoal Preserve privacy*.

The application could be realized by exploiting the microphones that form part of modern smartphones, whose owners volunteer to provide the data anonymously. The application could aggregate noise data from collocated volunteers. Thus the data is crowdsourced, and the volunteers' smartphones are the smart objects - the *things* - in a WoT. Finally, the Liveliness Indicator might be used as a Facebook plug-in helping people organize social events.

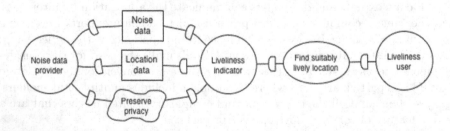

Fig. 1. i* Strategic Dependency Model for Liveliness App

4 WoT Requirements

As a first step towards identifying how RE needs to change to accommodate the needs of WoTs, we draw on experience from Ubicomp and WSAN applications. With Ubicomp systems, a key challenge is that of modeling context [9] [5] [13], which can be succinctly defined as "... partial state of the world that is relevant to an actor's goals" [1]. Krogstie decomposes context under six different headings:

- *spacio-temporal* context, including "location, ... place, the social arena";
- *environment* context, including "things, ... noise, persons and networks";
- *personal* context, including "mood, expertise, anger, stress";
- *task* context;
- *social* context;
- *information* context "... the global and personal information space ..." [9].

All of these types of context are relevant to actors in the Liveness Indicator application, particularly location, noise, mood (somewhere quiet or somewhere lively?), task (somewhere to study? somewhere to celebrate?), social (somewhere to meet friends?), information (need to avoid disclosing smartphone owner's identify). However, a fundamental feature of context is that while it should be possible to anticipate the kinds of context of relevance, not all types of context can be directly sensed at runtime or easily modeled. Further, there may be many different combinations of context, each of which may have a wide range of possible values. Thus enumeration of the system's required behaviour under each context state may be impractical.

Finkelstein and Savigni [5] proposed requirements reflection as a means for dealing with context. An implication of this was that the system would need to maintain run-time requirements models that permitted systems to introspect over the current degree to which their requirements were being satisfied. This in turn implies some kind of requirements monitoring [4]. Recent work has seen progress towards realization of Finkelstein and Savignis' vision, by employing goal models kept "live" for reasoning over and (to a lesser extent) updating at runtime. In [1] and [16], for example, context is sensed and when change is detected, an adaptation is triggered to optimize satisfaction of those requirements that are context-dependent.

Context is also important for WSANs, although it is typically less rich than that for Ubicomp systems. For example, the relative priorities of the non-functional requirements (NFRs) of the GridStix [6] flood prediction WSAN changed according to whether the river in which the sensing nodes were located was quiescent (energy conservation was prioritized) or in flood (network resilience was prioritized). GridStix further illustrated the problem of incompletely understood context and its impact on the system. Thus how the weather affected wireless signals and battery life proved to be hard to predict; an example of design-time uncertainty that could only be resolved at runtime. The key point is that, to date, the Ubicomp, WSAN and RE communities have focussed on a subset of context types, particularly spacio-temporal and environmental context.

For these types of context, significant progress has been made, particularly by the Ubicomp research community.

Integrating physical objects with information objects is a significant challenge to RE, and stems partly from the sheer variety of functions of the physical objects that may become part of the WoT, and partly from the range of information that they may hold. For example, a smart phone is a composite of phone, web client, GPS device, repository of text notes, music, photo and film library, and many more. It has a physical affordance for its user and sometimes a virtual one (e.g. as a router for other network devices, as an aggregator of noise data) and has relationships to several human, social and organizational entities; owners and service provider(s), music and app virtual marketplaces. Applications for which some subset of this information is important needs to deal with it as context. Domain ontologies and semantically-extended web standards [15] are likely to have a role to play, and current realizations of requirements-awareness will need to be augmented to exploit them.

To take information context as an example; it has been almost completely unexplored by RE. There is significant interest in modeling security and privacy requirements [11] and this is certainly important for the WoT, but is only one aspect of information context for WoT applications. For example, access to information context will enable new social networking possibilities. Were the Liveliness Indicator to be a Facebook plug-in, modeling of personal and social context would also become important. Sentiment analysis [10] allied to recent work on emotional requirements [14] might permit the application to infer the user's mood, but how to model and how to react to mood (does sad imply they will want to go somewhere quiet or somewhere lively?) is much less clear, and thus can't yet be sensibly specified.

5 Conclusions and Future Work

In this paper we draw on recent work on Ubicomp and WSANs to draw out some ways in which the WoT challenges existing RE practices. Our conclusion is that RE is currently poorly suited to the problems posed by WoT applications. In part this is nothing new; as new technology-driven classes of system emerge, the role of RE is limited until the technology matures and applications need to become requirements-driven to be useful or competitive. However, we believe that there are more fundamental inhibitors to the eventual utility of RE to developers of WoT applications.

Recent research on requirements-awareness [12], [1], [16] has shown that RE for many new classes of system spans design- and runtime, and reasoning with context for WoT applications will be no exception. We are far from ready to define a research roadmap for RE for WoT applications, but some waypoints might include research on modeling, sensing and reasoning over personal, social and information context [9].

References

1. Ali, R., Dalpiaz, F., Giorgini, P.: A goal-based framework for contextual requirements modeling and analysis. Requirements Engineering 15, 439–458 (2010)
2. Casagras, R.: RFID and the inclusive model for the Internet of Things report (2011)
3. Dillon, T.S., Talevski, A., Potdar, V., Chang, E.: Web of Things as a Framework for Ubiquitous Intelligence and Computing. In: Zhang, D., Portmann, M., Tan, A.-H., Indulska, J. (eds.) UIC 2009. LNCS, vol. 5585, pp. 2–13. Springer, Heidelberg (2009)
4. Fickas, S., Feather, M.: Requirements monitoring in dynamic environments. In: Second IEEE International Symposium on Requirements Engineering, RE 1995 (1995)
5. Finkelstein, A., Savigni, A.: A framework for requirements engineering for context-aware services. In: First International Workshop From Software Requirements to Architectures (STRAW 2001), pp. 2–7 (2001)
6. Hughes, D., Greenwood, P., Coulson, G., Blair, G.: Gridstix: Supporting flood prediction using embedded hardware and next generation grid middleware. In: Proc. the 2006 International Symposium on World of Wireless, Mobile and Multimedia Networks (WOWMOM 2006), pp. 621–626 (2006)
7. Jackson, M.: Defining a discipline of description. IEEE Software 15(5), 14–17 (1998)
8. Kortuem, G., Kawsar, F., Fitton, D., Sundramoorthy, V.: Smart objects as building blocks for the internet of things. IEEE Internet Computing 14(1), 44–51 (2010)
9. Krogstie, J.: Requirements engineering for mobile information systems. In: Proceedings of the Seventh International Workshop on Requirements Engineering: Foundation for Software Quality (REFSQ 2001), Interlaken, Switzerland (2001)
10. Pang, B., Lee, L.: Opinion mining and sentiment analysis. Found. Trends Inf. Retr. 2(1-2), 1–135 (2008)
11. Price, B., Adam, K., Nuseibeh, B.: Keeping ubiquitous computing to yourself: A practical model for user control of privacy. International Journal of Human-Computer Studies 63(1-2), 228–253 (2005)
12. Sawyer, P., Bencomo, N., Whittle, J., Letier, E., Finkelstein, A.: Requirements-aware systems: A research agenda for RE for self-adaptive systems. In: 18th IEEE International Requirements Engineering Conference (RE 2010), pp. 95–103 (2010)
13. Schmidt, A., Beigl, M., Gellersen, H.W.: There is more to context than location. Computers and Graphics 23(6), 893–901 (1999)
14. Sutcliffe, A., Thew, S.: Analysing "people" problems in requirements engineering. In: ACM/IEEE 32nd International Conference on Software Engineering (ICSE 2010), vol. 2, pp. 469–470 (2010)
15. Toma, I., Simperl, E., Filipowska, A., Hench, G., Domingue, J.: Semantics-driven interoperability on the future internet. In: IEEE International Conference on Semantic Computing (ICSC 2009), pp. 551–558 (2009)
16. Welsh, K., Sawyer, P., Bencomo, N.: Towards requirements aware systems: Runtime resolution of design-time assumptions. In: 26th IEEE/ACM International Conference on Automated Software Engineering (ASE 2011), pp. 560–563 (2011)
17. Yu, E.: Towards modelling and reasoning support for early-phase requirements engineering. In: Third IEEE International Symposium on Requirements Engineering (RE 1997), pp. 226–235 (1997)

Automatic Test Case Generation
from Functional Requirements in NDT

Javier Gutiérrez, Gustavo Aragón, Manuel Mejías, Francisco Jose Domínguez Mayo,
and Carmen M. Ruiz Cutilla

IWT2 Research Group, University of Seville, Seville, Spain
{javierj,risoto,fjdominguez}@us.es,
{gustavo.aragon,carmen.ruiz}@iwt2.org

Abstract. Navigational Development Techniques (NDT) is a Model-driven framework focused on defining Web requirements and obtaining related artefacts from them by means of transformations. Testing is one of the key elements in a software development process, however NDT neither include models to define artefacts nor transformations to obtain them from requirements. This paper presents how NDT improves with new models and transformations in order to generate test cases.

1   Introduction

Model-Driven Engineering (MDE hereinafter) is a Software Engineering paradigm focused on creating and exploiting domain models [19]. In the last years, this paradigm was used in several domains of Software Engineering providing relevant results.

Web Engineering constitutes one of these domains [5]. Research groups are using MDE for requirements treatment, design, development and several aspects of Web development. This field is commonly named Model-Driven Web Engineering.

However, one of the less treated phases is the testing and validation phase. In the survey presented in [5] relevant conclusions about the suitability of applying MDE in this context are stated. This paper presents the application of MDE in a Web context. It focuses on the first phases of the lifecycle and it studies how functional testing can be deeply improved by means of *early testing*. Thus, this paper analyses an approach that uses the MDE context and illustrates such uses in a concrete environment, NDT approach (Navigational Development Techniques)[6].

NDT was initially defined to deal with Web development requirements, but it has evolved in the last years and nowadays it offers a complete support for the complete lifecycle. NDT covers viability study, requirements treatment, analysis, design, construction or implementation as well as maintenance and test processes. Additionally, it supports a set of processes to bear out project management and quality assurance.

This paper describes how NDT has been extended to incorporate functional system test cases. These test cases verify that the system under test commits the behaviour defined in its functional requirement [12]. NDT models the functional requirements as use cases, thus, both terms will be used as synonyms in this paper.

M. Grossniklaus and M. Wimmer (Eds.): ICWE 2012 Workshops, LNCS 7703, pp. 176–185, 2012.
© Springer-Verlag Berlin Heidelberg 2012

This paper is organised as follows. Section 2 introduces a motivating example from a real project that enhances us to extend NDT. Then, section 3 cites related work dealing with generating test cases from use cases. Section 4 puts forward how NDT has been extended by means of metamodels and transformations so as to generate test cases from use cases. Finally, Section 5 states the conclusions and ongoing work.

2   A Motivating Example

During 2.008, the IWT2 research group participated in a technological migration of EMASESA information systems. EMASESA is a public company that manages the urban water cycle, providing and ensuring water supply to all citizens in Seville. IWT2 members' collaborative work focused on using NDT for the quality management of the methodological process.

AQUA-Web-Services project (also called AQUA-WS) consists in developing an application of an integrated business system for customer management and involvement in water distribution, cleaning, and net management. The software system was composed of three subsystems, each one representing a legacy system. There was a subsystem for managing the infrastructure of the pipe net, a subsystem for managing clients and another one for managing the whole organization. The total system includes 1.808 functional requirements, containing several scenarios and alternatives in each functional requirement.

The use cases were defined by means of Enterprise Architect tool, linked to an Oracle Database Server and a Subversion repository. This platform enables the parallel work of several teams: developers of the two software factories implied, EMASESA's managers and the group who works in quality assurance.

Use cases were modelled using two techniques: UML Activity Diagrams and text templates. Activities diagrams were modelled according to UML specifications. Text templates were modelled according to the previous work developed by the IWT2 group on functional requirements [6].

The estimate amount of time needed to generate the package structure, elaborate the test case suite that covers all scenarios from the functional requirements, design those test cases in Enterprise Architect and trace them with the functional requirement under test was vast. Estimating 5 minutes to create a test scenario in the modelling tool, the amount of time gained with NDT-Tool was 583 hours (73 days working eight hours a week). This was a big amount of time for a task that was repeated and systematic, so this tool support was proposed.

During the AQUA-WS project improvement teams used a software prototype to produce the test plan. This plan generated about 7,000 test cases from different scenarios of the use case in a few minutes, by repeating the package structure of the functional requirements and adding tracing relations to the functional requirements under test.

3   Related Work

Several approaches in the literature study how to generate functional test cases specifically from a functional requirements model defined as use cases. There are also two surveys analysing the existing literature. The most recent survey, which updates the original survey published in [4], has been published in [5] at the end of 2011. Some specific approaches studied in Escalona's survey are described in next paragraphs.

Ruder's [18] approach starts with functional requirements written in natural language. The result is a set of functional test cases obtained from a coverage criterion based on combinations that support Boolean propositions. Binder's book [1] describes the application of the Category-Partition Method in use cases. Categories are any points in which the behaviour of the use case may be different between two realizations of the use case. This application is named the Extended Use Case Pattern. Finally, Ibrahim et-al. [8] offers a tool, called GenTCase, which generates test cases automatically from a use case diagram enriched with each use case tabular text description.

Frölich et-al. [7] introduces an approach describing how to translate a functional requirement from natural language into a state-chart diagram in a systematic way, as well as how to generate a set of functional test cases from that diagram. Naresh [13] presents an approach dealing with translating a functional requirement from natural language into a flow diagram and performing a path coverage technique to generate test cases. Mogyorodi [10] introduces an approach analysing functional requirements as cause-effect graphs that generate test cases from diagrams. Boddu et-al. [2] presents an approach divided into two blocks: the first one describes a natural language analyzer generating a state machine from functional requirements, and the second one shows how to create test cases from such state machine.

Escalona's survey claims that there is no definitive approach that closes the problem of generating functional text cases automatically in a satisfactory way. Thus, there are some aspects to be improved, for example, the use of standards for inputs and outputs, the application of standards and more formal methods to describe the process itself, the need for empirical results or measuring the possible automation and a profitable tool supporting, among others. Conclusions of Denger's survey goes in the same line.

4   Extension of NDT

This section describes the extension of NDT with new metamodels and transformations. Section 4.1 describes the two testing techniques used for generating functional test cases identified in previous work (Section 3). Then, section 4.2 introduces the metamodel selected to define the results of the previous testing techniques. Section 4.3 analyses both testing techniques as a set of relations between previous models and their implementation in QVT code. Finally, section 4.4 describes the implementation of the new transformations in the existing set of supporting tools of NDT.

4.1   Techniques for Test Cases Generation

After mentioning the existing work in the previous section, it is worth mentioning that there are two techniques emerging as the most important ones for generating test cases from use cases: Round-Strip Strategy and Extended Use Cases (names given by Binder in [1]). Both techniques are described in next paragraphs.

The Round-strip strategy consists in applying a classic algorithm of path-finding in a state machine. The behaviour described in a functional requirement may be managed as a graph or as a state machine despite its concrete syntax. Hence, a path searching allows identifying all the different paths through behaviour. Each path will be a scenario designed together with the system. At the same time, each scenario is a potential test case for assessing the right implementation of such scenario in the tested system. Generation of test cases from state-machines is a widely described topic in research literature. Previous section presented several references about this topic in the specific use cases context, like [7], [13] or [2]. Figure 1(a) shows an example of the Round-Strip Strategy using the behaviour of a use case defined as an activity diagram.

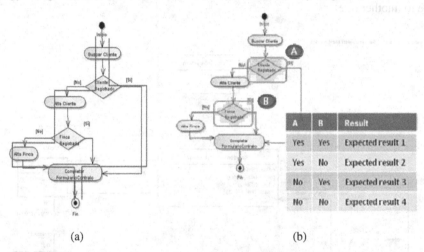

Fig. 1. Examples of Round-Strip Strategy (a) and Extended Use Cases (b) techniques

The Extended Use Case pattern consists in applying the Category-Partition Method [17] to use cases. The Category-Partition Method is a technique based on identifying categories and partitions to then generate combinations among such partitions (Figure 1(b)). In the context of functional requirements, a category is any point for which the functional requirement defines an alternative behaviour (Figure 1 (b)). Besides, a partition is defined as a subset of the domain of the condition evaluated in the category which decides whether a concrete piece of behaviour is executed or not. Once all categories and partitions are identified, a combination among them is performed and each combination becomes a potential test case. The previous section presented several references about this topic in the specific context of use cases, like [18] or [1]. Figure 1(b) shows an example of the Category-Partition Method (as described in [1]) using the same behaviour as Figure 1(a).

4.2   Metamodels

Due to the Model-driven nature of NDT, the concepts involved in functional test cases should be identified and defined as metamodels. A metamodel defines the concept in terms of its attributes and its relationships with other concepts [19]. Four metamodels were designed. These metamodels are described in next paragraphs.

The first one (Figure 2) defines the necessary elements from functional requirements to generate test cases. The *Subsystem* element represents a package or a container for functional requirements and other related elements (as *SysteActor*).

The key concept in this metamodel is the *FunctionalRequirement* element. The behaviour of a functional requirement is modelled using the elements *Step* and *ExecutionOrder*. The *Step* element models a concrete chunk of behaviour of the functional requirement, such as requesting information or calculating a result. The *ExecutionOrder* element defines the order in which steps are executed. Using a metaphor, the functional requirement may be seen as a finite-state machine (usually called FSM), the steps as states and the execution order as the transition from one state to another one.

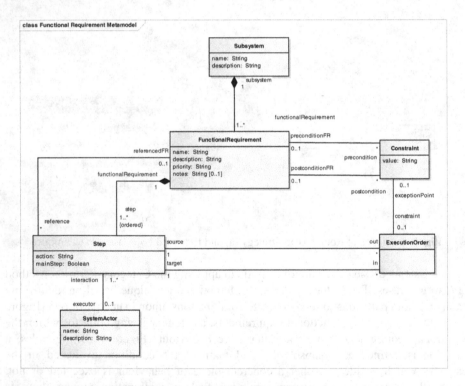

Fig. 2. Metamodel for Functional Requirements

The *SystemActor* element models an external entity that collaborates with the system during the steps performance.

The introduction of additional functional requirements as part of the behaviour of a functional requirement has been considered by using the relation *reference-referencedFR* (from *Step* to *FunctionalRequirement*). This mechanism allows defining the semantic expressed through inclusion and extension relations as defined in UML Use Case metamodel.

The metamodel in Figure 2 directly matches with the functional requirement model defined in NDT. This means that each functional requirement defined with NDT has the concepts exposed in Figure 2, and it may be used with the transformations and tools described in next sections.

The second metamodel (Figure 3) defines the concepts resulting from the Round-Trip technique (Figure 1(a)). Each path is called test scenario (element *TestScenario* in Figure 3) and the traverse steps are classified into actions, (element *ActionFromTestScenario* in Figure 3) when performed by an external actor or into verifications, (element *VerificationFromTestScenario* in Figure 3) when performed by the system and, therefore, it is suitable to introduce a assert during the test.

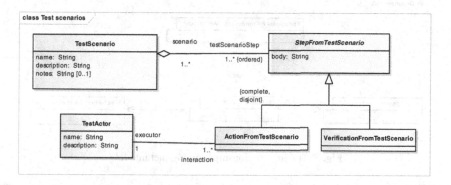

Fig. 3. Metamodel for test scenarios

The third metamodel (Figure 4) defines the concepts resulting from the Category-Partition Method. Categories are modelled by means of the element *OperationalVariable* (as named in [1]) whereas partitions are modelled through the element *Partition*. The element *Instance* points out an evaluation of an operational variable, for example A or B cells in Figure 1(b), and allows distinguishing it from other evaluations of the same operational variable, in case the behaviour of the functional requirement has loops. A *Quantum* element models a value transfer from a partition into an instance. A combination (a row in Figure 1(b)) is modelled using the element *InstanceCombination*.

Finally, the last metamodel introduces artifacts that combine the results of the two previous techniques in the same model. This last metamodel does not introduce any new information. However, it offers linking elements to represent the information through a common artifact (called test case), the steps from a functional requirement as well as a combination of partitions. Figure 5 shows the tracing relation between the four metamodels. Tracing enables knowing which test artifacts have been generated for each functional requirement.

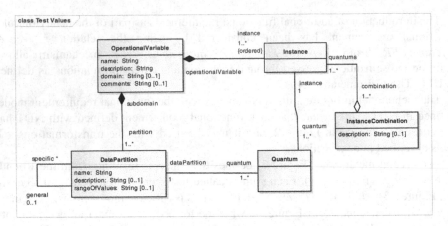

Fig. 4. Metamodel for test values

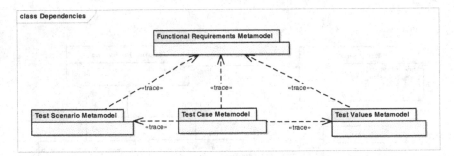

Fig. 5. Tracing relationships among metamodels

Former metamodels have been added to the set of metamodels managed and supported by NDT as part of its MDD development process.

4.3   Transformations and QVT

This section describes how to apply the two techniques presented in Section 2 (Round-Trip and Extended Use Cases) taking the information from functional requirements metamodels (in the previous section) as a source and the information from testing metamodels as a target.

The process of applying both techniques is analysed according to the identification of a set of relations between source concepts (functional requirements) and target concepts (test scenarios and operational variables combinations), as observed in Figure 6. The task of identifying these relations consists in detecting how one target element is built up, for example a test case, by means of the source elements and their information. Next paragraphs provide an overview of the three relations (named T1, T2 and T3 in Figure 6) defined to create test scenarios, combinations of operational variables and test cases from functional requirements.

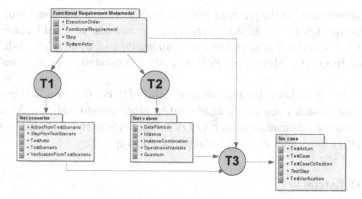

Fig. 6. Transformations among models

Relation T1 involves functional requirements and the Round-Strip strategy. As it was represented in Figure 1(a), the functional requirement behaviour may be modelled as a state-machine, the concept *Step* from Figure 2 models states, and the concept *ExecutionOrder* models transitions. Thus, a classic coverage criterion may be selected to traverse the functional requirement and generate test scenarios. The all-loops criterion, in which all combinations among loops are traversed at least once, is the one selected to extend NDT. Test scenarios steps are generated from all the functional requirements steps. Action (element *ActionFromTestScenario*) and verification (element *VerificationFromTestScenario*) classifications depend on whether there is a relation with a system actor. Finally, test actors are generated from actors, which, due to their attributes are the same ones.

Relation T2 in Figure 6 involves functional requirements and the Category-Partition Method. Operational Variables are created from steps that have more than one output transition (modelled as an ExecutionOrder *element). The outputs of the steps generate the different partition. Again, combinations may be calculated using several criteria, ranged from calculating all possible solutions to calculating only a subset.*

Table 1. Metrics for QVT-Operational code

	T0	T1	T2	T3
Total lines	124	118	290	170
Lines of codes	104	97	238	124
No. of Mappings	1	4	5	3
No. of Helpers	1	2	3	1
No. of Queries	3	2	1	3
No. of Input models	1	1	1	3
No. of Output models	1	1	1	1

Relation T3 (Figure 6) combines both techniques results. Test scenarios and combinations of operational variables merge using test cases.

The relations stated in the previous paragraphs (T1, T2 and T3 from Figure 6) were defined through QVT Operational language as a necessary step to know how to implement the transformation process into an automatic tool. QVT code may be downloaded from [20]. Metrics of QVT code are represented in Table 1 and defined in [16].

Table 1 adds an additional transformation, called T0, not included in Figure 6. This transformation contains common a code used in other transformations. As reference, the Umls2Rdb transformation written in QVT Operational and included in the QVT reference [15] has 65 lines of code, 6 mappings, and 1 query.

4.4   NDT Extension

Nowadays, several companies in Spain work with NDT. This is possible due to the fact that NDT is completely supported by a set of free tools, mainly grouped in NDT-Suite [9]. This suite enables the definition and use of every process and task supported by NDT (Figure 1) and offers relevant resources for quality assurance, management and metrics with the aim of developing software projects. The suite was also extended to implement the first technique for test case generation using activity diagrams as the concrete input for functional requirements, and for the concrete syntax of the test scenarios generated. The implementation of the second technique is still an ongoing work.

However, the MDD perspective allows the concrete notations independency. Thus, the metamodels and transformations defined in previous section may be used out of the scope of NDT. The only request is that the source functional requirements must include the concepts defined in the functional requirements metamodel used as the basis for the process. To remark this independency, a second tool, called MDETest was created. The main differences between this tool and NDT-Suite are that MDETest implements the three target metamodels and it generates the tool uses instances only for metamodels, so that, it does not impose any restrictions on the concrete notations of the functional requirements input. Nowadays, this tool supports activity diagrams such as the syntax for functional requirements, although it does not support any concrete syntax for the output. This tool is also available in [20].

5   Conclusions and Ongoing Work

This paper presents an extension of NDT, based on metamodels and transformations, with the aim of generating test cases from functional requirements. The extension has been tested in several projects and it opens new research lines. Firstly, we have to work in test cases prioritization mechanisms, consisting in giving relevance to functional requirements, as well as in redundant test cases detection. The practice concludes that it continues producing a high number of redundant test cases that the test teams have to detect by hand. One last ongoing work would deal with supporting the semantic of the inclusion and extension relations defined in UML [14] for use cases.

Acknowledgements. *This research has been supported by the Tempros project (TIN2010-20057-C03-02) and Red CaSA (TIN 2010-12312-E) of the Ministerio de Ciencia e Innovación, Spain, and NDTQ-Framework project of the Junta de Andalucía, Spain (TIC-5789).*

References

[1] Binder, R.V.: Testing Object-Oriented Systems. Addison Wesley (1999)

[2] Boddu, R., Guo, L., Mukhopadhyay, S.: RETNA: From Requirements to Testing in Natural Way. In: 12th IEEE International Requirements Engineering, RE 2004 (2004)

[3] Cutilla, C.R., García-García, J.A., Alba, M., Escalona, M.J., Rodríguez-Catalán, L.: Aplicación del paradigma MDE para la generación de pruebas funcionales. In: Experiencia Dentro del Proyecto AQUA-WS, ATSE 2011, Chaves, Portugal (2011)

[4] Denger, C., Medina, M.: Test Case Derived from Requirement Specifications. Fraunhofer IESE Report, Germany (2003)

[5] Escalona, M.J., Gutiérrez, J.J., Mejías, M., Aragón, G., Ramos, I., Torres, J., Domínguez, F.J.: An Overview on Test Generation from Functional Requirements. The Journal of Systems and Software (2011)

[6] Escalona, M.J., Aragón, G.: NDT. A Model-Driven Approach for Web Requirements. IEEE Transaction on Software Engineering 34(3), 370–390 (2008)

[7] Fröhlich, P., Link, J.: Automated Test Case Generation from Dynamic Models. In: Bertino, E. (ed.) ECOOP 2000. LNCS, vol. 1850, pp. 472–491. Springer, Heidelberg (2000)

[8] Ibrahim, R., Saringat, M.Z., Ibrahim, N., Ismail, N.: An Automatic Tool for Generating Test Cases from the System's Requirements. In: 7th International Conference on Computer and Information Technology, Fukushima, Japan (2007)

[9] García-García, J.A., Cutilla, C.R., Escalona, M.J., Alba, M., Torres, J.: NDT-Driver, a Java Tool to Support QVT Transformations for NDT. In: 20th International Conference on Information Systems Development, Edinburgh, Scotland, August 24-26 (2011)

[10] Mogyorodi, G.E.: What Is Requirements-Based Testing? In: 15th Annual Software Technology Conference, Salt Lake City, USA, April 28-May 1

[11] Gutiérrez, J.J., Nebut, C., Escalona, M.J., Mejías, M., Ramos, I.M.: Visualization of Use Cases through Automatically Generated Activity Diagrams. In: Czarnecki, K., Ober, I., Bruel, J.-M., Uhl, A., Völter, M. (eds.) MoDELS 2008. LNCS, vol. 5301, pp. 83–96. Springer, Heidelberg (2008)

[12] Myers, G.: The Art of Software Testing, 2nd edn. Addison-Wesley, USA (2004)

[13] Naresh, A.: Testing From Use Cases Using Path Analysis Technique. In: International Conference on Software Testing Analysis & Review (2002)

[14] Object Management Group, Unified Modelling Language 2.4 (2011), http://www.omg.org (last visit June 24, 2011)

[15] Object Management Group. Query View Transformation Specification 1.0 (2010), http://www.omg.org (last visit June 24, 2011)

[16] Kapová, L., Goldschmidt, T., Becker, S., Henss, J.: Evaluating Maintainability with Code Metrics for Model-to-Model Transformations. In: Heineman, G.T., Kofron, J., Plasil, F. (eds.) QoSA 2010. LNCS, vol. 6093, pp. 151–166. Springer, Heidelberg (2010)

[17] Ostrand, T.J., Balcer, M.J.: Category-Partition Method. Communications of the ACM, 676–686 (1988)

[18] Ruder, A.: UML-based Test Generation and Execution. Rückblick Meeting, Berlin (2004)

[19] Schmidt, D.C.: Guest Editor's Introduction: Model-Driven Engineering. Computer 39(2) (2006)

[20] Supporting web, http://www.iwt2.org/mdetest (last updated April 15, 2012)

Reasoning about Knowledge from the Web

(Extended Abstract)

Gjergji Kasneci*

Hasso-Plattner-Institute,
Prof.-Dr.-Helmert-Str. 2-3,
14482 Potsdam, Germany
Gjergji.Kasneci@hpi.uni-potsdam.de

In the presence of a vast amount of user generated content evolving around entities such as people, locations, products, events, etc., it seems that document-oriented retrieval is rather old-fashioned. Imagine an HIV-relevant search task that with the goal of finding drugs that may interfere with HIV protease inhibitors. Retrieving an exhaustive list of explicit results (i.e., drugs that may interfere with HIV protease inhibitors) can be crucial for people suffering from HIV, whose health depends on the unmediated effect of protease inhibitors. Moreover it might be desirable to have the drugs in the result list ranked by their probability of interfering with protease inhibitors. In order to automatically retrieve such an exhaustive list of ranked answers, there are two subtasks that have to be addressed: (1) knowledge about drugs that stand in an interference relationship to protease inhibitors needs to be extracted from various web pages and appropriately combined, (2) the drugs need to be ranked by their probability of interfering with protease inhibitors. Neither of these tasks can be addressed by state-of-the-art search engines. Expecting the user to manually inspect retrieved documents to construct an exhaustive list of answers is simply unrealistic. As a matter of fact, major players in the search engine industry have recognized these issues and are attempting to shift the focus towards knowledge retrieval. For example, in 2010, Google acquired Metaweb, the company behind Freebase, one of the largest knowledge bases with explicit facts about real-world entities. In 2011, Google's search group was restructured and renamed into "knowledge group" [6]. Another example is Microsoft's Bing, which has undergone similar changes in recent years. By the end of 2009 Bing was returning Wolfram Alpha results to entity-related and scholarly queries [8], and by the end 2010 Bing announced the new "health search experience" with the focus "on further enabling people to get relevant information and make better decisions" [7].

Some years earlier, two outstanding academic efforts [3,4] proved the concept of knowledge base construction with facts extracted from semi-structured information sources in Web 2.0 platforms. The information in such sources is typically contributed and curated by many different users, thus reflecting the "Wisdom of the Crowds". The most well-known example in this realm is Wikipedia, which provides infoboxes, categories, and other kinds of tabular information about the

---

* I am grateful to Thore Graepel and Jurgen Van Gael for many insightful comments and discussions on this topic.

M. Grossniklaus and M. Wimmer (Eds.): ICWE 2012 Workshops, LNCS 7703, pp. 186–188, 2012.
© Springer-Verlag Berlin Heidelberg 2012

entities described by the articles. Such assets mitigate the need of Natural Language Processing and Statistical Learning techniques for information extraction and allow instead the adoption of much simpler techniques such as regular expressions, lexicons, and pattern matching algorithms. Although the knowledge bases derived by the latter extraction techniques from Web 2.0 sources have a relatively high coverage and quality, much of the knowledge they contain is inherently uncertain. Quantifying this uncertainty is a major concern, which, to a large extent, has been ignored by the semantic web community.

To address the above concern, we propose a probabilistic knowledge representation model that quantifies uncertainty by exploiting user feedback on the truth values of statements in the knowledge base [1]. In this model the truth value of each statement is represented by a binary random variable and the logical interdependencies between statements, such as transitivity (e.g., if Potsdam is located in Brandenburg and Brandenburg is located in Germany then Potsdam must be located in Germany too), are represented as a Bayesian network connecting the binary random variables. In order to capture feedback on the statements we introduce binary random variables standing for the user feedback and continuous variables representing the reliability of users. The latter feedback components are directly connected with the random variables representing the truth values of statements. Note that the user feedback initiates and enables updates on the beliefs of the variables in the network. A sample subgraph from the Bayesian network is presented in Figure 1.

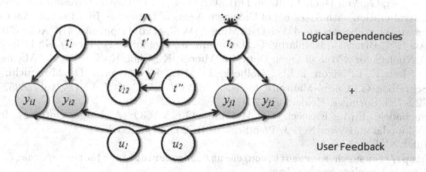

Fig. 1. Belief updates through feedback propagation

Figure 1 illustrates how the model enables joint reasoning on the reliability of two users (represented by the variables u_1, u_2) and the truth values of two statements (represented by the variables t_i, t_j) on which they provide feedback. Additionally, the truth value of a statement t_l that is deduced from the former statements is learned through the probabilistic conjunction (represented by t') of t_i, t_j and its disjunction with a variable t'', which accounts for incomplete knowledge, i.e., any deductions which might not be captured by the knowledge base.

As the reliabilities of users vary across knowledge domains, we also propose an extension of the above model, in which the user expertise is measured by means of a collaborative-filtering-style probabilistic model [2]. More specifically, in this model, users and statements are represented by feature vector variables (e.g., user features are: id, gender, country, etc., and statement features: id, topic, relationship type, etc.), which are mapped into a lower dimensional latent space where the similarity between users and statements can be measured.

For the probabilistic inference in the above models we have used Expectation Propagation as implemented by Infer.NET [5].

In experiments with a subset of YAGO statements [4] and feedback collected from Amazon Mechanical Turk[1], both models described above turn out to be far more accurate than a model that aggregates feedback based on majority voting[2]. Furthermore, a high prediction accuracy can be already achieved with relatively sparse feedback, thus avoiding unrealistic effort on the users' side. Finally, the model that captures the expertise of users excels in both accuracy and reduction of the amount of feedback needed.

Based on a distributed computing framework, we implemented an efficient, large-scale version of the above models, which can handle knowledge bases with hundreds of millions of statements. The result was presented at Microsoft's largest internal research and technology fair, TechFest 2011.

References

1. Kasneci, G., Van Gael, J., Herbrich, R., Graepel, T.: Bayesian Knowledge Corroboration with Logical Rules and User Feedback. In: Balcázar, J.L., Bonchi, F., Gionis, A., Sebag, M. (eds.) ECML PKDD 2010, Part II. LNCS, vol. 6322, pp. 1–18. Springer, Heidelberg (2010)
2. Kasneci, G., Van Gael, J., Stern, D.H., Graepel, T.: CoBayes: Bayesian Knowledge Corroboration with Assessors of Unknown Areas of Expertise. In: International Conference on Web Search and Web Data Mining (WSDM 2011), pp. 465–474. ACM (2011)
3. Auer, S., Bizer, C., Kobilarov, G., Lehmann, J., Cyganiak, R., Ives, Z.G.: DBpedia: A Nucleus for a Web of Open Data. In: Aberer, K., Choi, K.-S., Noy, N., Allemang, D., Lee, K.-I., Nixon, L.J.B., Golbeck, J., Mika, P., Maynard, D., Mizoguchi, R., Schreiber, G., Cudré-Mauroux, P. (eds.) ISWC/ASWC 2007. LNCS, vol. 4825, pp. 722–735. Springer, Heidelberg (2007)
4. Suchanek, F.M., Kasneci, G., Weikum, G.: YAGO: A Large Ontology from Wikipedia and WordNet. J. Web Sem. 6(3), 203–217 (2008)
5. Infer.NET,
   http://research.microsoft.com/en-us/um/cambridge/projects/infernet/
6. Google Dissolves Search Group,
   http://techcrunch.com/2011/05/03/
   google-dissolves-search-group-internally-now-called-knowledge
7. Bringing Knowledge into Health,
   http://www.bing.com/community/site_blogs/b/search/archive/
   2010/01/12/bringing-knowledge-into-health-search.aspx
8. Bing, Wolfram Alpha Agree on Licensing Deal,
   http://www.zdnet.com/news/
   bing-wolfram-alpha-agree-on-licensing-deal/333870

---

[1] For an exact description of the experimental setting, we refer the reader to [1].

[2] In the majority-based aggregation of feedback the truth value of a statement is estimated by a majority consensus; that is, a statement is assumed to be true if the majority thinks that it is true.

Toward the Improvement of a Measurement and Evaluation Strategy from a Comparative Study

Fernanda Papa

GIDIS_Web, Engineering School at UNLPam, General Pico, LP, Argentina
`pmfer@ing.unlpam.edu.ar`

Abstract. For evaluating web applications (WebApps) and other entities in a systematic way and further fostering robust data analysis among projects, measurement and evaluation (M&E) strategies are a valuable asset in any organization. However, the evaluation of the quality of the capabilities for an integrated M&E strategy –seen as a resource– has often been neglected. We regard a M&E strategy is integrated if three coexisting capabilities are supported, namely: i) a conceptual framework, ii) a well-established process specification, and iii) an explicit methodological support. Under this premise, we conducted a case study where GQM⁺Strategies (*Goal-Question-Metric*), and GOCAME *(Goal-Oriented Context-Aware Measurement and Evaluation)* strategies were evaluated. The results allowed us to understand the strengths and weaknesses of both strategies. From this understanding we have planned improvement actions and implemented some changes in GOCAME as well. This paper ultimately analyzes the achieved gains after recommended changes were performed.

Keywords: Measurement and evaluation strategy, Resource, Improvement.

1   Introduction

Regarding the Web Engineering discipline and its support process areas, quality measurement, evaluation and analysis for WebApps have been in the research forefront. Most of the published works and reported experiences are devoted to the evaluation of WebApps and its use –i.e. WebApp as a product, system or system in use–, and to lesser extent to the evaluation of used methods and tools. In a broad sense, evaluation is intended to assess a given information need and purpose e.g. "understand", "improve", etc. for different categories of entities such as product, system, system in use, among others such as service, process, resource or even a project. Oftentimes the evaluation is made specifying nonfunctional requirements by means of quality models. In a narrower sense, for a given category there are many sub-categories of entities of interest for evaluation. For example, for the resource category, we can identify more specific entity sub-categories such as "tool", "strategy", "software team", etc.; and, in turn, for a "strategy" we can identify a "development strategy", "testing strategy", "M&E strategy", among others. Furthermore, an entity is a concrete object that belongs to an entity category; for instance, in [11] we have recently evaluated two concrete entities, namely: GQM⁺Strategies [2, 3] and GOCAME [10] M&E strategies. In this way, the "M&E strategy" entity sub-category was considered as a resource for a software/web

M. Grossniklaus and M. Wimmer (Eds.): ICWE 2012 Workshops, LNCS 7703, pp. 189–203, 2012.

line of production, which can be employed in quality assurance activities. Based on our review of existing literature, the quality evaluation for an integrated M&E strategy has often been neglected.

With the aim to systematically carry out M&E projects and programs, organizations should establish clearly a set of activities and methods to specify, collect, store, and use trustworthy measures and indicators' values. Moreover, in order to make the analysis and decision-making process more robust, it is necessary to ensure that metrics and indicators are repeatable and comparable among the organization's projects.

In [10], GOCAME –an integrated M&E strategy that allows developing programs with these characteristics– was proposed. This strategy includes the following capabilities: i) a *M&E conceptual framework*, which is modular, flexible and terminologically consistent. A well-established conceptual framework should be built on a robust terminological base as for example a glossary, taxonomy or ontology; an ontology explicitly and formally specifies the main agreed concepts, properties, relationships, and constraints for a given domain, as well as their grouping into components. This capability ensures terminological uniformity and consistency among the other capabilities; ii) a *M&E process*, which describes what to do, by specifying the main activities to be planned and executed, their inputs and outputs, roles, interdependencies, among other aspects. A well-established M&E process not only facilitates the understanding and communication among stakeholders but also ensures repeatability and reproducibility in the implementation of activities; and iii) *methods and tools* that enable to perform and automate the activities' descriptions. Methods are allocated in a flexible way to perform the specified activities, which in turn can be instantiated by tools.

Under the premise that a M&E strategy is integrated if the three above mentioned capabilities are to a great extent achieved simultaneously, we recently conducted a case study [11] where the two quoted strategies (GQM⁺Strategies and GOCAME) were evaluated considering the *Capability Quality* focus. From the analysis of results we obtained a detailed list of strengths and weaknesses for both strategies. Then we elaborated recommendations and a plan with improvement actions. Based on the improvement plan, we performed some changes for GOCAME –especially for those weaker attributes– and we conducted the re-evaluation. Hence, a comparison between both evaluations –before and after changes– gave us quantitative evidence about the level of gain met for GOCAME.

The contributions of this research were documented in [11], namely: i) understanding the quality of integrated M&E strategies, ii) designing the nonfunctional requirements focusing on the capability quality of this resource; iii) developing a case study to analyze and provide conclusions/recommendations based on identified strengths and weaknesses. We overview in the present work these contributions for a better comprehension, and we go a step further by: iv) establishing and implementing actions aimed at improving GOCAME; and v) re-evaluating it based on some implemented recommendations in order to gauge the improvement gain in quantitative form.

The remainder of this paper is organized as follows. Section 2 discusses the research motivation and related work; also, it provides an overview of the two selected strategies. Section 3 summarizes design and implementation issues for the comparative study. Section 4 shows, considering the three capabilities, the analysis and recommendations to improve GOCAME and also discusses the actual impact of implemented change actions. Finally, Section 5 draws the main conclusions and future work.

2   Motivation and Related Work

The motivation for this work was driven by the purpose of continuously improving the capability quality of GOCAME looking at the strengths of other well-established and integrated M&E strategy. With this in mind, we selected two concrete entities to be assessed: GOCAME and GQM$^+$Strategies. The selection criteria used were basically: i) the M&E strategies are documented in the literature of public domain, i.e. there exists documentation –in English language– in digital libraries with recognized visibility such as IEEE Xplore, SpringerLink, ACM digital library, Scopus, etc.; ii) they have some impact in the academia or industry, and; iii) they have to great extent integrated the three capabilities simultaneously, i.e. the conceptual base/framework, process, and method/tool. With simultaneous compliance of these capabilities is meant that no input value to the conjunctive aggregation function (whose output is the value of the capability quality indicator) must be zero, as we see later on.

The systematic literature review showed there are many proposals published in the M&E area having some of the three capabilities, but they do not consider the integration of them simultaneously as a whole. Therefore, in the first selection process the following strategies were pre-selected: GOCAME, GQM [1], GQM$^+$Strategies, FMESP (*Framework for the Modeling and Evaluation of Software Processes*) [8], and CQA-Meth (*Continuous Quality Assessment*) approach [12].

GOCAME is the target entity to be evaluated since it is an integrated M&E strategy and our ultimate purpose is its improvement as well. The second entity considered was GQM. It is a strategy with some level of integration, with abundant level of documentation available, and widely referenced and used both in industry and academia. However, in the literature reviewed we found that GQM$^+$Strategies is an integrated M&E approach recently issued which includes GQM. So GQM$^+$Strategies was the second entity to be evaluated.

Another contribution is the CQA-Meth approach, a flexible methodology that allows the quality assessment of any software model. This methodology and its tool are part of the CQA integrated environment that can be used by companies to perform quality assessments of their own or third-party products. CQA-Meth defines the processes necessary to carry out the evaluation of UML models, and facilitate communication between the client (sponsor of the evaluation) and the evaluation team. CQA-Meth was not selected as an entity to be assessed because it does not meet the three criteria simultaneously; in particular, it lacks an explicit conceptual framework from a terminological base. While CQA-Meth comes from the same research group who developed the FMESP approach that does have a conceptual framework with an ontological base, in the literature or references provided by authors in [12] the relationship among the three capabilities is not explicit at all.

In summary, the two entities that were selected as part of the comparative study are GOCAME and GQM$^+$Strategies. Sub-sections 2.1 and 2.2 present an overview of both strategies to be assessed taking into account the three capabilities.

On the other hand, there are no other related works that document the evaluation-driven improvement of integrated M&E strategies as a resource.

2.1   GOCAME Overview

GOCAME is a multi-purpose M&E strategy which follows a goal-oriented and context-sensitive approach in defining M&E projects. It is based on the three above mentioned capabilities, which are summarized below.

GOCAME has its terminological base defined as an ontology. The metric and indicator ontology provides a domain model that defines all the concepts, properties and relationships which in turn helps to design the M&E activities. This way, a common understanding of data and metadata is shared among the organization's projects lending to more consistent analysis and results across projects. The C-INCAMI conceptual framework (*Contextual-Information Need, Concept model, Attribute, Metric and Indicator*) [10] emerged from the metric and indicator ontology.

C-INCAMI is structured in six components, namely: i) <u>M&E project definition,</u> allows specifying the management data for *M&E projects*; ii) <u>Nonfunctional requirements specification,</u> allows specifying the *Information Need* for a particular *purpose* and the *user viewpoint* related to an *Entity* and *quality focus*. The focus is represented by a *Concept Model* which includes *Concepts* (characteristics), *sub-concepts* and associated *Attributes*. Attributes are measurable properties of an *entity* under analysis; iii) <u>Context specification,</u> allows the description of the relevant *Context*, i.e. the situation of the entity to be assessed as regards the information need, through *Context properties,* which are attributes; iv) <u>Measurement design and implementation,</u> allows specifying *direct* and *indirect metrics* used in *Measurement* activities which produce *Measures*; v) <u>Evaluation design and implementation,</u> allows specifying the evaluation through *Indicators*, which interpret attributes and calculable concepts for a nonfunctional requirements tree. The *Indicator values* represent the degree of satisfaction achieved for a given information need. Two types of indicators are distinguished: *Elementary indicators* which evaluate lower-level requirements (attributes), and, *Partial/Global indicators*, which evaluate higher-level requirements, i.e. sub-characteristics and characteristics. The indicator *Scale* has *Decision criteria* in terms of acceptability levels; and vi) <u>Analysis and recommendation specification,</u> supports methods for data and information analysis in order to provide recommendations for improvement.

GOCAME has a well-defined M&E process [4], which is composed of six main processes: i) Define Nonfunctional Requirements; ii) Design the Measurement; iii) Design the Evaluation; iv) Implement the Measurement; v) Implement the Evaluation; and vi) Analyze and Recommend. These processes are broken down into activities, and sub-activities that are specified in SPEM language.

Lastly, GOCAME is supported by a methodology viz. WebQEM [9] and its C-INCAMI_Tool [10]. The methodology provides the 'how' to implement the requirements, measurement, evaluation, analysis and recommendation processes. It comprises a set of methods, techniques and tools to carry out the process activities accordingly.

2.2   GQM⁺Strategies Overview

GQM⁺Strategies is an approach built on GQM, which allows planning and implementing goal-oriented measurement programs. Taking into account GQM, GQM⁺Strategies adds a mechanism for explicitly linking software measurement goals to higher-level goals for the organization, as well as goals and strategies (tactics) to all business levels. This linkage helps to justify the efforts made in the software measurement and, in turn, the data collected contribute to make high-level decisions.

GQM⁺Strategies has its terminological base defined as a glossary [2, 3], reusing totally the GQM terms. In addition, terms are part of two primary components, namely: GQM⁺Strategies Element and GQM Graph. The former component includes a *single goal* and *derived strategies*, as well as all *context information* and *assumptions*, which explain how those goals and strategies are linked. On the other hand, the latter component reflects a single *GQM goal*, the corresponding set of *questions* and *metrics*, and an *interpretation model* that specifies how data items are to be combined and what criteria for determining the goal's success are.

Regarding the explicitness of the process, in [3] authors define basically two processes, which may be performed in parallel: one describing the tasks needed to define goals and related strategies, and the other describing the tasks needed to measure already defined goals and strategies. The first process involves activities such as: i) Elicit General Context and Assumptions; ii) Define Top-Level Goals; iii) Make Strategy Decisions; and iv) Define Goals. This process is iterated through all organizational levels. The other process involves activities such as: i) Define GQM goals for each selected GQM⁺Strategies goal at the appropriate level. The GQM goal template [3], which includes the object, purpose, quality aspect, viewpoint, and context terms, is used to formalize the measurement goal; ii) Specify the GQM graph for evaluating the achievement of the goal, i.e. GQM questions, metrics and interpretation models are defined; and iii) Identify relationships between the interpretation models on this level and the ones for the level above, if existing. Finally, it must be implemented the measurement and interpreted its results.

Lastly, in the reviewed literature no methodology is mentioned for GQM⁺Strategies; however, GQM explicitly defines one, covering several phases such as planning, definition, data collection and interpretation. Features of a tool that is configurable for each organizational measurement program is described in [13].

3   Evaluating Integrated M&E Strategies

In this section we summarize design and implementation issues for evaluating the two quoted strategies. GOCAME strategy was used in turn for conducting the evaluation itself. This evaluation allows understanding and comparing integrated strategies. Hereafter, using the same evaluation requirements and criteria, the re-evaluation of GOCAME allows gauging the improvement gain after recommended changes were made. Note that for didactic reasons activities are presented below in a bit different order that they were actually enacted. In fact, we performed first the design (i.e. nonfunctional requirements, measurement and evaluation), then the implementation of measurement and evaluation, and finally, the analysis and recommendation activities, as introduced in section 2.1.

Define Nonfunctional Requirements is the first activity. The purpose of the information need –for the first evaluation– is *"understand and compare"* from the *"quality assurance leader"* user viewpoint. The entity category is an *"integrated M&E strategy"* whose super-category is a *"resource"*, recalling that *GOCAME* and

GQM⁺Strategies are the concrete entities to be assessed. The focus of the evaluation is on their *"Capability Quality"*, which is defined as *degree to which a resource is suitable and appropriate for supporting and performing the actions when used under specified conditions*. Since in the related literature there is no ISO or *de facto* standard that specifies the capability quality model, we had to define our own concept model, as shown in the first column in Table 2.

The sub-characteristics associated to *Capability Quality* (coded 1) represent the three required capabilities of an integrated strategy, namely: *1.1 Process Capability Quality*, *1.2 Conceptual-Framework Capability Quality*, and *1.3 Methodology Capability Quality*. The sub-characteristics and attributes in the requirements tree –shown in the first column in Table 2– are all defined. For example, *1.1* represents *the degree to which a process is suitable and appropriate for supporting and performing the actions defined in it*; while the *1.1.1.5 Role-to-Activity Allocation Availability* attribute is defined as *the explicit indication of one or more role assigned to an enunciated activity* and its objective is *to find out the extent to which the activities have one or more roles allocated*.

The result of this activity is a nonfunctional requirements specification artifact, which has 48 definitions including 17 sub-characteristics and 31 attributes.

The second activity is Design the Measurement. For each attribute in the requirements tree a metric was assigned; e.g. the indirect metric *Role-to-Activity Allocation Availability Degree (RAAAD)* quantifies the *1.1.1.5* attribute. The metric objective is *to quantify how many process activities have an allocated role with regard to the total amount of enunciated activities*; also it has the following formula specification:

$$RAAAD = \begin{cases} \text{If } \mathbf{TEA} = 0 \rightarrow 0 \\ \text{If } \mathbf{TEA} > 0 \rightarrow (\#\mathbf{AAR} / \mathbf{TEA}) \times 100 \end{cases} \tag{1}$$

Where, *TEA* stands for *Total number of Enunciated Activities;* and *#AAR* for *Number of Activities with Allocated Role*. The metric scale is *numerical* and its unit is *percentage (%)*.

The metric specification document consists of 54 metrics (direct and indirect) to quantify the 31 attributes of the requirements tree.

Table 1. Measured values of direct metrics used for calculating the RAAAD indirect metric

	GOCAME	GQM⁺Strategies
Total number of Enunciated Activities (TEA)	47	101
Number of Activities with Allocated Role (#AAR)	0	18

Then, the next activity is Implement the Measurement. Data collection was performed from Sept. to Dec., 2010 based on published and accessible material as commented at the beginning of Section 2. We used the most relevant documents disregarding those that were not coauthored by at least one member of the authors of the original research. Moreover, we gave greater priority to the most current documents when they represented a contribution with regard to previous ones.

To our example, the indirect metric *RAAAD* result was *0%* for GOCAME and *17.82%* for GQM⁺Strategies. These values are calculated from measurement values in Table 1 and Eq. 1.

Table 2. Requirements tree -attributes are in italic (1st column). In the rest of columns, legend (1) shows the indicator values in % for GOCAME, and legend (2) for GQM+Strategies

	(1)	(2)
1.**Capability Quality** (for an integrated M&E strategy)	66.48	45.89
1.1.Process Capability Quality	58.88	54.34
1.1.1.Activities Suitability	46.67	38.37
1.1.1.1.Activities Description Availability	31.91	24.75
1.1.1.2. Activities Description Completeness	15.47	14.40
1.1.1.3.Process Breakdown Structure Granularity	70	70
1.1.1.4. Activities Description Formality	100	61.39
1.1.1.5.Role-to-Activity Allocation Availability	0	17.82
1.1.2.Artifacts Suitability	3	31.58
1.1.2.1.Artifacts Description Availability	0	27.59
1.1.2.2.Artifacts Description Completeness	0	26.96
1.1.2.3.Artifacts Breakdown Structure Granularity	30	70
1.1.3.Process Modeling Suitability	83.56	70.70
1.1.3.1.Functional View Suitability	88	76.42
1.1.3.1.1.Functional View Availability	100	100
1.1.3.1.2.Functional View Completeness	100	61.39
1.1.3.1.3.Functional View Granularity	70	70
1.1.3.2.Informational View Suitability	82.13	74.97
1.1.3.2.1.Informational View Availability	100	100
1.1.3.2.2.Informational View Completeness	90.32	72.41
1.1.3.2.3.Informational View Granularity	30	30
1.1.3.3.Behavioral View Suitability	88	60.42
1.1.3.3.1.Behavioral View Availability	100	100
1.1.3.3.2.Behavioral View Completeness	100	61.39
1.1.3.3.3.Behavioral View Granularity	70	30
1.1.3.4.Organizational View Suitability	0	63.78
1.1.3.4.1.Organizational View Availability	0	100
1.1.3.4.2.Organizational View Completeness	0	44.44
1.1.3.4.3.Organizational View Granularity	0	30
1.1.4.Process Compliance	85.79	71.11
1.1.4.1.Process-to-Concept-Base Terminological Compliance	94.74	88.89
1.1.4.2.M&E Process Standards Compliance	50	0
1.2.Conceptual-Framework Capability Quality	75.09	35.82
1.2.1.Conceptual Framework Suitability	75	25
1.2.1.1.Conceptual Framework Modularity	50	0
1.2.1.2.Conceptual Conceptual Framework Modeling Formality	100	50
1.2.2.Conceptual Base Suitability	68.53	18.53
1.2.2.1.Conceptual Base Completeness	21.33	1.33
1.2.2.2.Conceptual Base Structure Richness	100	30
1.2.3.Conceptual Framework Compliance	84.31	81.82
1.2.3.1.Framework-to-C-Base Terminological Compliance	84.31	81.82
1.3. Methodology Capability Quality	77.43	57.35
1.3.1.Methodology Suitability	83.19	51.88
1.3.1.1.Methodology Availability	100	100
1.3.1.2.Method-to-Activity Completeness	82.98	29.70
1.3.1.3.Methodology Automated Support Availability	50	0
1.3.2.Methodology Compliance	73.68	61.11
1.3.2.1.Methodology-to-C-Base Terminological Compliance	73.68	61.11

The next activity is Design the Evaluation –both elementary and global. For each attribute in the requirements tree, which represents an elementary nonfunctional requirement, an elementary indicator that interprets it was defined. For example, *Performance of Role-to-Activity Allocation Availability (P_RAAA)* is the indicator name for the *1.1.1.5* attribute, and its elementary model is specified as a direct mapping.

Regarding the global evaluation, we selected the LSP (*Logic Scoring of Preference*) model [6] for calculating the requirements tree partial/global indicators. LSP is a weighted multi-criteria aggregation model, which has operators for modeling simultaneity (C –conjunctive- operators) and replaceability (D –disjunctive- operators) relationships between attributes and (sub-)concepts. Thus, the C-+ weak conjunction operator lets modeling the simultaneity criterion among the *1.1*, *1.2* and *1.3* sub-concepts, yielding zero if one input was zero. It is worth remarking that this was one of the criteria for pre-selecting integrated strategies as indicated in the introduction of Section 2.

Regarding decision criteria we have used three acceptability levels for interpreting indicator values in percentage scale. A value between [0-50) represents an *unsatisfactory level* and means *that change actions must be taken with high priority*. A value between [50-75) represents a *marginal level* and means that *improvement actions should be taken*. While a value between [75-100] corresponds to a *satisfactory level*.

So the next activity is Implement the Evaluation. In this process we calculated each elementary indicator taking into account the measured value and its elementary model as well. For example, the elementary indicator value to *Role-to-Activity Allocation Availability* attribute is *0%* for GOCAME and *17.82%* for GQM$^+$Strategies. Finally, once calculated all elementary indicators, by enacting the LSP aggregation model, all partial/global indicators values are yielded. Table 2 shows in the 2nd and 3rd columns the resulting elementary, partial and global indicator values for both strategies.

The following section discusses in detail the results of the last activity named Analyze and Recommend. Once many of given recommendations were implemented in GOCAME during 2011, we carried out its first re-evaluation. For the re-evaluation we used the same M&E requirements with the aim yielded values were repeatable and comparable among studies.

4   Analysis, Recommendation and Improvement

The output of the Analyze and Recommend process is a conclusion and recommendation report comprised of tables, comparison charts, among other mechanisms. This report summarizes for instance strengths and weaknesses, and also recommends change actions to facilitate further improvements.

Below we address the analysis mainly for the GOCAME strategy considering those attributes that have to be improved in order to increase their satisfaction levels. Additionally, improvement recommendations arise not only from GOCAME indicators with weaker performance but also from GQM$^+$Strategies indicators with stronger score. Although the global satisfaction level achieved is lower for GQM$^+$Strategies, there are some well-scored elementary indicators that can be taken into account when planning improvements for GOCAME.

Based on Table 2, we can observe for the *Capability Quality* that GOCAME met a marginal satisfaction level for its global indicator (66.48%, which means that actions for improvement should be taken), while GQM⁺Strategies achieved an unsatisfactory acceptability level (45.89%, which means that must change).

Considering the simultaneity criterion for the three sub-characteristics of the *Capability Quality* focus concept, we observe for GOCAME that the *1.1 Process Capability Quality* falls in the marginal level (58.88); the *1.2 Conceptual-Framework Capability Quality* gets a satisfactory level (75.09); and for *1.3 Methodology Capability Quality* the indicator value is also satisfactory (77.43). As general conclusion, it emerges that GOCAME should strengthen its process. So to improve it we have to analyze and plan which change actions should be prioritized. Next four sub-sections discuss recommendations for each capability and actions taken (if any).

4.1   Process Capability Quality: Analysis, Recommendation and Improvement

The process capability quality sub-characteristics in the unsatisfactory level are namely *1.1.1 Activities Suitability* (46.67%), and *1.1.2 Artifacts Suitability* (3%). Let's start analyzing *1.1.1* and its three attributes which fall in the unsatisfactory level as shown in Table 2.

The attributes *1.1.1.1 Activities Description Availability* (31.91) and *1.1.1.2 Activities Description Completeness* (15.47) are quantified by indirect metrics composed of direct metrics (see Table 3) that deal with the total number of enunciated activities and the number of described activities (either minimally, partially, or completely described ones). We considered an activity is enunciated when it belongs to the process under analysis and has a unique name, or label; also, an activity is completely described when it is an enunciated activity and has explicit and textual specifications of *objective*, *description*, *pre-condition*, *post-condition*, *input* and *output* metadata. The design of these metrics was thoroughly specified in [11]. The metric specification and measured values for its direct metrics (e.g. as shown Table 3 for GOCAME), help us to understand the reasons why the elementary indicator ranks unsatisfactorily, and allow us to make recommendations for planning improvement actions.

Table 3. Measured values of direct metrics used for calculating indirect metrics for 1.1.1.1 and 1.1.1.2 attributes: In 1st column are direct metrics' names, 2nd column shows values gathered in the first evaluations (2010), and 3rd shows measures collected in the re-evaluation (2011).

	2010	2011
Total number of Enunciated Activities (TEA)	47	49
Number of Minimally Described Activities (#MDA)	5	45
Number of Partially Described Activities (#PDA)	10	45
Number of Completely Described Activities (#CDA)	0	31

The R1 recommendation in Table 4 shows two suggested actions to improve both attributes. Once change actions from R1 were planned and performed, the indicator value for *1.1.1.1* attribute will get a maximum level –if it were totally implemented– because its metric is a function of the enunciated activities and minimally described activities i.e. it has *objective* and *description* fields. The same applies to the *1.1.1.2* attribute once all abovementioned template fields for all the activities are filled.

It is worth mentioning that these improvement actions have already been done in

198   F. Papa

GOCAME. As shown in Table 5, the *1.1.1.1* indicator value increases from 31.91 to 91.84% (representing a positive impact, which in terms of difference is by 59.92), while the *1.1.1.2* indicator value goes from 15.47 to 81.45 (which represents a positive difference of 65.97).

Table 4. Summary of recommendations for the GOCAME process: 1ˢᵗ column represents the recommendation code; the 2ⁿᵈ shows its description; the 3ʳᵈ indicates the attribute to be improved and the 4ᵗʰ the change priority, i.e. MT means action must be taken and ST action should be taken. Last column shows if the change was made (R), it is pending (P), and not required (NR).

ID	Process Capability Recommendation	Attribute	Priority	Action
R1	1. Specify a template with the metadata required for a completely described activity. 2. Describe each enunciated activity filling the template.	1.1.1.1 1.1.1.2	MT	R
R2	1. Define used roles/responsibilities in the M&E process. 2. Assign one or more roles to each enunciated activity.	1.1.1.5	MT	R
R3	1. Analyze each process activity if can be divided in atomic activities.	1.1.1.3	ST	P
R4	1. Specify a template with the metadata required for a completely described artifact. 2. Describe each enunciated artifact filling the template.	1.1.2.1 1.1.2.2	MT	P
R5	1. Analyze each enunciated artifact to determine whether it can be divided in atomic sub-artifacts and be manageable from the configuration baseline standpoint.	1.1.2.3	MT	R
R6	1. Model processes from the organizational point of view considering all enunciated activities and roles are included.	1.1.3.4.1 1.1.3.4.2	MT	R
R7	1. Determine if models of the organizational view can be subdivided hierarchically into sub-views.	1.1.3.4.3	MT	R
R8	1. Determine if models of the informational view can be subdivided hierarchically into sub-views.	1.1.3.2.3	MT	R

As result of changes, GOCAME has currently two more enunciated activities (49) than before, being now 45 activities minimally described and 31 completely described activities (as shown in Table 3). The new data collection was made on the document published in [5].

On the other hand, the indirect metric that quantifies the attribute *1.1.1.5 Role-to-Activity Allocation Availability* uses the total number of enunciated activities and the number of activities with assigned roles as per Eq. 1. Considering that the indicator value was 0%, therefore the R2 recommendation emerged (see Table 4). In this case, GQM⁺Strategies helped us accomplishing this recommendation, since it has a set of enunciated roles –though seldom with their responsibilities defined. In order to perform R2, 13 roles and their responsibilities were defined in GOCAME. These roles were assigned to higher-level activities. As result of changes GOCAME has now 16 activities with allocated roles, however, the level of satisfaction met is still unsatisfactory, i.e. it upgraded by 32.56% as shown in Table 5.

Additionally, closer to the upper threshold of the marginal acceptability level is the indicator value for the *1.1.1.3 Process Breakdown Structure Granularity* attribute, which scored 70%. So we could work on it to improve it. The 100% of its satisfaction can be achieved when the whole process has fine-grained activity decomposition. Thus, in Table 4, R3 is the recommendation to reach that score. In GOCAME two activities were added, however, these do not represent an increase in the process granularity. So this improvement change was not tackled yet.

Table 5. Impact of changes for the process capability in GOCAME: 1st column shows process capability attributes (enhanced ones are shaded); 2nd and 3rd columns represent indicator values (in %) before and after improvements were made; last column indicates whether the change was positive (↑), negative (↓), or without variation (↔) and relative change values.

	2010	2011		Diff.
1.Capability Quality (for M&E strategy)	66.48	71.44	↑	4.96
1.1.Process Capability Quality	58.88	73.26	↑	14.38
1.1.1.Activities Suitability	46.67	80.29	↑	33.62
1.1.1.1.Activities Description Availability	31.91	91.84	↑	59.92
1.1.1.2. Activities Description Completeness	15.47	81.45	↑	65.97
1.1.1.3.Process Breakdown Structure Granularity	70	70	↔	0
1.1.1.4. Activities Description Formality	100	95.92	↓	-4.08
1.1.1.5.Role-to-Activity Allocation Availability	0	32.65	↑	32.65
1.1.2.Artifacts Suitability	3	7	↑	4
1.1.2.1.Artifacts Description Availability	0	0	↔	0
1.1.2.2.Artifacts Description Completeness	0	0	↔	0
1.1.2.3.Artifacts Breakdown Structure Granularity	30	70	↑	40
1.1.3.Process Modeling Suitability	83.56	89.26	↑	5.70
1.1.3.1.Functional View Suitability	88	86.78	↓	-1.22
1.1.3.1.1.Functional View Availability	100	100	↔	0
1.1.3.1.2.Functional View Completeness	100	95.92	↓	-4.08
1.1.3.1.3.Functional View Granularity	70	70	↔	0
1.1.3.2.Informational View Suitability	82.13	91.65	↑	9.52
1.1.3.2.1.Informational View Availability	100	100	↔	0
1.1.3.2.2.Informational View Completeness	90.32	94.12	↑	3.80
1.1.3.2.3.Informational View Granularity	30	70	↑	40
1.1.3.3.Behavioral View Suitability	88	86.78	↓	-1.22
1.1.3.3.1.Behavioral View Availability	100	100	↔	0
1.1.3.3.2.Behavioral View Completeness	100	95.92	↓	-4.08
1.1.3.3.3.Behavioral View Granularity	70	70	↔	0
1.1.3.4.Organizational View Suitability	0	94	↑	94
1.1.3.4.1.Organizational View Availability	0	100	↑	100
1.1.3.4.2.Organizational View Completeness	0	100	↑	100
1.1.3.4.3.Organizational View Granularity	0	70	↑	70
1.1.4.Process Compliance	85.79	85.79	↔	0
1.1.4.1.Process-to-Concept-Base Terminological Compliance	94.74	94.74	↔	0
1.1.4.2.M&E Process Standards Compliance	50	50	↔	0

As abovementioned, the *1.1.2 Artifacts Suitability* sub-characteristic met an unsatisfactory level (3%) as well. So, improvement actions for its attributes are analyzed and recommended. Particularly, for *1.1.2.1 Artifacts Description Availability* and *1.1.2.2 Artifacts Description Completeness* attributes, their indicator values were 0%. They are quantified by metrics which deal with enunciated artifacts and described artifacts. An artifact is completely described when it is enunciated and has explicitly specified the *objective*, *description*, and the *activity name* which create/modify it. The R4 recommendation (Table 4) gives the hint for planning the change, but the improvement actions at this moment are still pending of completion. However, by following R5 we have improved the *1.1.2.3 Artifacts Breakdown Structure Granularity* attribute raising the value from 30 to 70 (Table 5). In this case, we also considered as reference the GQM+Strategies elementary indicator which ranked 70%, as shown in Table 2.

Finally, the *1.1.3 Process Modeling Suitability* sub-characteristic ranked satisfactorily (83.56%). Table 2 also shows that the functional (*1.1.3.1*), informational (*1.1.3.2*) and behavioral process (*1.1.3.3*) views suitability are in the satisfactory level. However, the *Organizational View Suitability* (*1.1.3.4*) sub-characteristic is totally missing (0%). Table 4 shows the R6 recommendation whose improvement action embraces to *1.1.3.4.1 Organizational View Availability* and *1.1.3.4.2 Organizational View Completeness* attributes; also R7 is the recommendation for the *1.1.3.4.3 Organizational View Granularity* attribute. Note that for planning the improvement for these three attributes, the GQM+Strategies strengths were also considered. In [5], all enunciated roles assigned to main GOCAME activities, and a hierarchy of roles are documented. Consequently, the positive impact of improvement was very important for the *1.1.3.4 Organizational View Suitability* sub-characteristic going from 0 to 94% as shown in Table 5.

Lastly, Table 4 shows recommendations for the *Process Capability Quality* characteristic; however, some recommendation actions are still in progress. Note that also there were negative impacts, which it will be addressed in sub-section 4.4.

4.2   Conceptual-Framework   Capability   Quality: Analysis   and Recommendation

For the *1.2 Conceptual-Framework Capability Quality* sub-characteristic, its indicator value scored satisfactorily (75.09% in Table 2). Looking in turn at its sub-concepts only *1.2.2 Conceptual Base Suitability* fell in a marginal acceptability level (68.53%), while the others (*1.2.1* and *1.2.3*) reached the satisfactory level. Therefore, the most important recommendation for improvement arises from the analysis of the *1.2.2.1 Conceptual Base Completeness* attribute, which had low performance (21.33%). The recommendation statement emerges from the analysis of the metric specification, i.e., the indirect metric's calculation method that quantifies *1.2.2.1* is specified as a ratio of the level of correspondence between terms defined in the conceptual base and standards, and the total number of terms defined in standards. It is important to remark that the terms added to the terminological base –regardless whether be structured as glossary or ontology- should also be included in the conceptual framework, in order to not affect the *1.2.3.1 Conceptual Framework-to-Conceptual Base Terminological Compliance* indicator performance.

Additionally, in order to increase the score of the *1.2* capability quality evaluators can recommend improving the *1.2.1.1 Conceptual Framework Modularity* attribute, which scored 50%. This attribute is quantified by a direct metric that measures the degree to which the conceptual framework is divided into different modules or components. It is expected a conceptual framework includes components to manage projects, nonfunctional requirements, context, measurement, evaluation, and analysis/recommendations. Also several of them can be divided into design and implementation as well. GOCAME has considered this concern taking into account 6 mentioned modules. Nevertheless, an opportunity for improvement is that some modules can be split into design and implementation sub-modules.

Note that recommendations for this capability have not been implemented yet, so that the satisfaction level has not changed. Recall that first we have prioritized improvement actions for the *Process Capability Quality* (1.1), which was the weakest capability (58.88%) out of three.

4.3   Methodology Capability Quality: Analysis and Recommendation

For the *1.3 Methodology Capability Quality* sub-characteristic its indicator value scored also satisfactorily, i.e. 77.43% (Table 2). In addition, we can observe that the *1.3.1 Methodology Suitability* sub-characteristic met 83.19% even though the satisfaction level for its *1.3.1.3 Methodology Automated Support Availability* attribute scored marginally (50%). So, for improving this attribute the recommendation should considering two aspects, namely: 1) For the identified parts of the methodology without tool support, analyze for each part if automated support is feasible; 2) If feasible, implement the tool.

Additionally, in order to increase the score of the *1.3* capability quality evaluators can recommend improving the *1.3.2.1 Methodology-to-Conceptual Base Terminological Compliance* attribute, which scored in the upper limit of the marginal acceptability level, i.e. 73.68%. Hence, the following recommendation should be taken into account: Methodology descriptions should be documented adhering as much as possible to terms and definitions of the GOCAME terminological base.

Note that recommendations for this capability have not been implemented yet, so that the satisfaction level has not changed. In the next sub-section, we discuss the impact of performed changes after re-evaluation, which are summarized in Table 5.

4.4   Discussing Positive and Negative Impacts of Performed Changes

As discussed in sub-section 4.1, so far many improvement recommendations belonging to *Process Capability Quality* have been implemented either partially or totally. Therefore, change actions caused the process satisfaction level to increase by 14.38 points (considering the difference between the 2011 and 2010 results), while the global satisfaction level (i.e. the GOCAME *Capability Quality*) has increased by 4.96 points (see Table 5).

As expected, the performed change actions had usually a positive impact but in some attributes caused an undesired effect or negative impact. This was the case for attributes such as *1.1.1.4 Activities Description Formality*, *1.1.3.1.2* and *1.1.3.3.2* (which refer to the completeness of two process modeling views). The negative impact however was negligible due to our adding of two new activities for the M&E process (see TEA values in Table 3), which were not re-considered in the modeling of functional and behavioral views.

On the other hand, indicator values for *1.1.1.5 Role-to-Activity Allocation Availability* and *1.1.3.4.3 Organizational View Granularity* attributes have increased by 32.65 and 70 points respectively. However, the performed improvement was not enough to achieve the satisfactory acceptability level. More re-work is still necessary.

Regarding *Process Modeling Suitability* sub-characteristics the highest improvement gain was in *1.1.3.4* which increased 94 points. Besides, a small improvement gain of 9.52 points for *1.1.3.2 Informational View Suitability* has been met. This was caused mainly by improving the *1.1.3.2.3 Informational View Granularity* attribute.

Finally, it is worth mentioning that improvement changes made so far led to increases in the GOCAME *Capability Quality* indicator value but it has still not met the satisfactory acceptability level. To reach the [75-100] level, it remains to implement many of the improvement actions proposed by the original (2010) study.

However, performing recommended changes sometimes it is not an easy and fast job. For example, we have developed during 2002-2003 an ontology for metrics and indicators, which is the terminological base used in the C-INCAMI framework. This framework has 6 components –as commented in sub-section 2.1- in which this ontology was used totally in 4 modules. However, the <u>Analysis and recommendation specification</u> component has no ontological support until now, even though the process is well defined. Thus, for planning an improvement action for the *1.2.2.1 Conceptual Base Completeness* attribute, an ontology for the analysis and recommendation domain should be engineered. As the reader can surmise, this could take considerable effort and calendar time.

5   Conclusion and Future Work

To summarize, we would like to highlight the particular contributions of this research commented in the Introduction Section. This paper elaborates on the progress achieved using as foundation the comparative study made in 2010 on the *Capability Quality* evaluation of two concrete M&E strategies [11]. By using the same nonfunctional requirements, measurement and evaluation design, and identified strengths and weaknesses, we have gone a step further by: i) planning and implementing change actions aimed at improving GOCAME; and ii) re-evaluating GOCAME based on implemented recommendations in order to gauge the improvement gain in quantitative form.

It is important to remark that from the very beginning of this research our ultimate objective was the improvement of GOCAME, which is a strategy that can be used as an evaluation resource in different stages of a web engineering production line.

Regarding the former contribution, we have planned and implemented improvement recommendations not only considering GOCAME indicators with weaker performance but also GQM$^+$Strategies indicators with stronger performance. We have prioritized change actions mainly for the GOCAME *Process Capability Quality*, which had lower performance.

Regarding the latter contribution, we have re-evaluated GOCAME –using the same requirements and M&E design– after the actual change actions were carried out. Particularly, in sub-section 4.4, we have discussed not only expected positive impacts of changes but also their –negligible– undesired effects. So far, implemented improvement changes in *Process Capability Quality* enhanced its partial indicator from 58.88 to 73.26%. Even if this represents a moderate improvement in the process quality, the calculated *Capability Quality* global indicator increased from 66.48 to 71.44%. This is because many of the recommended changes in the other two capabilities are in progress, so they did factor in upgrading the global indicator value. We have also discussed that performing recommended changes sometimes it is not an easy and fast task.

Lastly, a future line of research is broadening the GOCAME scope in order to give support to M&E information needs (goals) at different organizational levels, following to some extent to GQM$^+$Strategies which does support them.

Acknowledgments. Thanks to the support given from the Science and Technology Agency, Argentina, in the PAE-PICT 2188 project, and to the 09-F047 project at UNLPam, Argentina.

References

1. Basili, V.R., Caldiera, G., Rombach, H.D.: The goal question metric approach. In: Encyclopedia of Software Engineering, vol. 1, pp. 528–532 (1994)
2. Basili, V.R., Heidrich, J., Lindvall, M., Münch, J., Regardie, M., Rombach, H.D., Seaman, C.B., Trendowicz, A.: GQM strategies®: A comprehensive methodology for aligning business strategies with software, pp. 253–266 (2007)
3. Basili, V.R., Lindvall, M., Regardie, M., Seaman, C., Heidrich, J., Jurgen, M., Rombach, D., Trendowicz, A.: Linking Software Development and Business Strategy through Measurement. IEEE Computer 43(4), 57–65 (2010)
4. Becker, P., Molina, H., Olsina, L.: Measurement and Evaluation as quality driver. Journal ISI (Ingénierie des Systèmes d'Information), Special Issue: Quality of Information Systems 15(6), 33–62 (2010)
5. Becker, P., Lew, P., Olsina, L.: Specifying Process Views for a Measurement, Evaluation and Improvement Strategy. Advances in Software Engineering Journal 2012, 28 (2012), Open Access at http://www.hindawi.com/journals/ase/contents/, doi:10.1155/2012/949746
6. Dujmovic, J.J.: A Method for Evaluation and Selection of Complex Hardware and Software Systems. In: 22nd Int'l Conference for the Resource Management and Performance Evaluation of Enterprise CS. CMG 96 Proceedings, vol. 1, pp. 368–378 (1996)
7. Lew, P., Olsina, L., Becker, P., Zhang, L.: An Integrated Strategy to Understand and Manage Quality in Use for Web Applications. Requirements Engineering Journal 16(3), 1–32 (2011), Loucopoulos P., Mylopoulos, J. (Eds.), doi:10.1007/s00766-011-0128-x
8. Mora, B., García, F., Ruiz, F., Piattini, M., Boronat, A., Gómez, A., Carsí, J.Á., Ramos, I.: Software generic measurement framework based on MDA. IEEE Latin America Transactions 6(4), 363–370 (2008)
9. Olsina, L., Rossi, G.: Measuring Web Application Quality with WebQEM. IEEE Multimedia Magazine 9(4), 20–29 (2002)
10. Olsina, L., Papa, F., Molina, H.: How to Measure and Evaluate Web Applications in a Consistent Way. In: Rossi, G., Pastor, O., Schwabe, D., Olsina, L. (eds.) Springer Book: Web Engineering: Modeling and Implementing Web Applications, ch. 13, pp. 385–420 (2008)
11. Olsina, L., Papa, M.F., Becker, P.: Assessing Integrated Measurement and Evaluation Strategies: A Case Study. In: IEEE Xplore, 7th Central Eastern European Software Engineering Conference, Moscow, Russia, pp. 1–10 (2011) ISSN: 978-1-4673-0844-1/11
12. Rodríguez, M., Genero, M., Torre, D., Blasco, B., Piattini, M.: A Methodology for Continuous Quality Assessment of Software Artifacts. In: 10th International Conference on Quality Software (QSIC 2010), pp. 254–261 (2010)
13. Solingen, R.V., Berghout, E.: The Goal/Question/Metric Method: a practical guide for quality improvement of software development. McGraw-Hill Co. (1999)

Evaluation and Comparison of Three Open Courseware Based on Quality Criteria

Monica Vladoiu and Zoran Constantinescu

UPG University of Ploiesti, Romania
{monica,zoran}@unde.ro

Abstract. In spite of the scale, popularity, and importance of the open courseware movement for users worldwide, there is yet no quality assessment framework that could support users on their quest for finding the most appropriate learning resource with regard to their educational needs. This paper presents both an evaluation and a comparison between three open courseware on databases offered by three major open courseware providers, which comply with three different open courseware paradigms. Both evaluation and comparison are based on our set of quality criteria that serve as general guidelines for development, use, modification, evaluation, and comparison of open educational resources and open courseware, from a social and constructivist perspective.

Keywords: open courseware, quality criteria, open courseware on databases.

1 Introduction

During more than one decade, we have been witnessing a paradigm shift of education, training, and learning, which has been triggered by the demands and challenges of emerging knowledge economy and learning society. Learning is now a continuous process that is no longer limited to dedicated spaces, times or modalities, in which borders between providers and consumers of knowledge are blurred. Users, communities, social construction of knowledge, 21st century's information and communication technologies, and open education models constitute the backbone of this paradigm shift that provide for lifelong and lifewide learning. Knowledge is more and more seen as public good that can be accessed, shared, used and reused, adapted etc.

Open courseware and open educational resources projects around the world have a significant contribution to this paradigm shift, as they open access to, otherwise closed, university-level educational materials. More than 10 years have passed since the launch of the MIT OpenCourseWare (OCW) program – now having more than 2100 courses online, which has triggered the emergence of numerous university programs that offer open access to some of their courses that have been developing in parallel with OCW: Stanford Engineering Everywhere, Carnegie Mellon Open Learning Initiative, Harvard's Open Learning Initiative and Harvard Medical School's My-Courses, Open Yale Courses, Webcast.Berkeley, Rice University's Connexions, Open University's OpenLearn, Open.Michigan, and so on. Besides these open courseware initiatives hosted by major universities, large open courseware reposito-

M. Grossniklaus and M. Wimmer (Eds.): ICWE 2012 Workshops, LNCS 7703, pp. 204–215, 2012.
© Springer-Verlag Berlin Heidelberg 2012

ries are available as well: OpenCourseWare Consortium, Open Education Resources (OER) Commons, and The Saylor Foundation's Free Education Initiative [1, 2].

Despite the magnitude, pervasiveness, and impact of the open courseware movement, on users worldwide, there is yet no quality assessment framework that could provide support for users. Thus, learners need guidance for choosing the most appropriate educational resources that fulfills their educational needs, while instructors are interested in support for instructional activities, which provide for achievement of learning goals, objectives, and outcomes, along with reflective learning. Faculty or institutions that are or want to become involved in the open courseware movement may be interested in the challenges and rewards of this process. Though, there is preoccupation about articulating a set of criteria for quality assessment, which may be used to support construction, evaluation and comparison of open courseware and open educational resources and repositories. However, the related work is extremely thin, with just a few works approaching the general subject of quality of open courseware and OERs in the context of assessing the impact of these paradigms in education nowadays. All these works emphasize on the importance of the quality of OERs and OCW, and on the need for continuous quality evaluation and assurance [3-10]. Still, none of these works has attempted to elaborate a set of quality criteria to be used for quality evaluation and assurance.

In this paper we evaluate and compare quality-wise three open courseware on databases offered by three major open courseware providers that comply with three different open courseware paradigms. The comparison is guided by our set of socio-constructivist quality criteria that serve as general guidelines for development, use, modification, evaluation, and comparison of open courseware and OERs [11]. Moreover, this work attempts to work those quality criteria on the chosen open courseware, and to learn, based on this experience, how to develop further the initial set of quality criteria.

The structure of the paper is as follows: the second section presents briefly our set of quality criteria, the third one introduces the three "candidates" for comparison, the fourth presents the evaluation and comparison of the three open courseware based on the quality criteria, and the last consists of some conclusions and future work ideas.

2   Criteria for Quality Assurance of OER and OCW

In this section, we present briefly a set of criteria for quality assessment of open educational resources and open courseware that has been introduced and presented in more detail in [11]. They may be used for quality evaluation of either small learning units or an entire courseware. These criteria have been grouped in four categories related with content, instructional design, technology and courseware evaluation. They correspond to quality characteristics of *quality in use*, *internal and external product quality* according to ISO/IEC 25000 SQuaRE standard, and cover the following user needs: effectiveness, efficiency, satisfaction, reliability, security, context coverage, learnability, and accessibility.

Content Related. This category includes criteria that reveal to what degree the educational resource allows learners having engaging learning experiences that provide for mastery of the content, such as: *readability, uniformity of language, terminology, and notations, availability of the course syllabus, comprehensiveness of the lecture notes, modularity of the course content, possibility to select the most suitable learning unit, opportunity to choose the most appropriate learning path, top-down, bottom-up or combined approach,* and *availability of assignments (with or without solutions).*

When considering only a particular learning resource - a small learning unit, a course module, a lesson etc., users may be interested in various aspects related to that resource: *accuracy, reasonableness, self-containedness, context, relevance, availability of multimedia inserts,* and *resource's correlation with the course in its entirety.*

Instructional Design Related. Criteria refer to *resource's goal and learning objectives, appropriate instructional activities, learning outcomes, availability of the evaluation and auto-evaluation means (with or without solutions), learning theory, the instructional design model* used for that particular educational *resource, and reflective learning* proneness. Outcome of reflective education is the construction of coherent functional knowledge structures adaptable to further lifelong learning [12-15].

Technology Related. In this category we find aspects of *compliance with standards for interoperability and accessibility, extensibility, reliability, user interface's navigational regard to the at user's end (both hardware and software),* along with *the prerequisite skills to use that technology, multi-platform capability, supporting tools,* and s*ecurity of user confidential information.*

Courseware Evaluation. In spite of the original statement of just offering high quality educational materials to users around the world, with no further aim to support them during their educational journeys, all major open courseware initiatives have recently become more involved with their learners. Therefore, regular assessment of effectiveness of open courseware becomes crucial. Moreover, the results of the evaluation may be used for further improvements. First criterion to be considered here is the *courseware overview,* which includes *information about the content scope and sequence, the intended audience, the grade level, the periodicity of updating the content, the author's credentials and the source credibility, its availability in multiple-languages, instructor facilitation or some kind of semi-automated support, suitableness for self-study and/or classroom-based study and/or peer collaborative study, the time requirements, the grading policy,* along with *instructions about using* the courseware and its components.

Other criteria included in this category are as follows: *availability of prerequisite knowledge, availability of required competencies, matching the course schedule with learner's own pace, availability of repository or institutional policies, bias and advertising freeness, option to provide a formal degree or a certificate of completion, user interface, appropriate design,* and *suitable presentation of educational content.* Some *participatory culture and Web 2.0* facets are also relevant when evaluating the quality of open courseware: contribution to the content, collaboration with fellow users, collection of users' feedback, sharing the development or using experience.

3   Three Open Courseware on Databases

In this section we provide a brief presentation of the three open courseware that offer educational materials on databases. We have chosen these particular educational resources because they are offered by three major open courseware providers, and because they comply with three different open courseware paradigms. The three candidates for quality evaluation and comparison are the MIT OpenCourseWare on *Database Systems* [16], The Saylor Foundation's *Introduction to Modern Database Systems* courseware [17], and Stanford's *Introduction to Databases* courseware [18].

3.1   MIT OpenCourseWare on Database Systems

MIT OpenCourseWare is a web-based free publication of virtually all MIT course content. OCW is open and available to the world and it is a permanent MIT activity. The course materials reflect almost all the undergraduate and graduate subjects taught at MIT. However, OCW does not stand for a formal MIT education, and it does not grant university degrees or certificates. Moreover, the course materials may not mirror the entire content of a course [16].

The *Database Systems* course is one of the 2100 MIT courses that have been made freely available via the MIT OCW site [19]. It is an introductory course on foundations of database systems that addresses to graduate students with no prior database experience. Courseware overview includes the course topics, the prerequisites, information about grading, and the course readings. While some of this information is of interest only for MIT students, other is also useful for MIT OCW users. Selected lecture notes, assignments without solutions, and exams with solutions are available too.

3.2   The Saylor Foundation's Introduction to Modern Database Systems

Saylor.org has been launched by The Saylor Foundation as a free online university. *The saylor.org is seen as a zero-cost alternative to those who lack the resources to attend traditional brick-and-mortar institutions, and as a complement to mainstream education providers that will both motivate people around the world to pursue personal growth and career ambitions, and lead to institutional change amongst education providers* [20]. The Foundation's goal is to offer to many individuals the opportunity to overcome the barriers of attending mainstream college education: fixed class schedule, physical distance to a campus, rising costs related to tuition, fee, and textbooks etc. For now, saylor.org offers appropriate content that a student needs to know in order to earn the equivalent of a degree in any of the top majors in the USA.

Introduction to Modern Database Systems is one of the 200 courses freely available at The Saylor Foundation site, which is mandatory for the Computer Science program [17]. This course provides students with an introduction to modern database systems. The courseware overview includes learning outcomes, course requirements, and learning units. Syllabus, readings, web media lectures, automated assessments and final exam are also available from the course home page.

3.3   Stanford's Introduction to Databases

Stanford's Professor Jennifer Widom has taken the challenge of a "flipped classroom" and has made freely available the online version of the *Introduction to Databases* course. While courses at Stanford are normally videotaped for internal purposes, the challenge consisted of "purpose-building" better videos, which were shorter, topic-specific segments that were spiced with in-video quizzes that allowed learners to check their understanding. That approach would have made the class more attractive for students and instructors, providing for interactive activities, interesting topics, and guest speakers [21]. The online version of the *Introduction to Databases* course is the result of taking that challenge. Available courseware may be used either on learner's self pace, in a "self-serve" mode, or by sticking to the tight course schedule. Course materials and video lectures, automated assignments and exams, extra exercises, software quick guides, Q&A Forum, and weekly "screenside" chats are offered.

4   Comparison between Three Open Courseware on Databases

This section includes an evaluation of each of the three open courseware on databases that have been presented in brief in the previous section. The three courseware have been evaluated based on the quality criteria introduced in [11], and presented here in a few words in Section 3. For the time being, the inspection procedure is informal and each criterion has been evaluated in a qualitative manner based on the evaluators' perspective and experience on teaching Databases for more than 20 years. A comparison between them follows the evaluation.

4.1   MIT OCW on Database Systems vs. The Quality Criteria

This section includes our quality evaluation based on the proposed quality criteria for the MIT OCW on *Database Systems*.

Content-Related. The *readability* of the course material is very different as the learning units have different authors. The selected lecture note available as .pdf files are the work of two instructors. One of them has written very telegraphic notes that are very valuable, of course, as the instructor is one of the most well-known names in databases (a true titan of the field), but they are very hard to read and comprehend for someone who has no previous knowledge of databases. The other, however, has provided textbook style lecture notes, which can be read and followed far more easily for inexperienced learners. The *uniformity* of the materials is also impaired by this dualism. The *course syllabus* for the course taught in Fall 2010 is offered. The courseware is *modular* and quite *comprehensive* with very few lecture notes unavailable, and providing both *assignments (no solutions)* and exams (with solutions). Selection of the *most suitable learning unit and learning path* can be done easily provided that the learner has previous familiarity with databases. The courseware may be approached *top-down, bottom up or combined.* Each instructional resource is *accurate, reasonable, self-contained, relevant in the context* of learning about databases, and *correlated* with the entire course. No *multimedia inserts* are provided. Only *links* to readings available on amazon.com are provided.

Instructional Design Related. The general *instructional goal* is presented in the course description. The *course syllabus* presents only the *learning objectives* and the *learning outcomes* of the entire course, there is no such offering for the learning units. The available instructional materials provide only for *basic instructional activities.* The only *auto-evaluation or evaluation* means are the exams of 2008, along with their solutions. *Reflective learning* has not been yet considered for this course. No information about *learning theory* or *instructional design* is given.

Technology Related. The courseware complies with *interoperability* standards. The *web accessibility* issues are detailed in the FAQ technology page of the OCW Help. However, a direct link to that page from the course page would be useful. Only the instructors may *extend the instructional resources.* The user interface is basic. *Prerequisite skills* of using the technology are not explicitly stated because they are, probably, considered too basic. The courseware may be used *reliably* on *multi-platforms*, and the *technical requirements* and *supporting tools* are described in Help FAQ Technology page. Privacy and Terms of Use page presents the issues of *privacy and security of confidential information.*

Courseware Evaluation. The *content scope and sequence* may be deduced from the Course Calendar page. The intended *audience* or *grade level* is explicitly affirmed in the course home page. No information about periodicity of updating is available. *Authors' credentials* and *source credibility* are, definitely, exceptionally high. No availability in *multiple languages* nor *support for learners* have been provided. The courseware may be used for *self-study or classroom based study. Time requirements* to cover the course materials are not available. *Grading policy* is presented, but it refers only to MIT students. Getting started section of the OCW Help provides *instructions on "how to"* use the courseware and its components.

The *prerequisite knowledge* and *required competencies* are revealed in the Syllabus page. The learners may use the courseware at *their own pace*, so there is no matching problem regarding the course schedule. *Repository policies* are presented in the Terms of Use page. The courseware is *free of bias and advertising.* For the time being, no *degree or certificate of completion* is obtainable. Learners may not *contribute* to the resources nor *collaborate* with fellow learners. *Feedback* from users may be given only via the Contact us form. Inside information about the OCW challenge and *development journey*, in general, are available in the About us page. No such information about the *Database Systems* courseware is given. The *user interface, design and presentation of the instructional content* are plain.

4.2   Saylor's Courseware on Database Systems vs. The Quality Criteria

We present here our quality assessment based on the proposed quality criteria for Saylor's Courseware *Introduction to Modern Database Systems*.

Content-Related. The *readability and uniformity* of the course materials is quite different as the learning units have different authors. The content is a particular combination of HTML readings, web media lectures, assignments (quizzes and animations) that includes the final exam as well. The instructional materials may come from other institutions, collections or repositories, but there are also some in-house developed ones. They all have been *selected, framed, and/or developed by our professors* so that they will enable the achievement of the stated learning goal is said on saylor.org. The detailed *course syllabus* is available. The courseware is *modular* and very *comprehensive* as shown above. *Assignments (with solutions)* are offered. Selection of the *most suitable learning unit and learning path* can be done easily as the courseware is very intuitively built. The courseware may be approached *top-down, bottom up or combined*. Each instructional resource is *accurate, reasonable, self-contained, relevant in the context* of learning about databases, and *correlated* with the entire course. *Multimedia inserts* are provided. Only *links* to the course readings are available.

Instructional Design Related. The general *instructional goal* is presented both in the *course syllabus* and in the course home page. The *learning objectives and outcomes* are available at two levels: course-wide and learning unit-wide. Diverse *instructional activities* provide for meaningful learning experiences and stimulate *reflective learning*. Dynamic and animated *auto-evaluation or evaluation* means are accompanied by either answer keys, guides to responding, or self-assessment rubrics (a list of criteria that can be used to determine the quality of a work) so that learners themselves can evaluate their own work. Each time the final exam is taken learners are offered different questions. No information about *learning theory* or *instructional design* is given.

Technology Related. *Interoperability* standards are fulfilled by the courseware. Accessibility is approached only in its larger sense rather than as *web accessibility*. Only the instructors may *extend the instructional resources*. The *user interface* is advanced and appropriate. The Saylor Student Handbook includes the supporting *technical requirements*, along with *some prerequisite skills* of using the technology. The courseware may be used *reliably* on *multi-platforms*, and the *supporting tools* are described in the handbook as well. Terms of Use page shows the issues of *privacy and security of confidential information*.

Courseware Evaluation. Starts with *courseware overview*. The *content scope and sequence* are presented in the course syllabus and course home page alike. Course *audience* and *grade level* is explicitly approached, but on saylor.org home page not on the database course's one. No information about periodicity of updating is on hand. For some learning units *author's credentials* are obvious, as they are professors at prestigious universities, while for others learners have to rely on *source credibility*, which is considerable in our opinion. The instructional resources are available in English only. The support for learners is semi-automated, being visible mainly on assignments. For now, the courseware may be used for *self-study* and *classroom based study*, but, taking into consideration the latest developments (forums, e-portfolios etc.), it seems that *peer collaborative study* is envisaged as well. Both syllabus and home page provide a *time advisory*, which show the needed time to complete each instructional resource. Student handbook details the *grading policy* and *instructions on "how to"* use the courseware and its components. The *prerequisite knowledge* and *required competencies* are presented in the course home page. Learners may use the courseware at *their own pace*.

Student Handbook includes also the community standards, i. e. the repository policies, along with the statement regarding the *freeness of bias*. The courseware is *free of advertising* as well. After passing the exam with more than 70%, the student is provided with a *certificate of completion* having a unique identification code. For the time being, learners may not *contribute* directly to the resources or *collaborate* with fellow learners. However, they may submit materials that might get chosen to be published on the saylor.org website. *Feedback* from users is collected via a user survey. Some hints about the *development journey* and saylor.org *experience* are presented in the student handbook as well. The *user interface, design and* presentation *of the instructional content* are well elaborated and attractive.

4.3 Stanford's Introduction to Databases vs. The Quality Criteria

We detail here our assessment of the open courseware of *Introduction to Databases* course of Stanford's Professor Jennifer Widom, against the proposed quality criteria.

Content-Related. The text materials that are available in two formats, namely .pdf and .pptx, are easy *readable* and very *uniform* in terms of language, terminology and notations, as they have a unique author. The course *syllabus* is not presented as such, but all the needed information is offered in the course home page. As for the *comprehensiveness of the lecture notes*, they do not include the Entity-Relationship approach for database design, being focused only on database normalization theory. Otherwise, plenty of quizzes, assignments, extra-exercises, demo scripts, quick-guides for relevant software, pointers to textbook readings, and other course materials, are on hand to be used for strengthening the learning process. As the online courseware has been designed from the very beginning as *modular*, the selection of the *most suitable learning unit* or *learning path* is straightforward. The course materials may be approached easily *top-down, bottom-up*, or in a *combined* way. The *assignments* are available without solutions. Professor Widom motivates this with the difficulty to construct so many meaningful assignments annually for each learner cohort. Each instructional resource is *accurate, reasonable, self-contained, relevant in the context* of learning about databases, and *correlated* with the entire course. *Multimedia inserts* are provided. No *links to related resources* are offered, only a list of textbooks.

Instructional Design Related. The general *instructional goal* is stated in the home page, but the *learning objectives* and the *learning outcomes* are not declared explicitly for the entire courseware nor for the learning units. They can be deduced, however, from the course syllabus. The educational materials provide for engaging multiple *instructional activities*, hence for rich opportunities for learning. They include: video lectures, in-video quizzes, course materials, and self-guided exercises, i.e. quizzes that generate different combinations of correct and incorrect answers each time they're launched, and interactive workbenches for topics ranging from XML DTD validation to view-update triggers [18, 21]. To *auto-evaluate* their learning progress learners may use automated assignments, both quizzes and exercises. Automated exams are available for evaluation. In our opinion, the courseware seeds the stimuli for *reflective learning*, especially due to Professor Widom's commitment and personal touch, and to the vibrant collaboration on the Q&A Forum. Moreover, to prevent rapid-fire guessing, the system enforces a minimum of ten minutes between each submission of solutions, so learners have some time to reflect. No information about *learning theory* or *instructional design model* is available.

Technology Related. The courseware complies with *interoperability* standards, and people with *accessibility* issues are invited to contact the support team on the last line of the About us page. Maybe a more visible invitation would be more practical. Instructional resources may be *extended* only by the members of the team. The *user interface* is basic. The supporting *technology requirements* at user's end are not available. *Prerequisite skills* of using the technology are not offered as they are probably considered to basic to mention. The courseware may be used *reliably* on various *platforms*, and the supporting tools are described in Software Quick Guides. The issues of *security of confidential information* are approached in the Terms of Service page.

Courseware Evaluation. *Courseware overview* criteria are considered further on. The *content scope and sequence* are deducible from the Course Schedule. No intended *audience* or *grade level* is explicitly affirmed. Despite the initial claim that it will not be a second database course offered in the immediate future, currently on the home page we learn that the next official offering will be likely in the latter part of 2012 – most probably then some content updating will be available as well. *Author's credentials* and *source credibility* are, of course, extremely high. The courseware is not available in any other language than English, however it has attracted students from 130 countries, top three being USA, India, and Russia. *Support for learners* is provided by instructor only by discussing during the weekly video the top unanswered questions on the Q&A forum. Some semi-automated support exists as well based on quizzes with Gradiance-style grading. Thus, after submitting a selection the system will score the quiz, and for incorrect answers will provide an "explanation" (sometimes for correct ones too), which is supposed to help learners get the right answer the next time around. Moreover, learners get a different variant of each problem of the quizzes on every attempt, so they are advised to continue taking them to reinforce their understanding, even after they have achieved a perfect score on one variant.

The courseware is suitable for *self-study, classroom based study, and peer collaborative study*. No *time requirements* to cover the course materials are available. However, in no "self-serve" mode, the time schedule was very tight, and the learners have been constantly struggling to meet the deadlines. FAQ page presents the *grading policy* and *instructions on "how to"* use the courseware and its components. Multiple-choice midterm and final *exams* are crafted carefully so that the problems are not solvable by just running queries or checking Wikipedia. *Creating these exams, at just the right level, turned out to be one of the most challenging tasks of the entire endeavor*, Professor Widom says.

The *prerequisite knowledge* and *required competencies* are shown in the FAQ page. The learners are allowed to use the courseware at *their own pace*, but the ones choosing that approach were not allowed to get the *statement of accomplishment* offered by Professor Widom. Terms of Service state the *repository policies* to comply with. The courseware is *free of bias and advertising*. Learners may not *contribute* to the resources. However, they may *collaborate* with fellow learners. *Feedback* from users is collected to be used for future improved versions. Professor Widom tells the story of the *development journey* and the *whole experience* in a very touching way on her ACM SIGMOD blog [21]. The *user interface, design and* presentation *of the instructional content* are basic.

4.4   Comparison of the Three Open Courseware Based on the Quality Criteria

We present here a comparison of the three open courseware that have been evaluated in the previous sub-sections. During this section, to make the exposition easier, we will be using three acronyms for the three open courseware: MITOCWDB, SaylorDB and StanfordWidomDB.

As a general idea, the most beneficial for learners in this moment is, in our opinion, StanfordWidomDB due to the commitment and enthusiasm of Professor Widom and her team. Saylor people are also very committed to the idea of offering valuable meaningful experiences, but what has made the difference between the two of them is, in our view, the fact that Professor Widom has involved herself personally (along with the team, of course) in the process, she has been keeping in touch with the learners, and she has confessed having "a grand time"[21], despite the challenges. MITOCWDB, despite the quality of the instructors and materials, lacks the direct connection with and support for its users.

However, both StanfordWidomDB and SaylorDB provide for engaging, reflective learning, based on personal touch only for the former, and on the powerful learning experiences triggered by the well designed instructional materials for both of them. Moreover, both open courseware have considered offering some sort of certificate of completion. Related to that, they have addressed also the cheating issues.

The user interface and supporting framework looks best in SaylorDB due, in our view, to the fact that Saylor.org is thought to become an open online university, where independent learners are ought to return with pleasure and confidence that the courseware materials are connected to them in a *meaningful, unique, transformative way* [20]. The main merit of MITOCWDB is that offers content provided by very high quality Professors, and, in a larger view, that with the OCW movement has started everything. Without it, the other "candidates" would have probably not existed. We conclude this section hoping that having many open courseware available, the struggle for quality will be encouraged for users' benefit, being them learners, instructors, faculty, developers, and even educational institutions.

5   Conclusions and Future Work

The main contribution of this paper consists in evaluating and comparing three open courseware on databases, using a set of quality criteria introduced in an earlier work. The three courseware have been chosen because they come from three major open courseware providers, and they comply with three significantly different open courseware paradigms. This work has tried to put into practice those quality criteria, and to learn from this experience how to develop further the initial quality model.

First thing learned is that there is no preoccupation yet for considering explicitly learning theories or instructional design models. Furthermore, new quality criteria have proven to be necessary. They include: support for learners coming from other learners, opportunity for peer collaborative learning, availability of quick guides of relevant software, and providing links to related relevant resources. Some criteria need to be extended. For example, accessibility needs to be seen at a higher level, not only as web accessibility, but as concerning access to as many people as possible to the open educational content. Security of confidential information has to be included in a larger subset of criteria regarding the terms of use (or service) for the open courseware that include: copyright and licensing issues, anonymity, age restrictions, netiquette, updating or deleting personally identifiable information, security for *primary, secondary* and *indirect users* in terms of ISO/IEC 25000 SQuaRE etc.

The quality criteria presented here, which may result in a quality model for open courseware and open educational resources, need significant future improvements. First they have to comply with existing quality standards (such as ISO/IEC 25000 SQuaRE standard), educational theories and best practice in the field. Each measurable criterion has to be evaluated in a quantifiable way, by devising an appropriate scoring or rubric system that will help "measuring" open courseware, helping this way both users and other evaluators to use the model. Moreover, the inspection procedure for quality evaluation and comparison needs to be taken to the next, more formal, level, aiming at providing a quality evaluation framework. Thus, learners and instructors may be provided with a valuable instrument for choosing the most suitable educational resource, and the learning path that fulfills their educational goals. In addition, developers may also use that framework to tailor their work.

Acknowledgements. The author is very grateful to the anonymous reviewers for their valuable comments and ideas to improve both the paper and the quality model.

References

1. Vladoiu, M.: State-of-the-Art in Open Courseware Initiatives Worldwide. Informatics in Education 10(2), 271–294 (2011)
2. Vladoiu, M.: Open Courseware Initiatives – After 10 Years. In: 10th International Conference Romanian Educational Network - RoEduNet, pp. 183–188. IEEE Press, Iasi (2011)
3. OTTER – Open, Transferable, and Technology-enabled Educational Resources, `http://www2.le.ac.uk/departments/beyond-distance-research-alliance/projects/otter/about-oers/Corre-web.pdf/view`
4. OpenCourseWare in the European HE Context, `http://opencourseware.eu/workpackages/wp2`
5. JISC Quality Consideration, `https://openeducationalresources.pbworks.com/w/page/24838164/Quality+considerations`
6. Schuwer, R., Wilson, T., Van Valkenburg, W., Lane, A.: Production of OER, a Quest for Efficiency. In: 7th Annual Open Education Conference, Open Ed 2010. UOC, OU, BYU, Barcelona (2010), `http://hdl.handle.net/10609/5103`
7. Blackall, L.: Open Educational Resources and Practices. Teaching English as a Second Language 11(4), 1–19 (2008), `http://www.tesl-ej.org/ej44/a8.pdf`
8. Schaffert, S.: Strategic Integration of Open Educational Resources in Higher Education. Objectives, Case Studies, and the Impact of Web 2.0 on Universities. In: Ehlers, U.D., Schneckenberg, D. (eds.) Changing Cultures in Higher Education – Moving Ahead to Future Learning. Springer, New York (2010)
9. Fleming, C., Massey, M.: JORUM Open Educational Resources Report (2007)
10. Vest, C.M.: Open content and the emerging global meta-university. EDUCAUSE Review 41(3), 18–30 (2006), `http://www.educause.edu/apps/er/erm06/erm0630.asp?bhcp=1`
11. Vladoiu, M.: Quality Criteria for Open Educational Resources and Open Courseware (submitted for publication)
12. Brockbank, A., McGill, I.: Facilitating Reflective Learning in Higher Education. SRHE and Open University Press Imprint (1998)
13. Light, G., Cox, R.: Learning and Teaching in Higher Education. The reflective professional. Paul Chapman Publishing (2001)
14. Loughran, J.J.: Developing reflective practice. In: Learning about Teaching and Learning through Modelling. Falmer Press (1996)
15. Schunk, D.H., Zimmerman, B.J.: Self-regulated learning – from teaching to self-reflective practice. Guilford Press (1998)
16. MIT OCW Database Systems, `http://ocw.mit.edu/courses/electrical-engineering-and-computer-science/6-830-database-systems-fall-2010/index.html`
17. Saylor-Introduction to Modern Database Systems, `http://www.saylor.org/courses/cs403/`
18. Introduction to Databases, `http://www.db-class.org`
19. MIT OpenCourseWare, `http://ocw.mit.edu`
20. The Saylor Foundation, `http://www.saylor.org`
21. Jennifer's Widom SIGMOD Blog – From 100 students to 100,000, `http://wp.sigmod.org/?p=165`

Maintenance of Human and Machine Metadata over the Web Content

Karol Rástočný and Mária Bieliková

Institute of Informatics and Software Engineering, Faculty of Informatics and Information
Technologies, Slovak University of Technology, Ilkovičova 3, Bratislava, Slovakia
name.surname@stuba.sk

Abstract. Semantics over the Web content is crucial for web information systems, e.g. for effective information exploration, navigation or search. However, current coverage of the Web by semantics is insufficient. Web information systems mostly create their own content based metadata (e.g., identified keywords) and user collaboration metadata (e.g., implicit user feedbacks) in a form of information tags – structured information with semantic relations to the tagged content. By information tags web information systems build a lightweight semantics over the Web content, in which they can store knowledge and information about the content and interconnections between information artifacts of the content. Crucial problem of information tags lies in dynamicity of the Web whose content is continually modified. This together with influence of time can lead to invalidation of information tags which are closely related to tagged content. We address this issue via maintenance approach based on automatically and semi-automatically generated rules that respect changes on the Web and time aspect. The maintenance utilizes a rule-based engine which watches changes in the tagged content, identifies dependencies among maintenance rules and builds optimal strategy of rules application. We evaluate proposed maintenance approach in two domains – programing repositories and digital libraries, which use shared information tags repository.

Keywords: metadata, information tag, maintenance, lightweight semantics.

1   Research Context

The Web was originally proposed as a hypertext – a repository of interconnected textual documents by links (references) straight from the document content [1]. This original idea has shifted from linked documents to linked data [2] nowadays. But these data are still mostly made accessible just in a human readable format (e.g., wrapped in the textual web page) which is not effective for a machine processing.

The problem is addressed by the Sematic Web initiative which is strictly oriented to data that are obviously stored in triple stores or ontologies [3]. Web information systems can use data from the Semantic Web repositories for an inference of new knowledge and to support users' information seeking and processing activities [4, 5]. Emergence of the Semantic Web for a support of users' activities often needs an in-

M. Grossniklaus and M. Wimmer (Eds.): ICWE 2012 Workshops, LNCS 7703, pp. 216–220, 2012.
© Springer-Verlag Berlin Heidelberg 2012

terconnection between the Semantic Web ontologies and the "wild" Web content. The interconnection is provided by semantic annotations which annotate parts of a natural text with their formal representations in ontologies [6] (e.g., a word "Berlin" in a natural text can be annotated by the URI of the "Berlin" entity in an ontology).

Although some semi-automatic ontology learning approaches [7] and approaches for creating semantic annotations [8] exist already, domain experts have to make a non-trivial effort to propose rules for ontology extraction from the "wild" Web, to filter out misidentified entities and to maintain ontologies. As the result of this complication only a small part of the Web is covered by ontologies [9]. An improvement can be achieved by lightweight ontologies which usually contain only basic elements as terms or concepts and "is-a" and "part-of" relations [10]. Lightweight ontologies can be extracted from the webpage content and from users' activities as annotating [11] and sharing which have become popular with an emergence of the Web 2.0 [12].

Similarly to user annotating activities, web information systems assign metadata to the Web content. These metadata describe particular aspect of an information artifact – a part of a webpage. We look on them as on structured tags which are generated by systems. These tags are based on the Web content (e.g., extracted concepts) or on users' activities (e.g., relevant terms identified in often read document parts).

Well-structured tags are created by users, too. These human tags can be processed by systems and they contain valuable users' information and knowledge e.g., explicit users' ratings or keywords. We group metadata of described type and well-structured human tags under term *information tags*. Formally, an information tag is a triple *(type, anchoring, body)*, where *type* defines a type and a meaning of the information tag, *anchoring* identifies a tagged information artifact and *body* represents structured information those structure corresponds to the type of the information tag.

An advantage of information tags over freeform human annotations is that information tags are already in machine readable format. In addition information tags are in a semantic relation to tagged aspect of an information artifact (they are assigned to tagged data with specific purposes), so they provide a lightweight semantics over the Web content. But existing systems obviously store their information tags in private repositories in a form which is understandable only for them. More crucial problem is a dynamicity of the Web whose content is continually modified. This with influence of a time affects validity and topicality of information tags which are closely related to tagged content. To support building of a lightweight semantic based on information tags, we propose information tags maintenance approach based on automatically and semi-automatically generated rules that respect changes on the Web and a time aspect.

2   Research Objectives

The main goal of our work is designing information tags maintenance approach which keeps information tags in a consistent form. To fulfill this goal we have to deal with:

- *Diversity of information tags formats and semantics* – each web information system generates information tags in different format and with different sematic relation to the source content.
- *Information tags accessibility* – web information systems have to be able find information tags assigned to the Web content.

- *Dynamicity of the Web* – the Web documents arise, are deleted and modified without a notice. In addition the Web users use the Web content differently over the time. These modifications, diversity in usage of the Web content and also time aspect invalidate information tags that have to be updated or deleted.

The first issue is not a direct part of the maintenance but, it falls to the scope of storages and data integration. Despite it, we have to deal with it for evaluation reasons. So we divide addressing of these issues to three parts whereby the last two parts represent main contribution of our research:

- *Information tags repository* – stores information tags in a flexible model which will be acceptable by wide range of web information systems. Current systems mostly preferred RDF-based models, e.g. Open Annotation (OA) model[1] which is currently in beta version but it is already used by a number of systems and projects [13–15]. Metadata in RDF-based format should be stored in triple stores that are good for inference but, they are not effective for manipulation with whole objects. But information tags have a meaning only as whole objects with information tags' anchoring and content together. We suppose that *information tags can be stored in a repository with RDF-based model, which stores information tags as a one entry and not fragmented to a set of entries (triples) and the repository still provides basic functionality of triple stores* (e.g., SPARQL querying).
- *Maintenance logic* – provides an automatic maintenance over information tags via maintenance rules that respect changes of the Web content and time aspect. We assume that if lightweight ontologies can be learned semi-automatically and automatically [10], their *maintenance rules can be semi-automatically and automatically learned by watching of a life cycle of information tags*. Because of some information tags are derived from other information tags, learned rules will not be independent and application of a one rule can lead to a complex cascade effect. These dependencies among maintenance rules can be identified, so we assume that *a rule-based engine can be used for the maintenance of information tags*.
- *Access provider* – provides an access to the information tags repository and notifies the maintenance logic about updates in the information tags repository and detected new versions of tagged documents. A detection of new versions of tagged document can be based on Memento framework [14].

3   Conclusions and Future Work Plan

We have proposed a repository of information tags, which stores information tags in a document database. Document databases store complete entry as a one document (object) and they often support indexes. Their properties predict them for fast access to whole information tags but, document databases do not provide functionalities of triple stores. For this reason we proposed to employ MapReduce algorithm for effective evaluation of SPARQL queries over entries of document databases.

---

[1] http://www.openannotation.org/spec/beta

For evaluation purposes we have chosen web-scale MongoDB[2] document database and we have implemented proposed SPARQL evaluation algorithm for MongoDB. After that we performed several performance tests on single node deploy. We also repeated these tests with a repository based on classic triple store – Bigdata[3] which was chosen for its web-scale possibilities. We noticed that [16]:

- The repository based on MongoDB is at least *hundred times faster* in testing cases that manipulates with whole information tags than repository based on Bigdata.
- SPARQL query evaluation took *approximately same time* in both realizations.

Performed information tags repository evaluations are promising but, they are not representative in the web-scale. For final repository evaluation, larger performance tests with the repository distributed over several nodes have to be performed.

We focus our next work for proposition of the information tags maintenance itself and evaluation of hypothesizes related to the proposed maintenance approach:

- Rule-based engines can be used for the maintenance of information tags.
- Maintenance rules can be semi-automatically and automatically learned by watching of a life cycle of information tags.

We plan evaluate hypothesizes within domains related to two research projects currently realized at the Institute of Informatics and Software Engineering, Slovak University of Technology in Bratislava, that employ a lightweight ontology based on information tags for as a basis for semantics representation:

- *Personalized Conveying of Information and Knowledge* – this project is focused on support of enterprise applications development by viewing a software system as a web of information artifacts. In the project several agents collect and process documentations, source codes, developer blogs, developer activities, etc.
- *Traveling in Digital Space* –main goals of this project are collaborative learning and support of novice researchers to orientate in new research domains. The core part of an employed lightweight ontology contains domain concept maps built from learning materials and from captured user activities with a studied content.

We currently work on a proposition of the rule-based engine for maintenance information tags. The engine updates information tags' anchoring to a tagged content, invalidate (delete) information tags when they become outdated and update information tags' content if it will be possible.

The next step is focused on a proposal of (semi-)automatic maintenance rules learning based on monitoring the life cycle of information tags. We plan to evaluate our approach by a comparison of information tags that are maintained by manually, semi-automatically and automatically created rules. We will also watch update activities provided by web information systems for an evaluation of accuracy and coverage.

---

[2] http://www.mongodb.org/
[3] http://www.systap.com/bigdata.htm

Acknowledgements. This work was supported by the grants VG1/0675/11, APVV-0233-10 and it is a partial result of the Research and Development Operational Program for the projects SMART, ITMS 26240120005 and SMART II, ITMS 26240120029, co-funded by ERDF.

References

1. Berners-Lee, T., Cailliau, R., Luotonen, A., Nielsen, H.F., Secret, A.: The World-Wide Web. Communications of the ACM 37, 76–82 (1994)
2. Handschuh, S., Heath, T., Thai, V.: Visual interfaces to the social and the semantic web (VISSW 2009). In: 13th Int. Conf. on Intelligent UIs, pp. 499–500. ACM Press, NY (2009)
3. Shadbolt, N., Berners-Lee, T., Hall, W.: The Semantic Web Revisited. IEEE Intelligent Systems 21, 96–101 (2006)
4. Ramachandran, V.A., Krishnamurthi, I.: NLION: Natural Language Interface for Querying ONtologies. In: 2nd Bangalore Annual Compute Conf., p. 4. ACM Press, NY (2009)
5. Elbassuoni, S., Blanco, R.: Keyword Search over RDF Graphs. In: 20th ACM Int. Conf. on Information and Knowledge Management, pp. 237–242. ACM Press, NY (2011)
6. Uren, V., Cimiano, P., Iria, J., Handschuh, S., Vargasvera, M., Motta, E., Ciravegna, F.: Semantic Annotation for Knowledge Management: Requirements and a Survey of the State of the Art. Web Sem.: Science, Services and Agents on the WWW 4, 14–28 (2006)
7. Hazman, M., El-Beltagy, S.R., Rafea, A.: A Survey of Ontology Learning Approaches. International Journal of Computer Applications 22, 36–43 (2011)
8. Reeve, L., Han, H.: Survey of Semantic Annotation Platforms. In: ACM Symposium on Applied Computing, pp. 1634–1638. ACM, NY (2005)
9. Sabou, M., Gracia, J.L., Angeletou, S., d'Aquin, M., Motta, E.: Evaluating the Semantic Web: A Task-Based Approach. In: Aberer, K., Choi, K.-S., Noy, N., Allemang, D., Lee, K.-I., Nixon, L.J.B., Golbeck, J., Mika, P., Maynard, D., Mizoguchi, R., Schreiber, G., Cudré-Mauroux, P. (eds.) ISWC/ASWC 2007. LNCS, vol. 4825, pp. 423–437. Springer, Heidelberg (2007)
10. Giunchiglia, F., Zaihrayeu, I.: Lightweight Ontologies. Tech. report, Univ. of Trento, p. 10 (2007)
11. Šimko, M.: Automated Acquisition of Domain Model for Adaptive Collaborative Web-Based Learning. Inf. Sciences and Tech., Bulletin of the ACM Slovakia 2(4), 9 p. (2012)
12. Bieliková, M., Barla, M., Šimko, M.: Lightweight Semantics for the "Wild Web". In: IADIS Int. Conf. WWW/Internet 2011 (keynote), pp. xxv–xxxii. IADIS Press (2011)
13. Gerber, A., Hyland, A., Hunter, J.: A Collaborative Scholarly Annotation System for Dynamic Web Documents – A Literary Case Study. In: Chowdhury, G., Koo, C., Hunter, J. (eds.) ICADL 2010. LNCS, vol. 6102, pp. 29–39. Springer, Heidelberg (2010)
14. Sanderson, R., Van de Sompel, H.: Making Web Annotations Persistent over Time. In: 10th Annual Joint Conf. on Digital Libraries, pp. 1–10. ACM Press, NY (2010)
15. Yu, C.-H., Groza, T., Hunter, J.: High Speed Capture, Retrieval and Rendering of Segment-Based Annotations on 3D Museum Objects. In: Xing, C., Crestani, F., Rauber, A. (eds.) ICADL 2011. LNCS, vol. 7008, pp. 5–15. Springer, Heidelberg (2011)
16. Bieliková, M., Rástočný, K.: Lightweight Semantics over Web Information Systems Content Employing Knowledge Tags. In: Castano, S., Vassiliadis, P., Lakshmanan, L.V.S., Lee, M.L. (eds.) ER Workshops 2012. LNCS, vol. 7518, pp. 327–336. Springer, Heidelberg (2012)

End-User-Development and Evolution of Web Applications: The WebComposition EUD Approach

Olexiy Chudnovskyy and Martin Gaedke

Chemnitz University of Technology
olexiy.chudnovskyy@cs.tu-chemnitz.de,
martin.gaedke@cs.tu-chemnitz.de

Abstract. End-user-development (EUD) has been a field of study for more than 30 years already. The results are visible – users, who have no or only little programming skills, have become active creators of Web applications, developing new tools to meet their situational needs, sharing them with colleagues and combining them into more complex solutions. Recent trends, like maturation of cloud computing, mass customization and changing demographics resulted in even higher demand for flexible, feature-rich and extensible platforms for end-user development. While the potential of involving end-users into developing task is extremely high, a clear need for new systematic methods has emerged, which would take both the new technological opportunities but also risks resulting from non-professional application development into account. In this paper, we present our research towards systematic, end-user-oriented Web application development. We identify relevant research challenges; derive requirements on EUD-oriented development process and show how the WebComposition approach can be extended to support end-users during the whole life-cycle of Web applications - from requirements elicitation to evolution.

1 Introduction

The opportunities of end-user-development have become much greater in the last years. Not only technological foundation has advanced, but also social conditions have changed [1]. Nowadays end-users are much more skilled in dealing with IT. Motivated by ubiquitous internet access and pervasiveness of mobile devices providing rich user experience, users have become active shapers of the Web [2]. Many end-user-oriented platforms and new development paradigms have emerged. One of the most promising are so called mashups [3], i.e. Web applications, which let end-users combine data, application logic and UI coming from different sources on the Web.

The EUD trend has also moved to enterprises. The new generation of workforce is willing and able to create tools for their everyday needs, avoiding long-lasting feature requests to IT departments. In addition, end-users are better domain experts and know exactly how software should support their tasks, even if they can't always explain it properly. Giving end-users an opportunity to develop their own solutions can save significant costs to the company and unburden IT department with numerous feature requests.

M. Grossniklaus and M. Wimmer (Eds.): ICWE 2012 Workshops, LNCS 7703, pp. 221–226, 2012.

Though the potential of EUD is extremely high, it also bears some risks and in worst case can have negative impact on the whole enterprise. The recent Gartner report on so called "citizen development" predicts that at least a third of businesses without formalised citizen developer governance policies will encounter substantial data, process integrity and security vulnerabilities [4]. One of the main problems identified is an inadequate application life-cycle management, resulting in plenty almost identical applications exposing many security vulnerabilities or performance drawbacks. Another problem is that if application becomes unmanageable, it is delegated to IT department, making its maintenance and evolution a cost-inefficient and time-consuming burden. Finally, end-users are simply not aware about best practises and governance rules to be applied during the application development process.

In this work, we address the above problems and propose a new method for end-user-development and evolution of Web applications. We build our work upon the WebComposition approach [5] and adapt its process model, tools and methods to the peculiarities of the EUD domain. The rest of the paper is structured as following: Section 2 gives an overview of the tackled research challenges. In section 3 we introduce the WebComposition approach and show how it can be extended towards the EUD domain. Finally, we conclude the paper and give an outlook into our future work.

2   Research Challenges

Consider the following example scenario, illustrating common problems and difficulties, which end-users face while developing new Web applications.

John is an employee of a medium-sized enterprise and works often with customer-relationship-management (CRM) systems, which help him in finding information about customers, performing data analysis or contacting them through various communication channels. John uses the system in his everyday work, but soon he discovers that many tasks are performed inefficiently – for example, the data should be collected from different areas of the system and can't be merged into one holistic view. John performs also many data lookup activities to find customer-related data on the Web. He can't enrich the system with other data sources rather than those foreseen by developers. Furthermore, he wants some system functionality to be available in other contexts, e.g. on desktop or embedded in his favourite portal application.

John decides to create his own application and takes the composition tool offered by the company IT department. The first hurdle John faces is the missing knowledge on how to start building an application. Most of the tools follow a bottom-up approach, giving end-users a toolkit to compose data, application logic or user interfaces. The requirements specification phase and corresponding modelling tools haven't gained much attention so far and lead to a unsystematic and time-consuming development process [6]. John starts to play with the given toolbox and encounters next problems - this time in finding relevant data sources or parts of application he should use. The building blocks are usually not fine-grained enough to be shared between applications or lack adequate semantic descriptions to be found among plenty of available artefacts. John creates his own data specifications, defines presentation and navigation aspects of the new application. The procedure takes him quite some time due to the missing expertise in Web application development. Unwittingly John doesn't consider security and performance aspects as his main purpose is to fulfil the current needs without taking possible future reuse of artefacts or application evolution into account. Having created several applications, John uses them quite often but later on encounters incompatibility problems if his applications should be integrated with the ones developed by his colleagues.

The presented scenario reveals several problems and research challenges, which will be tackled in this work:

- How end-users can be supported during the whole Web application life-cycle including requirements engineering and evolution?
- Which concepts and development paradigms are appropriate for EUD? Which expertise can be expected from end-users nowadays?
- Which interactions between IT experts and end-users are needed to guarantee a required quality of produced software artefacts and compliance to company policies?
- How development expertise and application artefacts can be shared among end-users? Which artefacts can be reused during the application life-cycle?
- How models and tools can be adapted to establish a systematic and efficient development process? Which EUD-platforms offer the best trade-off in simplicity and expressive power?

In the following section, we present our proposed extension of the WebComposition approach, which is adapted to tackle the aforementioned problems.

3   Research Methodology and Approach

The WebComposition approach was first introduced in 1997 as an object-oriented approach for development and evolution of Web applications [7]. The Web-based solution is seen as a set of fine-grained application components, which deal with different perspectives of a Web application, such as content [8], distributed system and architecture [9] or user interface experience perspectives [10]. The WebComposition process model focuses on systematic development and reuse of application artefacts, taking continuous application evolution into account. To take the peculiarities of EUD domain into account, we propose an extension of the WebComposition approach, illustrated in Figure 1.

The WebComposition approach considers a Web-based solution as a set of areas or so called "domains", which are continuously evolving and extending the original application. The first step within the development process is the domain analysis, which is focused on identification and description of envisioned application domains. Already existing domains are analysed with respect to their further evolution. The planning process is supported by the so called WebComposition Reuse Repository, containing artefacts, which can be reused and adapted to the current needs. In our work we are going to identify a set of artefacts specific to EUD, which can be produced during domain analysis and reused later on. These could be, for example, conceptual domain descriptions, user-interface-mockups, or user stories. Furthermore a set of services from IT experts as well as tools to support the domain analysis step will be elaborated.

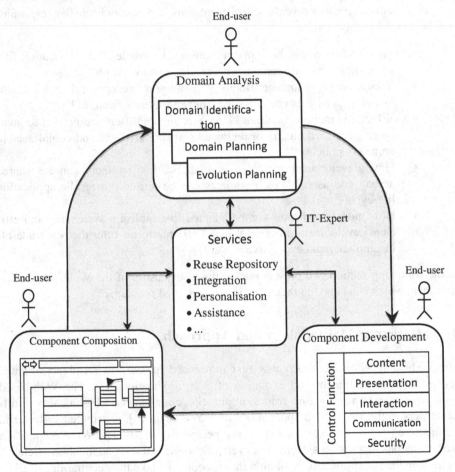

Fig. 1. The WebComposition process model for end-user- development of Web applications

The next phase focuses on specification and development of building blocks required to implement the envisioned domain. One identifies already existing components and creates the missing ones. In our work we will refine the component model originally defined in the WebComposition approach to take security, system integration and distribution requirements into account. We believe that components would provide much higher value both in terms of reusability and efficiency if appropriate packaging and distribution aspects are considered [11]. We will identify required IT-expert services, which would assist end-user in the development tasks, e.g. by providing consistency or policy compliance checks. A well-balanced cooperation between skilled and unskilled developers is needed to guarantee an efficient and maintainable development. We will develop a dedicated environment, which would let end-users implement the aforementioned components and access the identified IT-expert services.

The last step of the development cycle is the assembly of identified components into one solution, which would satisfy the requirements of the envisioned domain. Similar to the previous step, the composition process should happen in an end-user-friendly way, i.e. hiding the complexity of underlying technologies and providing assistance in such tasks as dependency resolution or establishing of component interoperability. We envision a dedicated run-time environment, which would enable graphical composition and provide end-user assistance facilities, e.g. recommendation and automatic composition engine. We will build upon well-adopted Web mashup technologies [3] but additionally cover security and user-experience aspects.

The working plan of our research is focused on tackling the research challenges stated in Section 2. In particular, we will continue with the following steps:

- Detailed requirements elicitation and use case definition for EUD-oriented process model and supporting tools.
- Profound state-of-the-art analysis of principles, methods and tools aiming to support EUD. We are going to cover the Web mashups domain, visual programming techniques, EUD suits as well as Web Engineering approaches.
- Specification of a EUD approach based on WebComposition process model, which would result in appropriate communication between different stakeholders and efficient development process.
- Development of a dedicated platform, supporting different phases of adapted WebComposition approach. End-user-friendly models, tools and run-time environments will be developed in this step.
- An evaluation of the proposed approach within several case studies. Applicability of tools and efficiency of the introduced process will be analysed.

4   Conclusions and Outlook

As recent studies showed, the risk of security vulnerabilities and poor maintainability of end-user-created products becomes high, if the development happens unsystematically and is not supported by IT departments. In this paper we presented a dedicated process model, tools and techniques to avoid the aforementioned risks. We described how WebComposition approach can be adapted towards the needs of EUD domain and elaborated our plan for the future research.

References

[1] Sarner, A.: How to Determine Levels of Engagement for Generation Virtual (2008)

[2] O'Reilly, T.: What Is Web 2.0. Design Patterns and Business Models for the Next Generation of Software (2005), http://oreilly.com/web2/archive/what-is-web-20.html

[3] Chudnovskyy, O., Nestler, T., Gaedke, M., Daniel, F., Ignacio, J.: End-User-Oriented Telco Mashups: The OMELETTE Approach. In: World Wide Web 2012 (2012)

[4] Finley, I., Knipp, E.: Citizen Developers Are Poised to Grow (2011)

[5] Gaedke, M., Rehse, J.: Supporting compositional reuse in component-based Web engineering. In: Proceedings of the 2000 ACM Symposium on Applied, pp. 927–933 (2000)

[6] Robles Luna, E., Rossi, G., Garrigós, I.: WebSpec: a visual language for specifying interaction and navigation requirements in web applications. Requirements Engineering 16(4), 297–321 (2011)

[7] Gellersen, H.-W., Wicke, R., Gaedke, M.: WebComposition: An Object-Oriented Support System for the Web Engineering Lifecycle. In: Electronic Proc. of The 6th International WWW Conference (1997)

[8] Chudnovskyy, O., Gaedke, M.: Development of Web 2.0 Applications using WebComposition/Data Grid Service. In: The Second International Conferences on Advanced Service Computing (Service Computation 2010), pp. 55–61 (2010)

[9] Gaedke, M., Meinecke, J.: The Web as an Application Platform. In: Rossi, G., Pastor, O., Schwabe, D., Olsina, L. (eds.) Web Engineering Modelling and Implementing Web Applications, pp. 33–45. Springer, Berlin (2008)

[10] Chudnovskyy, O., Brandt, S., Gaedke, M.: Integrating Human-Services using WebComposition/UIX. In: ACMIFIPUSENIX 12th International Middleware Conference (2011)

[11] Spahn, M., Wulf, V.: End-User Development of Enterprise Widgets. In: Pipek, V., Rosson, M.B., de Ruyter, B., Wulf, V. (eds.) IS-EUD 2009. LNCS, vol. 5435, pp. 106–125. Springer, Heidelberg (2009)

A Description-Based Mashup for Cooperation
of Mobile Devices

Korawit Prutsachainimmit and Takehiro Tokuda

Department of Computer Science, Tokyo Institute of Technology
Meguro, Tokyo 152-8552, Japan
{korawit,tokuda}@tt.cs.titech.ac.jp

Abstract. Recently, the study of mobile mashup has become important in mobile computing. Mashup approaches were proposed to allow users to create mashup for mobile devices. However, existing approaches still lack attention to enable mashup for cooperation of mobile devices. We present a description-based mashup construction approach for cooperation of mobile devices. Our approach allows end-users to create mobile mashup applications by integrating mobile applications, Web applications and Web services. We define a mashup description language for describing logic of mashup. We use a mashup generator to simplify mashup construction. We also present a mashup execution environment to automate information sharing for cooperation of mobile devices.

Keywords: Mobile mashup, Cooperation mashup, Description language.

1 Introduction

Mobile mashup has recently become an important trend in mobile computing. Mashup solutions and tools emerged to assist end-users to compose mashup applications for mobile environment. Yahoo! Pipes and Intel Mash Maker focus on data integration and filtering. TELAR mashup platform [1] presents a way to combine mobile devices' features such as GPS with existing Web resources. Kaltofen et al. presents an end-users' mobile mashup for cross-platform deployment [2]. Most of the proposed solutions share a common characteristic where they focus on mashup development for single device. The proposed solutions also have limited capabilities to develop mashup for cooperation of multiple devices.

The usage style of mobile application is changing from individual use to collaborative use. Collaborative applications such as groupware or social applications which are commonly used on desktop computers are adapted to the mobile platform. Hence, mashup development for cooperation of mobile devices is taken into account. With cooperation of devices, different information from multiple mobile devices can be integrated with existing mashup components to produce new mashup output. Thus, mashup with cooperation of mobile devices is an interesting research topic in mobile mashup.

M. Grossniklaus and M. Wimmer (Eds.): ICWE 2012 Workshops, LNCS 7703, pp. 227–231, 2012.
© Springer-Verlag Berlin Heidelberg 2012

In our previous work [3], we proposed a mobile mashup approach for end-users by using a description language and a mashup generator. We also presented Tethered Web service (TeWS) to support cooperation of mobile devices. However, the previous work still has limitations. Then, this research aims to find an optimal mashup approach for cooperation of mobile devices. To achieve this goal, the following objectives were set:

1. To develop a mobile mashup construction system dealing with cooperation of mobile devices.
2. To enable integration of mobile applications, Web applications and Web services in flow-based and event-based execution.
3. To allow automatic generation of typical database mobile applications for mashup.
4. To analyze and optimize efficiency of the mashup approach.
5. To evaluate usability of the mashup approach by conducting user-based test.

2   Mashup Approach

The general concept of our approach is using a description language for mashup construction. The description language allows mashup composers to define mashup components and detail of its integration. The mashup components can be Web applications, Web services and mobile applications. We also apply the description-based construction technique to create typical data-centric mobile applications which can be integrated into mashup. To leverage mashup composition effort, we use a GUI mashup designer tool to help mashup composers in creating mashup description files. The description files will be used with a mashup generator to build mashup applications. To enable cooperation of devices, we use a mashup execution environment which helps in data exchanging among participating devices.

2.1   Mashup Description Language

The mashup description language is an XML-based description language which is designed for describing mashup components and its integration. The description language provides a way to describe mashup components which can be used in a mashup application. Mashup components consist of:

1. *Web Application Component (WA)*. This component can extract a part of a Web page or a query through an HTML form. Mashup composers are provided with a Web extraction assistant tool [4] to indicate part of required information on a Web page. The description of this component will be generated to JavaScript code and executed in the runtime environment on a mobile device.
2. *Web Service Component (WS)*. This component is used for describing a Web service API. The target Web service will be invoked to extract a whole or a part of the result.

3. *Mobile Application Component (MA)*. This component allows a mobile application which implemented Intent and Service [5] messaging protocol to be integrated in mashup.
4. *Mobile Application Generator (MG)*. To expand integration capability of mobile applications, this component helps composers in creating a typical data-centric mobile application by using a description. The generated applications can be integrated and reused as a mobile application.
5. *Data Manipulation Component (DM)*. Output from one or more components can be transformed and filtered by using this component.
6. *Cooperation Component (CC)*. This component will be used for cooperation of multiple devices. Required information from participating devices can be described in this component. The description of this component will be generated to code for communicating with the execution environment to exchange information with other devices.

2.2 Mashup Construction Process

The mashup construction process is shown in Figure 1. To compose a mashup application, a mashup composer creates an abstract model of mashup by defining components and detail of its integration. The mashup designer tool will assist the mashup composer in transforming the abstract model into the description language. Output from the mashup designer tool is an XML description file. The description file will be used as an input of the mashup generator to generate Java source code. This generated code will be compiled into a mobile application which can be deployed on target devices. The mashup application can be used as an ordinary mobile application.

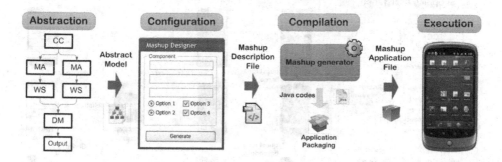

Fig. 1. Mashup Construction Process

2.3 Mashup Execution Environment

To achieve mashup for cooperation of devices, participating devices need a capability to communicate with other devices for exchanging mashup required information. We use an execution environment to automate this task. Our execution environment allows exchanging information between devices by using a custom mobile application called *Cooperation Agent*. The cooperation agent will be installed on the participating devices to take care of devices' connectivity and information sharing. With the cooperation agent, the participating devices can send messages to request mashup required information from other devices. To reduce data transmission among devices, messages that are sent in our execution environment use RESTful Web services and JSON [6].

3   Mashup for Cooperation of Mobile Devices

To demonstrate a mashup for cooperation of mobile devices, we implemented a mashup scenario with our approach. This scenario simulates a shopping situation in a department store for 3 or more users. Mashup for this scenario will help users in comparing prices on a local store with prices from online stores. The mashup also creates a summary of selected products shared to all users.

We show mashup model and screenshots in Figure 2. For this mashup, the cooperation component requests for a barcode from all client devices. Each client device reads a barcode of a selected product and submits it to the server device. Each barcode is given to the Web service component of Google's Search API for Shopping [7] to find available online stores and prices. The data manipulation component extracts the lowest price and stores' information. The lowest price is converted to target currency with Web services component of Exchange Rate API [8]. The converted price and stores' information are combined into a list on the server. After all clients finish sending the barcodes, the summary list of selected products can be shared among all devices.

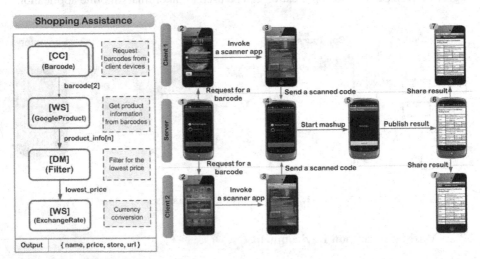

Fig. 2. Mashup model and screenshots of *Shopping Assistance*

In order to study cooperation of different mobile platforms, this example is implemented by using an Android device as the server and iOS devices as the clients. The mashup application was generated and deployed in the server device while the cooperation agent is pre-installed to all clients device. Mashup users can use this mashup application as an ordinary mobile application.

4   Conclusion and Future Work

This paper has presented goals and the current state of our research. We propose a description-based solution for mashup construction on single and cooperation of devices. The mashup created by our approach is capable for integration of mobile applications and Web information. We have also presented a solution for devices' connectivity by using the mashup execution environment. We have demonstrated capabilities of our approach with the example scenario. However, our current work is designed for flow-based mashup, where the mashup components are executed in sequences. In addition, some parts of mashup construction still require manual operations.

Our future research is targeted towards designing, implementing, and evaluating a novel mashup construction system for cooperation of mobile devices. The following specific contributions are planned:

- To enable event-based mashup where mashup components are executed by events.
- To allow automatic generation of typical database mobile applications in mashup.
- To analyze usability by conducting a user-based evaluation.
- To optimize efficiency of mashup execution on mobile devices.

References

1. Brodt, A., Nicklas, D., Sathish, S., Mitschang, B.: Context-Aware Mashups for Mobile Devices. In: Bailey, J., Maier, D., Schewe, K.-D., Thalheim, B., Wang, X.S. (eds.) WISE 2008. LNCS, vol. 5175, pp. 280–291. Springer, Heidelberg (2008)
2. Kaltofen, S., Milrad, M., Kurti, A.: A Cross-Platform Software System to Create and Deploy Mobile Mashups. In: Benatallah, B., Casati, F., Kappel, G., Rossi, G. (eds.) ICWE 2010. LNCS, vol. 6189, pp. 518–521. Springer, Heidelberg (2010)
3. Chaisatien, P., Prutsachainimmit, K., Tokuda, T.: Mobile Mashup Generator System for Cooperative Applications of Different Mobile Devices. In: Auer, S., Díaz, O., Papadopoulos, G.A. (eds.) ICWE 2011. LNCS, vol. 6757, pp. 182–197. Springer, Heidelberg (2011)
4. Guo, J., Chaisatien, P., Han, H., Noro, T., Tokuda, T.: Partial Information Extraction Approach to Lightweight Integration on the Web. In: Daniel, F., Facca, F.M. (eds.) ICWE 2010. LNCS, vol. 6385, pp. 372–383. Springer, Heidelberg (2010)
5. Android Developers, http://developer.android.com/index.html
6. Tsai, C.-L., Chen, H.-W., Huang, J.-L., Hu, C.-L.: Transmission reduction between mobile phone applications and RESTful APIs. In: Proceedings of the 2011 ACM Symposium on Applied Computing, SAC 2011 (2011)
7. Search API for Shopping, http://code.google.com/apis/shopping/search/
8. Exchange Rate API, http://www.exchangerate-api.com/

Model Based Simulation and Evaluation of Mobile and Web 2.0 Applications for Users with Special Needs

Philip Ackermann

Fraunhofer Institute for Applied Information Technology FIT
Schloss Birlinghoven, 53757 Sankt Augustin Germany
philip.ackermann@fit.fraunhofer.de

Abstract. The accessibility of modern Web 2.0 applications for people with disabilities continues to be a problem [1,2,3]. Recent research has shown that even the Web Content Accessibility Guidelines 2.0 only cover half of the accessibility problems that users encounter when interacting with those kind of web applications [4].

Those guidelines do not consider the fact that people with disabilities use special interaction patterns when interacting with web applications [5]. Analysing these interaction patterns and integrating them into the development process of web applications by providing tool support seems promising to help improving the accessibility of those web applications and also to reduce the time and costs for user trials [6,7].

The purpose of this thesis is to simulate interaction patterns of people with disabilities and to analyse how those interaction patterns have effects on the time and efficiency to complete given tasks in web applications. It will also analyse how effective this simulation will be in helping to design web applications, both accessible and usable.

To achieve this, a model based simulation framework will be designed that take into account different models involved in the interaction of users with web applications. A software tool will be developed that implements these models and the simulation.

Keywords: Web Accessibility, Web Usability, User Interactions, Web Simulation, Interaction Patterns, Model Based Simulation.

1 Problem Statement

Over the last years the web has evolved from a static hypertext system into a platform for rich internet applications [8,9] that emulate the functionality of desktop applications. However the accessibility of such applications for people with disabilities continues to be a problem [1,2,3]. Recent research has shown that even the Web Content Accessibility Guidelines 2.0 only cover half of the accessibility problems that users encounter when interacting with those kind of web applications [4] and that implementing them does not guarantee the usability of a web application [10,11].

M. Grossniklaus and M. Wimmer (Eds.): ICWE 2012 Workshops, LNCS 7703, pp. 232–237, 2012.
© Springer-Verlag Berlin Heidelberg 2012

One example of rich internet applications are social networks like Facebook[1]. Those social networks are intended to build relationships with other people on a private or a professional level [12]. Participating in such communities would be important especially for people with disabilities. However a recent survey by WebAIM on the usage of screen-readers revealed that Facebook is avoided by most of the screen-reader users because of accessibility issues[2]. One user commented that

> "Facebook is becoming especially annoying. I can force it to work, but it's TOTALLY inefficient and not a pleasure to use. It's becoming critical for business visibility, though."

This comment highlights the problem that users with disabilities are currently excluded from participating in social network activities, because of inaccessible and unusable design of web applications. This problem is not limited to social networks and is observed in other rich internet applications as well [13].

Another observation is that users with disabilities have developed different interaction patterns when interacting with web applications [14,11,15,5], partly to compensate some of the accessibility problems they encounter. Those interaction patterns are not taken into account in current accessibility guidelines. The interaction patterns that an user applies depend on different components like the task the user wants to perform, the assistive technology and device she is using and the application itself.

Analysing those interaction patterns can reveal how people with disabilities interact with web applications. It is important to analyse them to understand the behaviour of those user groups on web applications and how they effect the time and efficiency to complete tasks in web applications. Integrating them into the development process of web applications by providing tool support for web developers seems promising to help improving the accessibility of those web applications and to reduce the time and costs for user trials [6,7].

2   Purpose Statement and Research Questions

The purpose of this study is to simulate interaction patterns of people with disabilities in the context of mobile and Web 2.0 applications and to identify the effects of those interaction patterns on the time and efficiency to complete given tasks in web applications. It will also analyse how effective this simulation will be in designing web applications that are both accessible and usable. The work will try to answer the following research questions:

1. How effective is model based simulation to simulate interaction patterns of users with disabilities?

---

[1] http://www.facebook.com
[2] WebAIM. 2009. Survey of Preferences of Screen Readers Users, Retrieved July 30, 2012, from http://webaim.org/projects/screenreadersurvey/

- What components need to be taken into account to simulate interaction patterns?
- How can those components be integrated into the simulation?

2. How does simulating user interactions support web developers in designing accessible and usable web applications?
   - How can the simulation be integrated to work on real HTML based web applications instead of an abstract application model?
   - What kind of feedback is effective to explain accessibility and usability problems to the web developer?

The proposed simulation framework will take into account the following models: (i) the user model, (ii) the device model including user agents and assistive technologies, (iii) the application model under test, (iv) the tasks model and (v) the interaction patterns model. A proposal for the user model and the device model has been published by the author in [16]. The application model that is going to be used is the *Document Object Model* (DOM) [17] extended by the specification for *Accessible Rich Internet Applications* (ARIA) [1]. All those models have to be taken into account, because they influence the interaction patterns that an user would and could apply. Another reason is that the efficiency of performing tasks can differ significantly between different versions of an application, for example between the smartphone version and the desktop version [18].

3   Literature Review

This section describes different relevant existing approaches for simulation of interaction patterns and/or model based simulation in the context of accessibility and usability evaluation. The state of art in user preference and device modelling has been briefly described by the author in [16]. Due to space restrictions this section does not represent a complete review of the state of the art. Instead it highlights the most relevant existing work, their limitations and how the proposed work will differ.

Biswas [19] created an environment to simulate the interactions of people with low vision or motor impairment with a graphical user interface. The approach focus on graphical user interfaces in general and does not consider interactions that are specific to web applications. Furthermore instead of a real application the input for the simulation consists of a sequence of bitmap images and information about the location of different objects in that interface.

Schrepp [6] proposes models for (i) keyboard navigation in web sites, (ii) keyboard navigation in web applications and (iii) interaction of blind users in web pages. The models are based on the GOMS (Goals, Operators, Methods and Selection rules) model but extend it to take into account random errors made by the user. The approach has not been implemented in a software tool, although the author mentions that it would be an important part of future work, because performing a GOMS analysis without tool support would be time consuming and also not trivial from a technical point of view.

Tonn-Eichstädt [20] proposes an extension of GOMS to model the user interaction patterns and uses it to calculate the task execution time on a web page. The model has not been verified and it does not take into account parameters like speech rate of a screen-reader or Braille reading times. A tool that visualizes the interaction patterns is not provided but mentioned as future work.

Trewin et al. [14] observed different patterns that screen-reader users apply when interacting with web applications. Their goal is to create a tool for developers that simulate screen-reader users and report usability problems. Later the same authors [7] uses CogTool [21] as a start point to build a KLM (Keystroke Level Model) for one task and one user using JAWS[3] as screen-reader. Because CogTool only uses storyboards for simulation the goal remains to have a tool that works on a real web application. Until now no such software has been implemented.

MeMo tool [22] is a workbench for conducting semi-automatic usability evaluations by simulation. It simulates an user interacting with the *system interaction model* implemented by the software developer. The system consists of different models including those for the tasks and the user interactions. However MeMo does not focus on the following aspects that the proposed work will address: (i) interactions of users with disabilities and (ii) simulation on real web applications.

Based on the use of skip-links and heading tags the Accessibility Designer tool [23] calculates the time to navigate to an element on a web page using a screen-reader. Colors are used to visualize how fast a region on a web page can be reached by screen-reader users. However this tool does not take into account new semantic tags like those introduced in the HTML5 [24] or the ARIA [1] specifications. Newer screen-readers like JAWS 12[4] are able to interpret those semantics as well. Therefore the interaction patterns of screen-reader users have changed accordingly. This change must be considered when creating the models for the simulation.

4   Research Methodology and Research Plan

Based on existing studies about interaction patterns of users with disabilities the requirements for modelling such interaction patterns are collected. According to those requirements the model will be developed in an iterative process. The task and goals model and the simulation framework itself will be developed in iterative processes as well. The plan is to finish a first prototype of the simulation and the models after different iterations until November 2013.

The interaction of users with disabilities with web applications is quite complex, therefore we foresee the need to validate the prototype with user testing.

---

[3] Freedom Scientific. 2010. JAWS, Retrieved July 31, 2012, from
http://www.freedomscientific.com

[4] Freedom Scientific. 2010. Features and Enhancements in JAWS 12, Retrieved July 31, 2012, from
http://www.freedomscientific.com/downloads/
jaws/JAWS12-previous-enhancements.asp

Based on those user tests the models and the simulation will be calibrated as necessary. The plan is to finish the user testing and the validation until April 2014.

After the simulation framework has been validated a software will be designed that implements the framework. The purpose of this software is (i) to verify the applicability of the simulation framework and (ii) to provide tool support for web developers. According to the plan a prototype of the software will be finished in September 2014. The software will be validated with user tests until December 2014. The plan is to defend the thesis in January 2015.

References

1. Pappas, L., Schwerdtfeger, R., Cooper, M.: WAI-ARIA 1.0 Primer - An introduction to rich Internet application accessibility challenges and solutions, W3C Working Draft 16 September 2010. Technical report, World Wide Web Consortium, W3C (2010)
2. Zajicek, M.: Web 2.0: hype or happiness? In: Proceedings of the 2007 International Cross-Disciplinary Conference on Web Accessibility, W4A 2007, pp. 35–39. ACM, New York (2007)
3. Chadwick-Dias, A., Bergel, M., Tullis, T.S.: Senior Surfers 2.0: A Re-examination of the Older Web User and the Dynamic Web. In: Stephanidis, C. (ed.) HCI 2007. LNCS, vol. 4554, pp. 868–876. Springer, Heidelberg (2007)
4. Power, C., Freire, A., Petrie, H., Swallow, D.: Guidelines are only half of the story: accessibility problems encountered by blind users on the web. In: Proceedings of the 2012 ACM Annual Conference on Human Factors in Computing Systems, CHI 2012, pp. 433–442. ACM, New York (2012)
5. Petrie, H., Power, C., Swallow, D.: I2web deliverable 3.1: User requirements analysis in ubiquitous web 2.0 applications (2011)
6. Schrepp, M.: GOMS analysis as a tool to investigate the usability of web units for disabled users. Universal Access in the Information Society 9(1), 77–86 (2009)
7. Trewin, S., John, B.E., Richards, J., Swart, C., Brezin, J., Bellamy, R., Thomas, J.: Towards a tool for keystroke level modeling of skilled screen reading. In: Proceedings of the 12th International ACM SIGACCESS Conference on Computers and Accessibility, ASSETS 2010, pp. 27–34. ACM, New York (2010)
8. Allaire, J.: Macromedia flash mx-a next-generation rich client. Technical report, Macromedia (2002)
9. Duhl, J.: White paper: Rich internet applications. Technical report, IDC (Sponsored by Macromedia and Intel) (2003)
10. Schrepp, M.: On the efficiency of keyboard navigation in web sites. Univers. Access Inf. Soc. 5(2), 180–188 (2006)
11. Borodin, Y., Bigham, J.P., Dausch, G., Ramakrishnan, I.V.: More than meets the eye: a survey of screen-reader browsing strategies. In: Proceedings of the 2010 International Cross Disciplinary Conference on Web Accessibility, W4A 2010, pp. 1–10. ACM, New York (2010)
12. Skeels, M.M., Grudin, J.: When social networks cross boundaries: a case study of workplace use of facebook and linkedin. In: Proceedings of the ACM 2009 International Conference on Supporting Group Work, GROUP 2009, pp. 95–104. ACM, New York (2009)

13. Wentz, B., Lazar, J.: Usability evaluation of email applications by blind users. J. Usability Studies 6(2), 8:75–8:89 (2011)
14. Trewin, S., Richards, J., Bellamy, R., John, B.E., Thomas, J., Swart, C., Brezin, J.: Toward modeling auditory information seeking strategies on the web. In: Proceedings of the 28th of the International Conference Extended Abstracts on Human Factors in Computing Systems, CHI EA 2010, pp. 3973–3978. ACM, New York (2010)
15. Francisco-Revilla, L., Crow, J.: Interpretation of web page layouts by blind users. In: Proceedings of the 10th Annual Joint Conference on Digital Libraries, JCDL 2010, pp. 173–176. ACM, New York (2010)
16. Ackermann, P., Velasco, C.A., Power, C.: Developing a semantic user and device modeling framework that supports ui adaptability of web 2.0 applications for people with special needs. In: Proceedings of the International Cross-Disciplinary Conference on Web Accessibility, W4A 2012, pp. 12:1–12:4. ACM, New York (2012)
17. Le Hors, A., Le Hégaret, P., Wood, L., Nicol, G., Robie, J., Champion, M., Byrne, S.: Document Object Model (DOM) Level 3 Core Specification. Technical report, World Wide Web Consortium, W3C (2004)
18. Wentz, B., Lazar, J.: Are separate interfaces inherently unequal?: an evaluation with blind users of the usability of two interfaces for a social networking platform. In: Proceedings of the 2011 iConference, iConference 2011, pp. 91–97. ACM, New York (2011)
19. Biswas, P.: Inclusive User Modeling - A simulator to design Accessible User Interfaces. PhD thesis, University of Cambridge Computer Laboratory (2010)
20. Tonn-Eichstädt, H.: Measuring website usability for visually impaired people-a modified goms analysis. In: Proceedings of the 8th International ACM SIGACCESS Conference on Computers and Accessibility, ASSETS 2006, pp. 55–62. ACM, New York (2006)
21. Bellamy, R., Kogan, S., Street, R.: Deploying CogTool: Integrating Quantitative Usability Assessment into Real-World Software Development. In: Human-Computer Interaction, pp. 691–700 (2011)
22. Engelbrecht, K.P., Kruppa, M., Möller, S., Quade, M.: Memo workbench for semi-automated usability testing. In: INTERSPEECH 2008, pp. 1662–1665 (2008)
23. Takagi, H., Asakawa, C., Fukuda, K., Maeda, J.: Accessibility designer: visualizing usability for the blind. SIGACCESS Access. Comput. (77-78), 177–184 (2003)
24. Hickson, I.: HTML5 - A vocabulary and associated APIs for HTML and XHTML, W3C Working Draft 25 May 2011. Technical report, World Wide Web Consortium, W3C (2011)

Decision Support for Off-the-Shelf
Software Selection in Web Development Projects

Widura Schwittek and Stefan Eicker (PhD supervisor)

paluno – The Ruhr Institute for Software Technology
University of Duisburg-Essen
Universitätsstr. 9, 45141 Essen, Germany
{widura.schwittek|stefan.eicker}@paluno.uni-due.de

Abstract. Reusing off-the-shelf (OTS) components (including commercial and open source software) has become a key success factor in software development projects leading to reduced costs, faster time-to-market and better software quality. This especially holds true in the field of web engineering, where software engineers are faced with a steady proliferation of new technologies and standards. But there are upfront and ongoing efforts and risks attached to the adoption of OTS components which makes decision-making very difficult. Such difficulties are for example a large and intransparent market, incompatibilities between components and architectural mismatches. In this paper, a plan towards a novel platform concept is proposed that can improve the situation for software engineers coping with the adoption of OTS components during web-based systems development.

One key contribution is an empirically derived ontology to describe software artifacts on a feature level allowing a better description and identification of OTS components in the domain of web development. Another key contribution is a concept for a lean experience sharing mechanism. The goal of both contributions is to improve OTS component decision-making.

The concept will be implemented as a platform prepopulated with OTS components from the domain of Java web development. A cross-case study is planned to evaluate the concept.

Keywords: off-the-shelf components, open source software, web engineering, web-based systems development, decision support, experience management.

1   Introduction

Reusing off-the-shelf (OTS) components has become a key success factor in software development projects [1] leading to reduced costs, faster time-to-market and better software quality [2]. This especially holds true in the field of web engineering, where architects and developers are faced with the steady proliferation of new technologies and standards [3]. The term "OTS components" is considered as an umbrella term which includes commercial off-the-shelf (COTS) components and Open Source Software (OSS), such as in [4]. OTS components are ready-to-use software components

M. Grossniklaus and M. Wimmer (Eds.): ICWE 2012 Workshops, LNCS 7703, pp. 238–243, 2012.

which can be acquired commercially (COTS) or free of charge (OSS) and are easily reusable because of their cohesive nature. OTS components are being reused in software development projects and therefore address software engineers rather than end-users. In my work, I consider OTS component types such as frameworks, libraries, or UI component sets.

If software engineers decide to build upon OTS components, they are confronted with a large and vibrant OTS component marketplace, especially in the domain of web-based systems development. This provides many opportunities, but difficulties as well:

- Information about OTS components is cluttered around several sources (websites, brochures, etc.) and has often not the quality to serve as a foundation for decision-making.
- Many alternatives to the same problem exist with slight differences which need to be identified.
- OTS component decisions can impact other decisions leading to complex interdependencies.

In all, OTS component selection becomes a time-consuming and tedious activity.

In this paper, a plan towards a novel platform concept is proposed that can improve the situation for software engineers coping with the adoption of OTS components during web-based systems development and evolution. In the following, this group of software engineers will be called "integrators".

2   Key Contributions

In the following two sections, the two key contributions of this research is described in more detail, each contributing to a "decision support for off-the-shelf software selection in web development projects" and addressing the shortcomings of the related work presented in the previous section.

2.1   A Feature Ontology for Enhancing OTS Component Descriptions

The main goal of this part of the research is the development of an ontology to be able to semantically enrich the description of OTS components from the domain of web-based systems development on a feature level. If OTS components are described in this way, they can be searched more elaborately solving issues such as the use of different but synonym search terms or inferring aspects the integrator was not aware of in the first place.

The ontology focuses on features of OTS components. Features comprise external and internal features. External features directly satisfy customer's requirements such as the feature "Scrollable Data Table" of a UI component suite. This allows a mapping of requirements onto OTS component features. Overlapping or missing features can be easily identified. Internal features are of interest for the actual integration of the OTS component such as "Dependency Injection" or "MVC". Internal features are also of use for discovering architectural mismatches.

In order to derive the ontology an empirical study is planned, for which a large and representative set of OTS components from the web development domain will be analyzed. The analysis process is repeated until additional OTS components do not significantly contribute to the feature ontology anymore. All harvested feature descriptions will then have to be harmonized according to the different terms used. I will focus on the OTS component market for Java web development which is known to be quite cluttered and in which the author already has practical experience. The study will be conducted systematically so that it can be repeated for other programming languages and even for software development domains other than web development.

The feature ontology will be implemented within a proof-of-concept tool serving two use cases. First, it will support describing OTS components on a feature level in an accurate and unambiguous way. Second, it will support identifying OTS components in this tool providing an exploratory (faceted) search and a comparison mechanism. The second use case will be evaluated as part of a cross-case study, proving or disproving the effectiveness of such an ontology for identifying OTS components.

2.2   Sharing OTS Component Selection Experience

During the time-consuming and tedious activity of OTS component selection, well-thought decisions as well as bad decisions are made over and over again. Experience about this is highly valuable but is not often shared, although it is available. Asking people who already solved a similar problem or developed a web application in a similar setting are a popular and welcomed source of information to prepare a decision.

The main goal of this part of my research is the extension of the tool described in the previous section. While it already provides means to enrich OTS component descriptions with ontology-based features, the tool should also incorporate OTS component selection experience. For this, the OTS component description facility will be extended by a "used by" statistic and inferred recommendations. It is assumed that the experience of one's OTS component decision is of interest for someone else. The "used by" data is generated by other integrators using the platform for managing their OTS component selection. Recommendations are generated from underlying data mining mechanisms.

Additionally, further means to provide feedback is planned allowing to rate relations between OTS components. As an example, these ratings might indicate incompatibilities between different components or successful integrations.

Rules can be generated on basis of this data, which is either provided upfront by experts or is inferred from existing combinations and feedback by other integrators. This makes it possible to automatically detect valid or invalid combinations, similar to a configurator used for cars.

A final OTS component selection can be marked as "final", thus contributing to the overall knowledge of successful OTS component combinations. This final selection can be enhanced by decision rationales contributing to the architectural knowledge which is of relevance during evolution and maintenance of the software system as well. As a byproduct, it serves as a starting point for a software architecture documentation, to be handed over to stakeholders for discussion or to be used in bulletin boards, so that people know, what OTS component set the integrator is talking or asking about.

The evaluation of these "experience sharing" features of the tool is difficult, since a critical mass of users is required to reach an amount of data which is generalizable. In the case the critical mass is reached, an online questionnaire will be used to evaluate the concept. If the critical mass is not reached, it is planned to provide experience data through investigating large Open Source projects and extract OTS component combinations out of these. Then, a cross-case study will be used to evaluate the concept.

3   Related Work

Many repository and search engine approaches have been proposed ([5],[6],[7]) to support finding the right OTS components within the numerous OTS components available and matching the requirements. Also, much research can be observed in the fields of component specification and standardization ([8],[9]). Nonetheless, studies have shown that rather than really using these approaches during OTS component identification, the most usual way in practice is to ask colleagues relying on the experience of experts or use general internet search engines [2]. Our platform implementing the feature ontology as well as the experience exchange mechanisms aims at enhancing the repository approach making it more useful and thus more attractive for practitioners.

Furthermore, most of the research which can be found in this context is dedicated to component models such as CORBA, EJB, JavaBeans etc. which is not the theme of this work. As already mentioned, I refer to a broader meaning of OTS components, also including frameworks, programming libraries, UI component suites etc.

An increasing body of knowledge on Semantic Web Enabled Software Engineering can be observed, which also becomes visible through an ISWC collocated workshop series. But only little research deals with semantically enriching OTS component descriptions: "KOntoR" [10] provides an extendable ontology for software reuse, but keeps quite general in terms of a specific domain and thus lacks of a concrete application. The "OTS wiki" focuses on sharing OTS knowledge following the Wiki approach [11]. Our research is seeking for a feature ontology for describing OTS for the web engineering domain and for knowledge sharing mechanisms other than offered by Wikis.

A huge body of knowledge exists in the context of "feature models" originating from Software Product Line Engineering (SPLE). While there are differences between "feature models" and "ontologies" [12], this research is strongly related when it comes to using our feature ontology for OTS identification. Further investigation towards this direction is therefore planned.

4   Work Already Done, and a Tentative Plan

The author already conducted research in the fields of architectural knowledge sharing [13] and ontologies for codifying bodies of knowledge [14]. Although the author has made no experience yet in the scientific field of web engineering, he already participated as software architect in industry projects, where he got the inspiration for this research.

This PhD work will be conducted cumulatively. While there are two big parts clearly defined (as described in section 3.1 and section 3.2) I see enough challenges for even smaller parts resulting in one paper each. Currently starting my third year as PhD student, I plan to finish my work in 2014.

Literature

1. Gartner: The Evolving Open-source Software Model (Predicts from December 2008)
2. Li, J., Conradi, R., Bunse, C., Torchiano, M., Slyngstad, O.P.N., Morisio, M.: Development with Off-the-Shelf Components: 10 Facts. IEEE Softw. 26(2), 80–87 (2009), doi:10.1109/MS.2009.33
3. Rossi, G.: Web engineering: Modelling and implementing web applications. Human computer interaction series, vol. 12. Springer, London (2008)
4. Ayala, C., Hauge, Ø., Conradi, R., Franch, X., Li, J.: Selection of third party software in Off-The-Shelf-based software development: An interview study with industrial practitioners. Journal of Systems and Software 84(4), 620–637 (2011), doi:10.1016/j.jss.2010.10.019
5. Clark, J., Clarke, C., de Panfilis, S., Granatella, G., Predonzani, P., Sillitti, A., Succi, G., Vernazza, T.: Selecting components in large COTS repositories. Journal of Systems and Software 73(2), 323–331 (2004), doi:10.1016/j.jss.2003.09.019
6. Wanyama, T., Far, B.: Repositories for Cots Selection. In: Canadian Conference on Electrical and Computer Engineering, Ottawa, ON, Canada, May 7-10, pp. 2416–2419. IEEE Service Center, Piscataway (2006), doi:10.1109/CCECE.2006.277301
7. Yanes, N., Sassi, S.B., Ghezala, H.H.B.: State of Art and Practice of COTS Components Search Engines. In: IEEE/ACS International Conference on Computer Systems and Applications, AICCSA 2010, Hammamet, Tunisia, May 16-19, pp. 1–8. IEEE, Piscataway (2010), doi:10.1109/AICCSA.2010.5587032
8. Cechich, A., Requile-Romanczuk, A., Aguirre, J., Luzuriaga, J.: Trends on COTS Component Identification. In: Proceedings of the Fifth International Conference on Commercial-off-the-Shelf (COTS)-Based Software Systems, ICCBSS 2006, Orlando, Florida, February 13-16, pp. 90–99. IEEE Computer Society, Los Alamitos (2006), doi:10.1109/ICCBSS.2006.31
9. Crnkovic, I., Sentilles, S., Vulgarakis, A., Chaudron, M.R.V.: A Classification Framework for Software Component Models. IEEE Trans. Software Eng. 37(5), 593–615 (2011), doi:10.1109/TSE.2010.83
10. Happel, H., Korthaus, A., Seedorf, S., Tomczyk, P.: KOntoR: An Ontology-enabled Approach to Software Reuse
11. Li, J., Ayala, C., Conradi, R.: Role-Based Wiki for Reuse of Off-the-Shelf Components
12. Czarnecki, K., Kim, C.H.P., Kalleberg, K.T.: Feature Models are Views on Ontologies

13. Schwittek, W., Eicker, S.: Communicating Architectural Knowledge: Requirements for Software Architecture Knowledge Management Tools. In: Babar, M.A., Gorton, I. (eds.) ECSA 2010. LNCS, vol. 6285, pp. 457–463. Springer, Heidelberg (2010)
14. Schwittek, W., Schmidt, H., Eicker, S., Heisel, M.: Towards a Common Body of Knowledge for Engineering Secure Software and Services. In: Filipe, J., Liu, K. (eds.) KMIS 2011 - Proceedings of the International Conference on Knowledge Management and Information Sharing, Paris, France, October 26-29, pp. 369–374. SciTePress (2011)

Author Index